Apostle of Taste

❧

Creating the North American Landscape

Consulting Editors

Gregory Conniff
Bonnie Loyd
Edward K. Muller
David Schuyler

Published in cooperation with the

Center for American Places
Harrisonburg, Virginia

Apostle of Taste

ANDREW JACKSON DOWNING

1815–1852

David Schuyler

The Johns Hopkins University Press
Baltimore and London

© 1996 The Johns Hopkins University Press
All rights reserved. Published 1996
Printed in the United States of America on acid-free paper
05 04 03 02 01 00 99 98 97 96   5 4 3 2 1

The Johns Hopkins University Press
2715 North Charles Street
Baltimore, Maryland 21218-4319
The Johns Hopkins Press Ltd., London

ISBN 0-8018-5229-3

Library of Congress Cataloging-in-Publication Data
will be found at the end of this book.

A catalog record for this book is available from the British Library.

Frontispiece: Andrew Jackson Downing, ca. 1851.
From a daguerreotype. Courtesy of The Athenaeum of Philadelphia.

For
Nancy Brimmer Sener
Marsha Sener Schuyler
Nancy Sener Schuyler

Contents

❧

Contents

8

The Metropolitan Landscape

9

Tastemaker to the Nation

Appendix:
Writings of Andrew Jackson Downing

Acknowledgments

In the course of writing this book I have incurred numerous obligations. Franklin & Marshall College generously granted me the sabbatical during which I wrote most of the following pages, while the college's Committee on Grants provided the funds that enabled me to conduct research and assemble the illustrations. I am grateful to the many people at the college who have made Franklin & Marshall such an exciting and pleasant place to teach. Not least am I indebted to librarians Thomas A. Karel, Charles J. Myers, Mary K. Shelly, and Andrew Gulati, who provided enormous help at every stage of the research and writing.

Many individuals beyond the campus have also helped. In Newburgh, New York, Helen Ver Nooy Gearn, long the City Historian, extended many kindnesses over a period of years, while James Halpin of the Newburgh Free Library, Bea Cornell of the City Engineer's Office, Tom Kyle, formerly director of the Historical Society of Newburgh Bay and the Highlands, and the Reverend Wayne Schmidt of St. George's Church, have made my research both pleasant and efficient. Richard Jenrette generously shared copies of Downing letters to Robert Donaldson in his possession. At one time or another over the years, Kenneth Ames, James L. Baughman, Whitfield J. Bell, Jr., Thomas Bender, Jane Censer, Walter Creese, James Curtis, Jane B. Davies, Robert Gross, Kenneth Hawkins, Kenneth T. Jackson, John Kasson, Elisabeth B. MacDougall, Eric L. McKitrick, Charles McLaughlin, Jon A. Peterson, Mary Corbin Sies, Leonard Wallock, Gwendolyn Wright, and John Zukowsky have generously shared information derived from their own research or otherwise provided important support.

For help in assembling the illustrations I am grateful to Charles E. Beveridge, Alan Gowans, Kenneth Hawkins, Harvey Flad, Morrison H. Heckscher of the Metropolitan Museum of Art, Nancy MacKecknie of Vassar College, Mark Renovitch of the Franklin Delano Roosevelt Library, Hyde Park, New York, Beverly Shank of the Medford Public Library, Medford, Massachusetts, and Alexander von Hoffman of Harvard University. Max Yela, formerly of Morris Library, University of Delaware, took a keen interest in my research and helped collect the many illustrations from that institution that enrich the text.

Numerous friends took time from their own work to comment on what

I had written at various stages of this project. I am grateful to Michael Birkner, Tom Daniels, Ted Pearson, and Tom Ryan for their comments on specific chapters, while Frank Kowsky's careful reading of the chapters concerned with architecture was most helpful. John A. Andrew III, Charles Beveridge, Mark Carnes, Alan Gowans, Elizabeth Mackey, and Alden T. Vaughan read the complete typescript and generously offered criticisms that helped me improve it. I am particularly indebted to George B. Tatum, the preeminent Downing scholar. More than twenty years ago I enrolled in the Winterthur Program in Early American Culture in the hope of studying with him. Over the course of two decades George has been a generous and supportive mentor and friend. I hope that *Apostle of Taste* is in some small way testament to his teaching and his friendship.

George F. Thompson, president of the Center for American Places, has been my editor for more than a decade. I am grateful for his continuing faith in this book, and its author, and for the care with which he oversaw the various stages of the publishing process. At the Johns Hopkins University Press, Henry Y. K. Tom and Robert J. Brugger have been supportive friends over the years, Anne Whitmore once again shepherded my text through copy editing. I was also fortunate to have Ed King design *Apostle of Taste.*

One of the real delights in writing this book was the opportunity it afforded me to revisit the community in which I grew up, to spend time with my mother, my brothers and sisters and their families, as well as friends whom I have known since childhood. I cherish those moments. Equally do I cherish the community of my adult years, Lancaster, Pennsylvania, and the many colleagues and friends there who enrich my life. The dedication, I trust, speaks to the center of that life.

Apostle of Taste

❧

Introduction

The lead article in the June 1849 *Horticulturist* began with the lament of a correspondent who had just moved to a community where, he declared, the residents were completely devoid of architectural taste. The church had a "huge pepper-box" for a spire, other buildings were little more than eyesores, and nary a tree graced the streets. "Is there no way of instilling some rudiments of taste into the minds of dwellers in remote country places?" the writer inquired. The editor of the *Horticulturist*, Andrew Jackson Downing, preached hope rather than despair: he ordained this reader an "APOSTLE OF TASTE" and charged him—and all his readers—with the responsibility of providing examples of architectural design worthy of emulation.[1] In this and in other essays, Downing described the individual who built a beautiful home or tended a handsome garden as a public benefactor. These words capture the significance of Downing's mission as well.

Andrew Jackson Downing was a horticulturist, landscape gardener, and prolific writer who, more than any other individual, shaped middle-class taste in the United States during the two decades prior to the Civil War. His name is indelibly if sometimes nostalgically identified with that era's taste in domestic architecture and landscape design. Edith Wharton's *Hudson River Bracketed* (1929), for example, took its title from the one of the building types he popularized, while a number of more recent books and articles have associated Downing's name with the architectural style of mid-nineteenth-century cottages or villas. Author of four important and widely read books and editor of the *Horticulturist*, a monthly journal devoted to "rural art and rural taste," Downing articulated the ideal of a society of refined individuals who lived in tasteful homes set within handsome landscapes. As he explained in 1848, Downing defined his mission as the responsibility to "teach men the beauty and value of rural life," to encourage all individuals, no matter what their occupation or income, to cherish gardens and orchards as well as homes "created by their own industry—embellished by their own taste—endeared to them by simple pleasures shared with their own families."[2]

Downing championed what he termed the modern or natural style of landscape design instead of the formal or geometric arrangement of gardens that was the legacy of the eighteenth and early nineteenth centuries in the

United States. Together with his longtime collaborator, architect Alexander Jackson Davis, he contributed to the revolution in American architectural taste from the near universality of the classical revival to Gothic, Italianate, Swiss, and other romantic or picturesque styles of domestic design. Downing interpreted this progression from classic to romantic not simply as a change in stylistic preference but as a reflection of the nation's evolution from a pioneer condition to a more advanced state of civilization. He promoted simple board-and-batten homes, bracketed cottages, and more ostentatious villas, all in styles consciously "adapted" to the United States. In calling for the development of an American architectural expression, Downing particularly cited the bracketed, which he described as the first style to take "a distinct shape and meaning in the hands of our countrymen."[3]

As both the testimony of his contemporaries and surviving houses indicate, readers across the United States eagerly welcomed Downing's advice and built dwellings or planted gardens following the principles he outlined in his various writings. Jonathan Baldwin Turner, a frequent contributor to the *Horticulturist* and a champion of agricultural education, asserted that Downing had "produced more lasting and salutary effect upon the real well-being of this continent" and deserved "a prouder and more lasting monument than any political or military man that has lived since the days of WASHINGTON."[4] Similarly, Luther Tucker, publisher of the *Horticulturist*, believed that Downing would figure prominently "in that unwritten history of social progress, in the councils of the fireside."[5]

The linking of Downing's name with that of Washington and other notable Americans of the revolutionary generation may seem extravagant, as might Tucker's claim that Downing would occupy an honored place in accounts of the social development of the nation. Senator Charles Sumner of Massachusetts, however, described Downing's reputation as "superior to that of any other citizen in the walk of life to which he had devoted himself," and asserted that he knew of "no man who at that early age had rendered services of such true beneficence to his country as he had done by the various works in his profession."[6] These and other laudatory assessments reflect the importance contemporaries attributed to the cause of culture that Downing exemplified and to his singularly influential role as an apostle of taste. Well-designed surroundings and other evidence of refined domestic life, they believed, would temper the excessive mobility of the American population, promote social order, and develop responsible citizens. Downing insisted that an appreciation of the beautiful in nature and the improvement of domestic architecture in the United States were keys to the nation's cultural development and accurate measures of "the progress of its civilization."[7]

A number of commentators attributed Downing's success as an apostle of taste at least in part to the timing of his arrival on the American scene. A reviewer of Downing's *Architecture of Country Houses* (1850) noted that when the author had published his first books, almost a decade earlier, the "*new* had by no means worn off of the new world." The initial stages of settlement had produced prosperity, but this was "only a step in a transition to a better state of things": the "desolation" of clear-cut forests had not yet been replaced by a taste for planting trees and gardens and building tasteful homes.[8] Similarly, Henry F. French, an agricultural reformer and educator, noted that Downing's first books appeared "just when the inhabitants of this western world had laid down the woodman's axe."[9] Having tamed the wilderness, at least in long-settled areas of the east, Americans had begun the task of beautifying their surroundings, and they turned to Downing's writings for inspiration. In the inaugural issue of the *Horticulturist,* Downing observed that his countrymen were "crying out loudly for more light, and more knowledge" about how to design their houses and gardens, yet he was heartened that so many individuals were devoting "the same zeal and spirit" once manifested by the pioneer in cutting down trees to the "refinements and enjoyments which belong to a country life, and a country home."[10]

Downing's success had as much to do with his message as it did with the generation in which he lived. He reached his greatest influence as an apostle of taste during the 1840s and early 1850s, an era generally described by historians as "Young America," an ambiguous term associated with the aggressively expansive ideology of Manifest Destiny as well as with the search for an American cultural identity. Ralph Waldo Emerson captured the more positive side of this sentiment in his 1844 essay "The Young American," his optimistic assessment of the nation's cultural aspirations. According to historian Neil Harris, the antebellum era was a time of "egalitarian self-confidence," when American society was awkwardly grappling with the social and cultural implications of democracy. Ironically, Downing became the preeminent authority on domestic architecture and landscape gardening during the same decade in which P. T. Barnum became the dominant figure in American popular culture. Whereas the showman appealed to the "vanities and conceits" that accompanied the emergence of "a new democratic sensibility," as Harris has argued,[11] Downing saw his calling as disciplining and refining the nation's taste and directed his prose to a different audience than Barnum's. His readers too were buffeted by tremendous technological and social change, by a revolution in the availability of books and consumer goods, but unlike habitués of Barnum's American Museum they yearned for certitude—confidence that they had chosen the most appropriate plans for their homes and gardens, assurance that the nation was evolving toward a more advanced state of society, above all a sense of place in a rapidly changing country. For these individuals, agriculturist George Jaques wrote, Downing represented the belief that improvements in taste signified "the advancement of civilization."[12]

The same attempt to promote a refined American culture was central to the efforts of the American Art-Union. Founded as the Apollo Association in 1838, the Art-Union emerged in the 1840s as a powerful engine of patronage for American artists. Annual dues enabled the Art-Union to acquire paintings and other works of art, which were distributed to members at a lottery. The Art-Union consciously promoted American themes—"subjects illustrating national character, or history, or scenery"—and urged artists to "cherish American simplicity and freshness." By the time of its demise in 1853, following a court ruling that declared its annual lottery illegal, the Art-Union had distributed hundreds of original works of art as well as handsome engravings.[13] Downing clearly sympathized with the goals of the Art-Union—he served as a teller at its 1844 lottery[14]—yet chose a different strategy in his crusade to influence American taste. Whereas the Art-Union urged painters to abandon European precedents,[15] Downing conceded that the development of an American expression in architecture would take years, and he instead attempted to adapt European building styles to American conditions. And whereas members of the Art-Union were consumers of culture, Downing thought of his readers as apostles, energetic citizens who would build tasteful houses and gardens and who, through their example, would influence others to improve their homes and grounds.

Although Downing's career obviously differed from Barnum's and from the evolution of the Art-Union, he too was a major figure in the democratization of culture. At a time when many of his contemporaries associated refinement and taste with wealth and leisure, Downing believed that taste was something that could be learned and that could extend to every income level in society. According to the popular essayist Nathaniel Parker Willis, in the last years of his life Downing had developed "quite a passion" for improving the "homes of The Many" and strove to bring "taste and refined comfort within reach of moderate means."[16] His designs for modest dwellings and farmhouses attempted to demonstrate that even the simplest working man's residence could be comfortable and tasteful. He also advocated the establishment of institutions of popular refinement—parks and gardens, museums, libraries, and other repositories of "intellectual and moral culture"—that would be attractive to and accessible by all citizens. Downing thus posited a vision of a society in which gentility was universal, where even the poorest working man could benefit from "the higher realms of art, letters, science, social recreations, and enjoyments."[17]

The democratization of culture involved two other issues that pervade Downing's writings—republicanism and class. Downing apparently avoided politics throughout his life. Indeed, in the first issue of the *Horticulturist* he observed, "Angry volumes of politics have we written none; but peaceful books, humbly aiming to weave something more into the fair garland of the beautiful, and useful, that encircles this excellent old Earth."[18] While Downing may have scorned the "excitement of politics" and the machinations of governance, and occasionally denounced demagogues who appealed to the "prejudices" of ignorant or self-interested citizens,[19] he nevertheless promoted a conservative nationalism and an attachment to place, both of which he allusively identified with republicanism.

Although Downing frequently claimed the mantle of republicanism as a justification for his ideas, he never defined precisely what he meant by the term. Most obviously, he referred to the absence of monarchy and a hereditary aristocracy. Though wary of the excesses of political democracy, he clearly favored an electoral system that invested power in the hands of the many and a government entrusted with promoting opportunities for the improvement of all citizens. According to the Swedish republican and champion of women's rights, Fredrika Bremer, Downing had "united himself with that great, true republican" spirit she found in many parts of the United States, "all of whose endeavors tend to 'leveling upward,' and whose watchword is 'all things for all.' "[20] While *republicanism* as he used the word included politics and economic opportunity, it also embraced broader questions of culture, especially access to knowledge and institutions that would promote taste and civility among all citizens. Historian Jean Baker has observed that during the antebellum years republicanism "had been overtaken by a political philosophy offering Americans individualism over community, majoritarianism over restraint, and liberty in the name of personal interests rather than virtue in the defense of civic humanism."[21] Downing's republicanism, however, reached back to original, or at least long-since displaced, meanings of the term—community, restraint, commitment to public good.

Just as Downing used *republicanism* in an almost archaic way, his understanding of class apparently derived from Tocqueville's formulation of the middle class as the representative and dominant group in American society. Above all, the American way was one in which a person's station in life was a product of individual effort and personal choice, not a status determined arbitrarily by birth. Thus, he criticized Gervase Wheeler's *Rural Homes* (1851) because it portrayed an ideal American village in terms that seemed to replicate a rigidly hierarchical English class structure.[22] Although the America Tocqueville visited in 1831 had changed dramatically during the intervening two decades and the stratification of class lines had become more pronounced, Downing continued to maintain an older image of the United States as a fluid society characterized by the honor of all labor and the widespread opportunity to improve one's condition, material as well as mental and moral. Indeed, while his writings indicate an awareness of social divisions, what is striking is the degree to which Downing avoided that reality: he used the term *class* to refer not to economic or ideological groups within society but to categories of houses.

Together, Downing's conceptions of republicanism and of class projected a vision of an ideal society, a community of equals united by refinement and taste. Convinced that the physical environment influenced patterns of human behavior, he believed that appropriately designed homes and gardens were "a powerful means of civilization." Improvements to the nation's homes, together with institutions of popular refinement, he predicted, would raise the level of "*social* civilization and social culture" in the United States and elevate the "working-man to the same level of enjoyment with the man of leisure and accomplishment."[23] At its best Downing's was an appealing vision of the possibilities of a republican society. But in important ways his understanding of the dynamics of class and republicanism was limited. Downing was the single most important early advocate of a public park for New York City, at least in the eyes of Frederick Law Olmsted; and the success of Central Park, which Olmsted designed in collaboration with Downing's former partner, Calvert Vaux, launched the public parks movement in the United States. Yet the public parks he promoted for the nation's cities included no space for the sports and popular entertainments increasingly favored by the working classes. Similarly, although Downing was, in historian Kenneth T. Jackson's words, "the most influential single individual in translating the rural ideal into a suburban ideal,"[24] the new communities he advocated proved to be beyond the economic means of most residents of the nation's cities. Despite a rhetoric of inclusiveness, Downing's designs masked a limited understanding or a limited acceptance of the differences that increasingly characterized American society. Downing thus shared important similarities with a small group of individuals in the 1850s who, according to historian John Higham, were "exploring new possibilities for organizing and disciplining a culture of rampant individualism."[25]

Downing died in the burning of the steamboat *Henry Clay* in 1852, when he was only thirty-six, so it is impossible to determine whether his ideas would have evolved to reflect the cultural and recreational interests of the emerging social order. At that time, many of his ideas remained only partially developed, his mission as an apostle of taste was left incomplete. For example, Downing was arguably the most articulate spokesman of his generation for the development of an American architecture. While he drew upon English examples, he insisted on adapting those designs to the climate, social structure, and republican institutions of the United States. But Downing's modifications—most often a reduction in the scale of the dwelling and the addition of a porch or veranda—were "starting-points," in Calvert Vaux's words,[26] not the realization of the national architecture that he advocated, one that sprang from American experience. The quest for a national cultural expression, in literature and painting as well as in architecture, that so drove his generation gave way after the Civil War to what historian Daniel Walker Howe has termed the "international quality of Victorian culture." Howe suggests that many of the nation's cultural imperatives were derived from European standards,[27] a dramatic shift away from the antebellum search for an American culture that Downing sought in the nation's commitment to economic opportunity and republican social institutions. Moreover, the method of building that Downing advocated was essentially conservative. While he eagerly embraced certain new household technologies, such as the water closet, and believed fervently in the continual improvement of American homes, he was silent about two critically important innovations, the balloon frame house and the application of cast iron to building, that transformed construction technology in the second half of the nineteenth century.

Downing's career provides an important vehicle for studying several major developments that reshaped American culture during the antebellum years. Central to this study is his role in promoting the emergence of a picturesque aesthetic in architectural and landscape design—the new styles in building and gardening that he popularized and the public's reception of his ideas. Downing's life also serves as a valuable lens through which to examine both the aspirations and the limitations of cultural ideology during the 1840s and early 1850s. His writings contributed to the enshrinement of the single-family home, set amid handsome grounds, as a domestic utopia, yet Downing seemed unaware of how the private realm of domesticity contributed to a broader cultural withdrawal from the public sphere. He celebrated the opportunities for economic advancement that he considered a hallmark of America and educated the public about matters of taste so that they could acquire the ornaments of a genteel life, yet he fretted over his own finances and at times seemed dangerously close to losing the house and gardens that symbolized his cultural authority. In short, Downing personified many of the fears as well as the hopes of the very middle class he instructed in matters of refinement and taste.

Downing's legacy was, in one respect, extraordinarily broad: the range of his activities and interests ran the gamut from practical subjects, such as fruits and improvements in horticulture, to agricultural education, from domestic architecture and extensive ornamental pleasure grounds to promoting popular taste. His legacy was also remarkably persistent, as many of his ideas continued to resonate in the popular press and in architectural pattern books long after his death. In another sense, Downing's legacy is very limited: he designed only a handful of buildings and even fewer gardens that are reasonably intact or even well documented in photographs, which makes a detailed study of his works impossible. Moreover, he left few manuscripts, and most of those are unrevealing of the full range of his various activities, so a biographer is unable to present a nuanced portrait of his personal and psychological development.

Downing's published writings are the principal basis for this study, not simply because they constitute the bulk of his ideas that have survived, but because the printed word and the widely reproduced design were Downing's chosen vehicles for influencing American taste. The following pages analyze Downing's career as an apostle of taste and the gospel of refinement and taste that he preached to his fellow citizens.

1

Downing's Newburgh and the Spirit of Place

He was no merely "lucky" man to whom Fortune had been kind though he was undeserving, but he was slowly elaborating, step by step, the life which from his youth he had determined to lead. . . .　　　　　　　　—Clarence C. Cook

Andrew Jackson Downing was born in Newburgh, New York, on October 31, 1815.[1] The village was located on the west bank of the Hudson River, just north of the Highlands, a setting Washington Irving described as "abounding with transcendent beauties."[2] Newburgh's small population of 2,370 lived and worked largely in wood structures: seven years later a local census revealed that there were 372 frame dwellings and stores in the village, while only 85 buildings were of brick or stone. Whatever their material, most of these structures must have been of Germanic or Anglo-American vernacular design, reflecting the European antecedents of the community's population. The visiting Englishman Henry Bradshaw Fearon noted the presence of "many new and excellent buildings" in the village, but what he found praiseworthy was probably their size and quality of construction rather than design.[3] In 1850 George P. Morris and N. P. Willis's *Home Journal* characterized the state of American architecture a generation earlier as a "*barn* style—the main features of which seemed to be *squareness, hugeness,* and most *un-fig-leaved nakedness* of all external decoration." Clarence C. Cook similarly asserted that at the time of Downing's birth, extant buildings yielded "no proof" that Americans had "any taste or skill in architecture." Ignoring the surviving buildings of the colonial and early national period, Cook trenchantly asserted that, save for a few notable estates in Massachusetts and along the Hudson River, there was little evidence of "any graceful or elegant design" in American homes or their grounds.[4]

Downing's life was inextricably linked to Newburgh and the cultural landscape of the mid-Hudson Valley. With the exception of a brief sojourn at Montgomery Academy, a boarding school in nearby Montgomery, New York, he continued to live in the cottage in which he was born until 1838, when he designed and superintended construction of a large residence on the property he inherited from his parents. Although Downing traveled extensively—throughout the Northeast in the 1830s and 1840s, to Europe and then to Washington, D.C., in the early 1850s—he lived his entire life in Newburgh. Indeed, he both benefited from the prosperity of his birthplace and actively supported its nascent cultural institutions. This attachment to place stood in stark contrast to the "spirit of unrest" Downing and other commentators attributed to so many of their contemporaries. "Unable to take root anywhere," Downing wrote of the prototypical migrating American, "he leads, socially and physically, the uncertain life of a tree transplanted from place to place, and shifted to a different soil every season."[5]

If throughout his career Downing demonstrated a commitment to the village in which he was born, his parents represented the surging tide of American migration. Samuel Downing traced his lineage to Puritan forebears, but about 1800 he left home, wife, and children in Lexington, Massachusetts, and, together with his second wife, the former Eunice Bridge, established a new household in Newburgh. The senior Downing was part of a substantial influx of New Englanders who settled in the mid-Hudson village around the turn of the nineteenth century. A number of these settlers became successful merchant freighters, who invested in real estate and thereby increased their prosperity as the town grew.[6] Several would, in future years, become clients of the younger Downing's nursery or of the professional services he offered in landscape and architectural design. Samuel Downing acquired property at the corner of Broad and Liberty streets and on it established a business as a wheelwright. This may well have been a lucrative occupation, for there was much cart and wagon traffic entering the village. As was true of other New Englanders, the elder Downing invested in Newburgh real estate: at the time of his death in 1822, Samuel Downing owned at least seven large lots adjacent to his residence, as well as three other properties, one of them strategically located along the Newburgh and Cochecton Turnpike (the modern Route 17K), which had been constructed by a group of Newburgh's wealthier merchants. Downing's will specified that the latter three properties be sold to pay his estate's debts, but Eunice and Charles Downing, his executors, apparently had to relinquish only the lot adjacent to the turnpike (for $140) for this purpose.[7]

The Downing family residence stood near the northeast corner of Broad and Liberty streets. Other than its location—evident on several maps of the village (see fig. 1)—and its red color, little is known about the structure. The frequent designation "cottage," however, suggests that it was a modest dwelling. The family properties included a 4½ acre lot on which the dwelling stood, located north of Broad Street between Liberty and Second (later Grand) streets, a 4½ acre lot north of Broad Street between Grand and Hasbrouck (later Montgomery) streets, a 2¾ acre lot south of Broad Street between Grand and Montgomery streets, and a smaller lot at the southeast corner of Broad and Liberty streets that contained a barn and, presumably, Samuel Downing's wheelwright shop. By 1810 the elder Downing had established a commercial nursery on the acres surrounding the cottage and begun advertising "trees engrafted and inoculated, of the following kinds: apples, pears, peaches, apricots, cherries, &c."[8]

Andrew Jackson Downing was the fifth and last child of Samuel and Eunice Downing.[9] Surely he was named after the hero of the Battle of New Orleans, as were so many sons born in the months following Jackson's stunning victory, but otherwise, relatively few details of his youth have survived. Shortly after Downing's death, Caroline DeWint Downing, his widow, and Charles Downing, his brother, shared their recollections of his early experiences with Marshall P. Wilder, the eminent president of the Massachusetts Horticultural Society, who was preparing a eulogy. Wilder incorporated these written re-

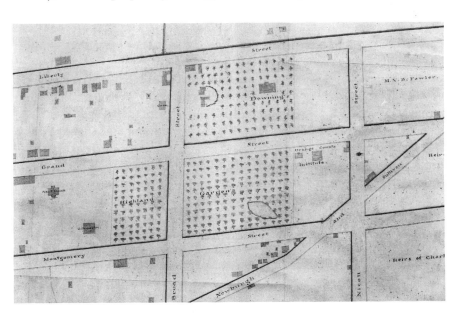

Figure 1. The Downing family properties in 1846. Detail of "Map of Part of the Village of Newburgh, Showing the Location of the Streets, Wharves, Buildings, Public Springs, Reservoirs, Hydrants, Water Logs, Iron Pipes, Drains, &c. &c. in the said part of the village.—made pursuant to a Resolution of the Board of Trustees, by Stephen C. Parmenter, Corporation Surveyor. 1846." Courtesy of the City Engineer's Office, City of Newburgh, N.Y.

membrances, together with material provided by friends such as Asa Gray and Calvert Vaux, in the eulogy, which he delivered at the annual meeting of the American Pomological Congress in September 1852 and published in the *Horticulturist* two months later. These reminiscences, as well as information Downing's widow and brother must have conveyed orally to other biographers, such as Clarence Cook and Mary E. Monell, are essential clues to Downing's formative years.

Based on the information Wilder and Cook published, on conversations with surviving members of the family, and on his own knowledge of Downing in the six years before his death, George William Curtis wrote what became the standard biography, the "Memoir" that serves as the introduction to *Rural Essays*. Curtis inferred that Downing's early years must have been a lonely, unhappy time for a misunderstood boy growing up in a poor family. In addition, Curtis wrote, the family's straitened finances forced Andrew to leave school at age sixteen, when, despite his mother's wish that he clerk in a dry goods establishment, he joined his brother Charles in the family's nursery business.[10] Some of Curtis's conclusions about Downing's youth, however, appear to be mid-nineteenth-century literary conventions. The Downing family was not poor, and despite his father's death in 1822, Andrew did not leave school for financial reasons: Samuel Downing's will required that his son George, a physician, provide for Andrew's education as a condition of accepting the bequest of the lot at the southeast corner of Broad and Liberty streets. Moreover, the Downings were well-respected in the community, and Samuel had served for a period of years as a trustee of the village.[11]

Curtis's assertion that Downing's youth was an unhappy one may also have been a common biographical device. An 1853 description of Downing's home and gardens, however, hints at a different interpretation of his childhood. Although much of the article documented the handsome improvements to the grounds that Downing had undertaken in recent years, a paragraph paid homage to two elements of the gardens which survived from his youth. One was a wisteria that "formerly climbed up the front of the little dwelling" where Downing was born, and which, as an adult, he trained into an arbor. An engraving drawn by Calvert Vaux (fig. 98 in this volume) depicts the arbor, with its delightful view of the Hudson and the mountains to the east. The other was a large balsam fir, clearly indicated on the map accompanying the article, which the author, Clarence Cook, described as "one of the few trees planted" during Samuel Downing's life "still remaining in its original place." The seventy-foot tree was "a specimen of remarkable beauty," Cook concluded, and "was always a pleasant memorial with Mr. DOWNING of his early days." Downing did not try to escape from his past but continued to live in the midst of it, building a house and laying out a garden on "the spot which of all others on earth was dear to him," and enshrining a surviving vine and tree as "pleasant" reminders of boyhood and family.[12]

Downing's education, his brother Charles recalled, was "only a good english one & mostly in this village." He could have attended Newburgh Academy, a private school founded in the eighteenth century, or the publicly supported Glebe School. Then, at the age of fourteen, Downing became a boarding student at Montgomery Academy, one of the oldest and best secondary schools in New York State. During the years of Downing's residence there the school was located in a Federal-style brick building erected in 1818. The private school boasted a library of a thousand volumes and a rigorous curriculum that included courses in Roman and Greek antiquities as well as "Drawing, Landscape and Perspective."[13]

In 1831 or 1832, Downing's formal education ended. His schooling had prepared him well for later professional endeavors: within a few years he was regularly publishing articles in horticultural journals and had translated a French horticultural notice. Moreover, from the course in drawing he learned to make architectural and landscape sketches that, while clearly not the work of a professional draughtsman, are accurate and nicely executed. College was not a realistic option, given his decision to join Charles in the nursery business, because no institutions of higher education in the United States then provided practical training in horticulture, pomology, or landscape gardening. Thereafter Downing continued his professional education "through his own industry," his brother recalled. This emphasis on careful study, theoretical as well as practical, shaped Downing's mature view of the purposes of education. The "well-educated agriculturist," he wrote in 1849, "should combine in himself both the science and the art which he professes." Knowledge, whether gleaned in the fields or studied in the classroom or laboratory, had to be put in action. Downing envisioned an educational program for farmers that would combine the classroom with practical application in the fields, promoting what he termed "that *agricultural wisdom* which involves both, and which can never be attained without a large development of the powers of the pupil in both directions."[14] In effect, Downing used his own education— both at school and in the nursery—to define the optimal experience for the next generation of students.

About the time Downing completed his formal education and returned to Newburgh, the village was beginning to recover from a period of economic distress. Completion of the Erie and the Delaware and Hudson canals had diverted to other river towns much of the trade that had accounted for the village's economic vitality. But beginning roughly in 1831, the New England–born merchant freighters, who had consolidated their wealth through intermarriage, solidified their control over a reduced hinterland. Although the streets of the village were dirt, the near constant rumble of carts disturbing, and the herds of animals heading to market unsightly, trade once again powered the city's growth.[15]

With the return of prosperity, the merchants began building a new community. A local newspaper, the *Telegraph,* surveyed the changes these families had wrought in an article published in 1835. By that time, approximately six hundred buildings huddled in a dozen or so blocks adjacent to the riverfront, the town had become a community of 5,118 persons, and numerous tradesmen catered to the wants of residents. Among the most notable improvements cited by the paper were handsome new mansions that ornamented "many of the beautiful points in our landscape which render it the admiration of the traveller"; new dwellings erected in the "compact part of the town" (fig. 2); a new financial institution, the Highland Bank; and an impressive number of new commercial buildings and docks. Several churches had recently been constructed or were nearing completion, as was the theological seminary of the Associate Reformed Synod, which was initially scheduled to open in 1836. The new United States Hotel, a five-story brick structure with three spacious "piazzas" and an observatory overlooking the Hudson, stood near the ferry wharf, while Alexander Jackson Davis's design for the Dutch

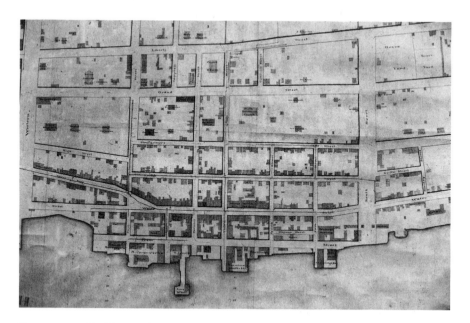

Figure 2. Detail of "Map of Part of the Village of Newburgh . . . 1846," showing dock area and adjacent blocks. Courtesy of the City Engineer's Office, City of Newburgh, N.Y.

Reformed Church, a handsome Greek Revival temple topped with a cupola, was taking shape near the corner of Grand and Third streets.[16] So great was the material progress of the community, the *Telegraph* reported in 1835, that "upwards of 60 buildings have been erected here within the *past year,* upwards of 1500 feet of dock built; and something like a million of dollars in stocks taken up by our citizens."[17]

Newburgh's increasing prosperity, the construction of numerous large dwellings, and the organization of a local horticultural society ensured a ready clientele for the Downing nursery. In 1832 it was still clearly associated with Charles Downing. A description published that year attributed its success to Charles but noted the presence of "his equally meritorious and not less modest brother and coadjutor." Within a year the business bore the name "Botanical Gardens and Nursery." By 1833 the nursery had begun attracting the notice of numerous customers from distant places, as the brothers were successfully cultivating 150 kinds of apples and more than 200 varieties of pears. Three years later the New York City author and publisher Freeman Hunt visited the nursery of "C. and A. J. Downing" and reported, "[M]any strangers are drawn hither by the increasing taste for horticulture, to view the improvements in cultivation, or to draw from the rich resources of fruit and ornamental trees collected here, for the improvement and embellishment of their own estates." The Downing brothers possessed "a profound knowledge, both theoretical and practical," and maintained a constant correspondence with European horticulturists.[18]

While Andrew Jackson Downing was becoming deeply involved in the operations of the business and beginning to write articles for publication in the horticultural and agricultural press, he also formed several friendships that, according to Charles Downing and Caroline DeWint Downing, contributed to his scientific and artistic development. The first of these was with Alois Freiherr von Lederer, the Austrian Consul-General in New York between 1820 and 1838, who maintained a summer residence near Newburgh. Charles Downing described Baron von Lederer as "a man of eminent purity & dignity of mind, with great refinement of manner & mental cultivation." An amateur mineralogist and botanist, the elderly baron found a kindred spirit in young Downing. Together they often roamed the picturesque hills near Newburgh, outings Caroline Downing termed "excursions in search of specimens illustrating their favorite studies." Downing must have found the times he spent with the baron rewarding, for later in life he kept a cabinet, prominently positioned in the hall of his residence, displaying many of the items he had collected during their long walks together.[19]

A second important friend was Raphael Hoyle, an English-born landscape painter whose family had settled in Newburgh as early as 1823, when Hoyle's father, William, established a business there as a draper and tailor. Although the painter was more than a decade older than Downing, he was an "intimate friend" to the young horticulturist, according to Charles Downing. The two men shared a strong interest in nature, and they became companions on frequent expeditions through the Hudson Highlands, Hoyle sketching picturesque scenes and Downing studying and collecting native plants. Hoyle was elected an associate member of the National Academy of Design in 1829 and a full member two years later. Thomas S. Cummings, secretary and historian of the academy, described Hoyle as "an artist of merit" who contributed twenty paintings to its annual exhibitions. Upon studying his *View of the Susquehanna River,* an anonymous reviewer observed: "Mr. Hoyle is one who never oversteps the modesty of nature. His landscapes have a quiet in them, that is delightfully characteristick; and they possess the charms of truth's sweetness, (we know no other word that will better convey our meaning,) softness, and a retiringness of distance with obscurity, that we do not remember in the works of any other painter." Another contemporary described Hoyle's paintings as "true to nature, and of remarkable delicacy of coloring."[20]

Hoyle cultivated Downing's "sensibility to artistic beauty," Marshall P. Wilder wrote in 1852. At the time of his death, Hoyle had been selected as an artist to accompany the U.S. Exploring Expedition of 1838–42. His death in 1838 left "a void which many years may not fill," observed the *Newburgh Telegraph.* "Amiable, generous to a fault, affable, and conciliating, as a son brother and friend, few will be more sincerely mourned." Hoyle bequeathed to his friend Downing an oil painting of the Green Mountains, which for the rest of Downing's life hung in the parlor of his residence—fitting testament to the memory of a boyhood friend and also a reminder of the close relationship between landscape painting and gardening.[21]

In retrospect, von Lederer and Hoyle seem representative of two aspects of Downing's professional development. The baron apparently also provided the young man entry into the realm of wealth and gentility. Caroline Downing recalled that the "attraction of the Baron's family circle was enhanced by the society of his wife & daughter, two most accomplished & cultivated women, who made the home & the table of the interesting foreigner very attractive to the young man so kindly & gracefully received there." Another social influence, Wilder acknowledged, was Edward Armstrong, who lived in an elegant Greek Revival temple near Danskammer Point, north of Newburgh. Downing's manners, Wilder wrote, "were much improved and adorned by his familiar intercourse" with Armstrong, who was "a gentleman of refinement and wealth." Moreover, at Armstrong's home Downing "made the acquaintance of many other distinguished men, who subsequently became his correspondents and personal friends." According to Caroline Downing, these "associations had no doubt much influence in strengthening his naturally refined taste & generous nature."[22] This introduction of Armstrong as a significant influence on Downing, and especially the emphasis on wealth and taste, neglected an important point, however. The two men must have been drawn together by kindred interests, much as Downing and von Lederer had been. Armstrong was an active member of the Horticultural Society of Newburgh and delivered an address at its fifth anniversary gala.[23]

The descriptions of Downing's early years, by family, friends, and acquaintances, present a composite of an ambitious youth who was generously aided by men who usually were significantly older but who nevertheless took a keen interest in the young man. Predictably, each account focuses on areas that would be important to the mature Downing's career: the scientific knowledge he would display in numerous writings, but most notably in *The Fruits and Fruit Trees of America* (1845); the aesthetic development that contributed to his work as a landscape gardener and popularizer of artistic taste; and the self-educated individual who nevertheless acquired the social graces that were essential to collaboration with a wealthy clientele and central to his conception of the role of a gentleman of taste in a democratic society. Perhaps because of propriety, these accounts failed to mention the person who undoubtedly exerted the most important influence on Downing, Charles Downing, whose careful research informed the pages of *Fruits and Fruit Trees*, whose management of the nursery enabled his younger brother to devote considerable time to study and writing, and whose love and respect must have been of incalculable value. These reminiscences are nevertheless important, both because they represent efforts by persons who knew him well to understand the factors that contributed to his later success and because they have shaped virtually everything written about Downing since his death.

ﹾ During the mid-1830s, when he was actively involved in the nursery, Downing published the first of his essays directed to a general audience. The two pieces, published in the *New-York Mirror* in 1835, celebrate scenes of natural beauty and historic interest in the vicinity of Newburgh that may well have been places he visited with von Lederer and Hoyle. The prose style combines matter-of-fact descriptions of landscape with romantic allusions befitting a nineteen-year-old author, but the theme of the essays—the superiority of cultivated nature over the sublime, of pastoral civilization over wilderness—would remain central to Downing's writings, to his conception of the promise of American society, in later years. The first essay, "Beacon Hill," led readers to the summit of Mount Beacon, directly across the Hudson from Newburgh. Named for the beacon fires that had alerted Washington's troops to the movement of the British army during the waning days of the American Revolution, Mount Beacon was, to Downing's untraveled eye, one of nature's "most majestick thrones." He compared the view favorably to better-known prospects in the Catskills, which were too sublime for his taste. From Mount Beacon, he wrote, "in every direction the country is full of beauty, and presents a luxuriant and cultivated appearance."[24]

The second essay was a "reverie" at Dans Kamer, a flat rock that projected into the Hudson north of Newburgh. The northernmost point of Newburgh Bay, this was a locale celebrated by Washington Irving as a ceremonial pow-wow ground for Native Americans. Downing, who praised Irving for preserving the "rich old legends and antiquarian scraps" of the river's history, amply described the autumnal splendor of the vicinity. He then reflected on the history of the site, and particularly the plight of the Indians. Although he was saddened by the "extinction of the thousand tribes of our fellow-beings," Downing was hardly a sympathetic ethnographer: he gave credence to the suggestion that Native Americans were violent, barbaric "conquerers and destroyers of a former race far more advanced in the arts and conveniences than themselves," and whose "highest pleasure seems to have been the cruel scalping of their prisoners." The canoe had given way to the tall sloop and the steamboat, the "wild yell of the savage" had been replaced by the ringing of the church bell, and where wigwams once stood were "a thousand cheerful homes gleaming in the sunshine." What best characterized the changes wrought by civilization, Downing implied, was the domestication of the landscape, the establishment of homes, farms, and villages: the "once dense wilderness," he wrote approvingly, "has disappeared under the hands of civilized man."[25]

But civilization was not progressing quickly enough, even within the confines of the village of Newburgh. Thus, while continuing to work in the nursery and exploring his interests in landscape and aesthetics, Downing also began a period of intense involvement in efforts to raise the level of civilization and culture in his native village. Caroline Downing's words describing the purpose of Downing's better-known books and of the *Horticulturist*—"to direct attention to every practical opportunity for the social and artistic advancement of his countrymen"—were equally true of his efforts to establish cultural institutions and otherwise improve the quality of life in Newburgh.[26]

In March 1835, while still in his nineteenth year, Downing was one of twelve citizens named to study the "propriety of establishing a PUBLIC LIBRARY in connection with an association for the general diffusion of knowledge," as

the *Newburgh Telegraph* put it. The Newburgh Library Association was organized as a joint stock corporation the following December and began collecting books, but, during the first year of its existence, at least, accomplished
little else. In 1836, however, a new group of seven trustees elected Downing
president and the institution began a period of energetic activity.[27] Downing
hosted a fund-raising gala for the library at the nursery, which the *Telegraph*
described as featuring "numerous long aisles studded on either side with
plants of all seasons and climes, and with the beautiful dahlia and other
choice flowers in full bloom, all lighted at short intervals with arches of var-
iegated lamps." The overall effect was "a most enchanting scene," complete
with music from the West Point Band. In December 1836 the association
sponsored an address by the Reverend James R. Wilson at its first annual
meeting. Increased funding from such events and from memberships—at the
cost of $3 per share and unspecified quarterly dues—enabled the library to
take rooms at 29 Water Street and open to the public two afternoons and
evenings each week. Holdings included 1,200 volumes and current subscriptions to the "most valuable and popular of the Foreign and American periodicals."[28]

Although it was a membership organization supported by private subscriptions rather than governmental funds, Downing thought of the Newburgh Library Association as a public institution. The annual report that he
wrote on behalf of the trustees praised the "eagerness with which all classes of
our citizens have come forward to subscribe" to the library and patronize its
rooms. Equally important, the library would function as an extension of the
educational system. "The formal routine of school or college education,"
Downing wrote, perhaps thinking of his own intellectual development, "is
not the only desideratum in bringing out the latent faculties of the mind."
Pointing to recent efforts in France to establish libraries in every village, he
contrasted the benefit derived from the private collections of royalty with that
which he anticipated from "the possession of a well chosen selection of volumes in every little town and village and open to every class of the people."
Public libraries, he concluded, were the cornerstone of an enlightened citi-
zenry and the guarantor of America's republican institutions.[29]

Downing also became involved in the founding of the Newburgh
Lyceum, a related institution for popular education. On December 20, 1837, a
group of citizens met and recommended the "establishment in this village of
a Lyceum for the acquisition and diffusion of useful knowledge." Participants
at the meeting appointed a nine-member committee—including Downing
and several other trustees of the library association—to draft a constitution
and launch the society. An editorial notice in the *Telegraph* predicted that the
lyceum "would add greatly to the stock of information abroad among our

citizens, and of course measurably to the credit of our village."[30] The constitution of the lyceum, adopted in January 1838, called for public education through "lectures, essays, discussions, and experiments, with the gradual collection of a cabinet of natural curiosities, philosophical apparatus, and the requisite text books and scientific periodicals." Members paid an initiation fee of $3 and annual dues of $2.[31] Perhaps because of his continuing responsibilities as president of the library, perhaps because of his impending marriage or business commitments, Downing did not serve as an officer of the lyceum; but he surely attended its meetings, which included lectures on natural science, physical geography, moral philosophy, and agriculture, as well as discussions of such topics as the abolition of slavery in the District of Columbia and the question of public versus private education.[32]

Downing's involvement in the founding of the Newburgh Library Association and the Newburgh Lyceum were first steps toward creating the kinds of institutions of popular education he considered essential for the future of American society. In subsequent years he would continue to play an important role in Newburgh's cultural development—most obviously through the landscapes and buildings he designed, but also by contributing to the cost of acquiring and improving the grounds of the new county court house.[33] Each of these efforts anticipated Downing's clarion call for cultural reform, which he published as "The New-York Park" in the August 1851 issue of the *Horticulturist*: "Open wide, therefore, the doors of your libraries and picture galleries, all ye true republicans! Build halls where knowledge shall be freely diffused among men, and not shut up within the narrow walls of narrower institutions. Plant spacious parks in your cities, and unloose their gates as wide as the gates of morning to the whole people."[34]

❧ Downing's commitment to the Newburgh community was solidified by his courtship of Caroline Elizabeth DeWint, whom he married on June 7, 1838.[35] Caroline Downing was the oldest daughter of John Peter and Caroline Smith DeWint of Fishkill Landing (now Beacon), New York. Mrs. DeWint was the niece of John Quincy Adams. Her husband, an amateur horticulturist of note, had amassed substantial wealth through the Caribbean sugar trade and was also deeply involved in real estate speculation, both in Dutchess County, across the Hudson, and in Newburgh, where he owned a substantial business block on Water Street between Third and Fourth streets, as well as other properties.[36] DeWint was a stockholder in several Newburgh enterprises, including the Newburgh Whaling Company, and was an owner of the ferry service on the Hudson. A prominent booster of the local economy, he invested $25,000 in the construction of a Newburgh spur of the Erie Railroad and contributed the second largest amount toward the purchase and improvement of the court house grounds.[37]

The wedding of A. J. Downing and Caroline DeWint was "a grand affair, a dance and supper." Although on the surface it may appear that Downing, the son of a wheelwright, had gained wealth and social status through marriage, it is helpful to recall that the published announcement of the wedding identified Downing as "Esq."—gentleman—a designation used infrequently in such notices and the same standing attributed to the father of the bride. No pictures of Caroline Downing have come to light, but contemporaries who knew the Downings well invariably described her as a bright, convivial woman. Fredrika Bremer, for example, described her as "charming, merry, and amiable . . . of a highly cultivated mind, and equal to her husband."[38] She was not simply "the sweet wife" who filled his life with "days of peace and pleasantness." Caroline Downing was a talented woman in her own right, deeply interested in the arts, a devoted reader of the works of Ralph Waldo Emerson and the poems of William Cullen Bryant. These same traits were manifested by several of her sisters, who, like Caroline, married artistically inclined men—the transcendentalist, minister, and aspiring artist Christopher Pearse Cranch, art critic Clarence Cook, and architect Frederick C. Withers. Long after Downing's death, Caroline, who had subsequently married her first husband's longtime friend, John J. Monell, persuaded Frederick Law Olmsted to undertake revisions to Downing's *Cottage Residences* (a task he never completed) and spearheaded the creation of Andrew Jackson Downing Memorial Park in Newburgh.[39]

Soon after the wedding Downing began designing a house that would, simultaneously, be a testament of the standing he had achieved in the community and a powerful statement of a new architectural aesthetic. Until that time few buildings in Newburgh could claim architectural distinction. The Greek Revival Dutch Reformed Church designed by A. J. Davis was an important exception; other noteworthy structures included the chaste St. George's Church, with a small but handsome cupola attributed to Calvin Pollard, and five attached Greek Revival townhouses on First Street called Quality Row. The only structure exhibiting a new direction in taste was the Theological Seminary of the Associate Reformed Synod, designed by stonecutter Thornton M. Nevin and completed in 1839.[40] Unfortunately, most of the Gothic Revival details of the building—drip moldings, crenelations above the eaves, and vaguely Gothic chimneys—were incongruously grafted to a late Georgian block complete with projecting central pavilion and quoins. If an 1839 lithograph of the seminary is an accurate representation of its setting, Downing would have been appalled at the axial treatment of the landscape, especially for a "picturesque" building prominently located on a steep hillside overlooking the village. In short, there was little precedent in Newburgh for the kind of house Downing wanted to build. In designing an appropriate home for himself and his new bride, Downing may well have been attempting to provide precisely the kind of example of architectural excellence he believed would influence others planning to build their own dwellings.[41] His house, located just north of the cottage in which he was born, would champion a new, romantic aesthetic, and stand in juxtaposition to the blocks of vernacular and classical buildings that dominated Newburgh's townscape.

For the design of the new residence (fig. 3), Downing looked to English sources as inspiration. Clarence Cook believed that at the time he was preparing the plans Downing's "ideas of such matters were procured from one or two English books." These may well have been Francis Goodwin's *Rural Architecture* (1835) and John Claudius Loudon's *Encyclopaedia of Cottage, Farm, and Villa Architecture* (1832): Downing thought highly enough of these works to suggest them to "readers who desire to cultivate a taste for rural architecture."[42] The overall massing of the new house and the projecting entrance porch clearly derive from Goodwin's illustration of an "Elizabethan" villa (fig. 4), while other features bear strong resemblance to a design for a villa in the

Figure 3. Downing's residence, Newburgh, N.Y., built 1838–39 and demolished ca. 1922, from Downing, *A Treatise on the Theory and Practice of Landscape Gardening*, 2d ed. (New York, 1844). Courtesy of Shadek-Fackenthal Library, Franklin & Marshall College.

"pointed" style published in Loudon's *Encyclopaedia*.[43] What is important is that Downing assembled working plans by combining elements of at least two published building designs, and in doing so created one that was simpler and more harmonious than either of his models. Equally important, Downing consciously adapted English ideas to the climate and social conditions of the United States. A prominent example of this is the porch, or veranda, which extended across the façade and which Downing considered an essential accommodation to climate, because it provided shade for the principal rooms as well as a sheltered outside seating area. Verandas were also important as a means of uniting house and garden in a single composition and as an "expression of purpose" in a dwelling.[44]

Residents of Newburgh who observed Downing's house taking shape must have been startled by the design of the structure. Instead of the vernacular classicism that dominated local building the new house was aggressively Gothic, with two towers that flanked a boldly projecting entrance porch. The central pavilion, which contained the hall and library, was twenty feet wide by thirty-four feet deep, while the wings, which contained the parlor to the south and dining room and service areas to the north, were each roughly twenty-two by twenty-five feet. Drip moldings, belt courses, shields, and clustered chimneys all incorporated Gothic elements and contributed to the success of the building as a work of architecture. Moreover, Downing located the

Figure 4. "A Villa in the Elizabethan style," from Francis Goodwin, *Rural Architecture* (London, 1835). Courtesy of Special Collections, Morris Library, University of Delaware.

house so as to take advantage of views of the Hudson and the mountains, to the east, and included interior spaces designed to accommodate the various uses he and his wife must have anticipated.[45]

Contemporaries usually described Downing's house as built of stone, but at least one writer recognized the actual medium and noticed the artistry with which a less expensive material, stucco, had been substituted for a more costly one. Describing another Gothic Revival residence, designed by A. J. Davis, that used the technique, this author noted that the exterior walls were "laid off into courses, and colored in imitation of stone," and commended this as a "beautiful manner of building" as well as a durable one. This was amply demonstrated by similar use of stucco in other notable buildings, the author added, including Downing's residence at Newburgh. Downing was pleased enough with the result that he later recommended to others the man who had stuccoed this house, New York plasterer George Gill.[46] Cost may have been a factor in Downing's decision to use stucco rather than stone, because the house apparently was heavily mortgaged. Downing's estate carried at least two mortgages that derived from the construction—a $2,000 note dated October 15, 1839, and a $3,000 note dated November 15, 1841, the latter probably a refinancing of an earlier, short-term loan—while a third, a $4,000 loan issued by the Highland Bank, may well also have been a refinancing of another construction loan. During the months the house was under construction the Downings lived with Caroline's family in Fishkill Landing, and Downing made daily trips to Newburgh to superintend the construction and to conduct the nursery business.[47]

Downing's mother, Eunice, died at the end of October 1838. In March 1839, Charles and Andrew divided the family property. Andrew received the 4½ acre lot on which he was building his home, Charles the 4½ acre lot to the east, and the brothers retained joint ownership of a third lot, a 2¾ acre parcel south of Broad Street between Grand and Montgomery streets.[48]

As the house neared completion, Downing undoubtedly turned his attention to the grounds, which formerly had been part of the nursery. An 1853 description of the property noted that prior to the construction of Downing's house "by far the greater part of it was planted as a nursery; and in altering it . . . , a large proportion of the fruit trees had to be entirely given up or transplanted."[49] An 1841 plan of the grounds (fig. 5) demonstrates how effectively Downing combined a domestic landscape with the grounds of a working nursery. From Broad Street, an entrance drive led carriages into the property and then swept east in a gentle curve, providing a view of the house across a verdant lawn planted with flower beds, tropical plants in pots, and a sundial. Carefully placed plantings obscured the nursery grounds to the east, but because of the slope of the ground, the property retained views from the house to the river. South of the house were the buildings associated with the nursery—the cottage, then functioning as the residence of Downing's assistant, Andrew Saul, a greenhouse, stable, and packing house—all screened by a curving hedge of arbor vitae that the Downing brothers had planted about 1834.[50] The areas north and west of the residence continued to function as a nursery, as did the adjacent property owned by Charles Downing and the lot the brothers owned in common.[51] The grounds—ornamental garden and nursery—were at once a part of the village and yet removed from it: the plantings created visual barriers that obscured the commercial activity to the south and east. From Downing's property, wrote George William Curtis, "the enchanted visitor saw only the garden ending in the thicket, which was so dexterously trimmed as to reveal the loveliest glimpses of the river, each a pic-

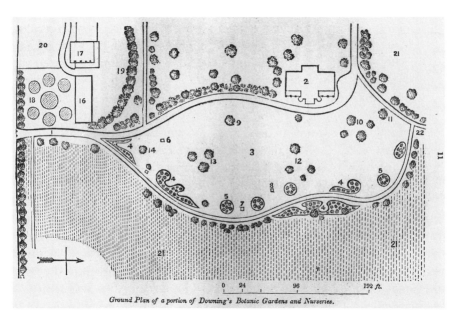

Ground Plan of a portion of Downing's Botanic Gardens and Nurseries.

Figure 5. Downing's garden in 1841, from the *Magazine of Horticulture* 7 (Nov. 1841), p. 404. Courtesy of Special Collections, Morris Library, University of Delaware. The numbers on the plan indicate the following features: *1*, carriage road; *2*, house; *3*, lawn; *4*, arabesque beds for choice flowers; *5*, circular beds; *6*, sun dial; *7*, large palms in pots, or Maltese vases; *8*, rustic basket for flowers; *9*, fine specimen of arbor vitae; *10*, group of magnolias; *11*, specimen of Wahoo elm; *12*, group of trees (Osage orange, American linden, weeping cherry, and Virgilia lutea); *13*, group composed of Sophora japonica, Acer striatum, A. Negundo; *14*, weeping ash; *15*, Salisburia adiantifolia; *16*, greenhouse; *17*, gardener's house; *18*, flower garden; *19*, hedge or screen or arbor vitae; *20*, stables, house for packing trees, etc.; *21*, nursery grounds; *22*, walk.

ture in its frame of foliage, but which was not cut low enough to betray the presence of road or town. You fancied the estate extended to the river; yes, and probably owned the river as an ornament, and included the mountains beyond."[52]

Downing's new home was a striking, imposing building. Its "bold yet unassuming" presence proclaimed that the owner was a person of substance and announced that Downing was an apostle of taste, ready to lead the vanguard of his disciples toward a new direction in taste. The decision to illustrate his new residence in the *Treatise,* as part of the chapter devoted to rural architecture, and also to allow C. M. Hovey to publish the same view in the November 1841 *Magazine of Horticulture,* was a measure of Downing's confidence that the house combined elements of Gothic architecture in a way that made them suitable for the American public.[53] The house was also a prominent landmark, visible to travelers on the Hudson River, which was an important transportation artery. A writer in 1845 described Downing's dwelling, seen from that vantage, as "a chaste and finished villa, in the Tudor gothic style, with growing trees surrounding it." The house and grounds were not only testament to Downing's taste but were "a fine practical illustration, as well as an acceptable theory, of both Architecture and Gardening."[54]

Downing's domestic landscape quickly became his most immediately recognizable aesthetic statement. Curtis, who considered the dwelling Downing's "finest work," asserted that it was designed as an attempt "to prove that a beautiful, and durable, and convenient mansion, could be built as cheaply as a poor and tasteless temple, which seemed to be, at that time, the highest American conception of a fine residence." To Clarence Cook, Downing's residence, designed in his early twenties and without any training in architecture, was "surprising evidence of . . . genius." Although Curtis believed that Downing's house did not "satisfy his maturer eye," and Cook expected him to make improvements to the garden, especially the enlargement of the lawn, the house and grounds were nevertheless an important cultural statement of the aesthetics, and the aspirations, of its owner.[55] This was a controlled landscape, far removed from the wilderness Downing decried in his essays about Beacon Hill and Dans Kamer, a landscape that bore the impress of civilization. The house and grounds were the designs of a young man confident in his taste, willing to translate his ideas into physical form, and eager to hold them up as an example, both to residents of Newburgh and, through engraving, to the American people.

ℐℴ When the Downings began living in the new residence, in late 1839, Andrew Jackson Downing was twenty-four years old. Professionally he was a successful nurseryman and widely published in the periodical press, while his involvement in the library and other cultural endeavors brought him into close association with the leaders of the community. Downing's home may well have asserted his place within Newburgh's elite, for, like the dwellings of the merchant freighters, it stood above and apart from the bustle of economic activity. From the south chamber on the second floor of his dwelling, where for the next thirteen years he would write books and essays that influenced the direction of American culture, Downing could look east, toward the river and mountains, or south, toward the town and the commerce that was essential to his own prosperity. The content of his writings and the screen of trees near the southern end of the property make clear that he preferred the view east, over a handsome garden and majestic landscape, emblems of the taste he had already begun to promote.

During the preceding decade, Downing had shaped a life for himself, just as Clarence Cook surmised he had. He had developed a broad knowledge of his profession as well as the literary skills that would enable his better-known books to reach a broad audience. He had established friendships with a number of individuals who would support his various activities in the years to come, including architect Alexander Jackson Davis, horticulturist and agricultural reformer Jesse Buel, and publisher Charles Mason Hovey. His correspondence extended widely throughout the United States and included John Claudius Loudon, the English landscape gardener and prolific writer. Downing had, through his various activities in Newburgh, developed an interest in virtually all the themes that would consume his professional life. He had, in short, established a role for himself as an apostle of taste; and the publication of the book he was writing, *A Treatise on the Theory and Practice of Landscape Gardening,* would bring Downing's considerable talents to the attention of the American public. Although in subsequent years his profession would lead him far from Newburgh, and he would not be able to maintain his earlier level of involvement with the community's developing institutions, Downing's youthful experiences in Newburgh nurtured his career.

2

The Making of the *Treatise*

*If ever writer incarnated his very nature in his work, truly and
entirely, it was done by A. J. Downing.* —Fredrika Bremer

In April 1841 Wiley and Putnam published Downing's first book, *A Treatise on the Theory and Practice of Landscape Gardening, Adapted to North America*. The author hoped to contribute to the "improvement of country residences," and so the topics listed in a lengthy subtitle included "Horticultural Notices and General Principles of the Art, Directions for laying out Grounds, and arranging Plantations, the Description and Cultivation of Hardy Trees, Decorative Accompaniments to the House and Grounds, the Formation of Pieces of Artificial Water, Flower Gardens, &c., With Remarks on Rural Architecture." Gracefully written and handsomely illustrated, the *Treatise* quickly became the best selling and most widely influential book of its type published in nineteenth-century America. Despite the expensive price of $3.50, it went through four editions and sold approximately 9,000 copies during the next twelve years; it remained in print well into the twentieth century.[1]

Although the *Treatise* eventually proved such a success, Downing experienced considerable difficulty securing a publisher. In July 1838 the *Cultivator* reported that Downing was "about to publish a work on our forest trees, and ornamental planting" and described the author as "eminently qualified" for the task. Six months later C. M. Hovey's *Magazine of Horticulture* noted the probable publication, in the spring of 1839, of a book by Downing on "the forest trees and shrubs of America and Europe, with observations upon their arrangement in both the picturesque and gardenesque styles, &c."[2] Neither prediction of the time of publication proved accurate. Landscape gardening was "completely unknown" as an art, Hovey recalled, and potential publishers had "little idea of the value of such a work." By late 1840, when Downing finally reached agreement with Wiley and Putnam, the *Treatise* had become a very different book from the one he had originally envisioned.[3]

It is impossible to reconstruct the precise evolution of the *Treatise*, but

Downing wrote several letters to Hovey that explained the purpose and content of the book in various stages of the preparation. In 1836, for example, he had given the work in progress the title "Arboriculture, or the Culture and Management of Forest, Ornamental and Fruit Trees, with their adaptation to Landscape Gardening, the Orchard, the Arts, &c." At this stage of Downing's conceptualization, the volume would have been a "little work," Hovey later surmised, and would have included information on "the principles of taste in arranging trees, the effect produced, &c." By October 1838 Downing had "nearly completed" a book of 270 pages, to be illustrated with twelve to eighteen lithographs, on "The Improvement of Country Residences, &c." Half of the text was devoted to "a description of all the finest hardy ornamental and forest trees of both hemispheres, with remarks on their effect in landscape gardening, both singly and in composition," while the remainder was "a short treatise on modern Landscape Gardening—the arrangement of plantations—disposition of grounds—architectural decorations, buildings, &c." Some time thereafter, probably 1839, Downing envisioned a still longer volume illustrated with "handsome wood engravings." The chapter on "rural architecture" would have included "views of some of our prettiest cottages and villas on the North [Hudson] River, Washington Irving's among the rest." In March 1839 Downing still expected that the book would be published no later than September.[4]

The evolution of the *Treatise* is an important indication of the development of Downing's ideas. Even in its earliest formulation he had intended to demonstrate how to apply the knowledge of plants to landscape gardening, but apparently this was secondary in importance to horticultural matters. As the text he was writing increased in length, and perhaps as Downing's interests matured, the emphasis changed: *Landscape Gardening* replaced *Arboriculture* in the tentative title, and the opening sections, which set the tone for the book, were devoted to discussions of the historical development of styles in the garden and the "beauties and principles of the art." By November 1840 Downing was referring to the forthcoming volume as "Landscape Gardening and Rural Architecture," which became its familiar title shortly after publication. Trees, once the central focus, had become elements of composition, part of the palette of the landscape gardener.[5]

Even as he reshaped the content of the *Treatise* Downing also struggled to determine the appropriate audience for his ideas. "One of the most perplexing difficulties I have met with in composing my essay," he informed Robert Donaldson in December 1840, "has been to adapt myself properly to the views of our countrymen and to the prospective scale of the art in this country." Some potential readers wanted a heavy dose of theory, others "practical observation"; some were interested in learning how to arrange a large estate, others grounds of moderate extent, while "a large number," he believed, wanted "*exact plans* for small places to be carried into execution in an easy and economical manner." Downing concluded that his role was to educate the public taste: Americans had no difficulty in following plans but needed instruction in "the leading principles of the art." Thus he determined his authorial strategy: "to raise the standard rather than come down entirely to the practical view and wants of many of our countrymen."[6]

✏ In its various stages of preparation, the *Treatise* reflected Downing's development both as a scientific horticulturist and as a landscape artist. Many of the ideas incorporated in the book Downing first explored in a series of articles written during the 1830s. Between 1835 and 1840, for example, he published in the *Magazine of Horticulture*, sometimes in collaboration with Charles Downing, at least seventeen articles and twenty-four notes that might be described as scientific or technical. Articles on similar subjects appeared in *Horticultural Register, New-York Farmer, New England Farmer,* and perhaps other periodicals as well. Although the frequent use of expressions such as "descriptive notice" or "observations on" or "remarks on" in the titles of these articles may suggest gentlemanly avocation or casual engagement with the subject, Downing was indeed scientific, at least in his emphasis on experimentation and the publication of findings. His articles are punctuated with phrases such as "we have never found it to answer our expectations upon trial," or "recent experiments have also proved," or "from many and repeated observations."[7] When Downing disputed a theory on the declining yield of fruit-bearing trees propounded by Thomas A. Knight, president of the Horticultural Society of London and one of Europe's leading horticulturists, and confirmed by Professor Jean Baptiste Van Mons, of Brussels, he did so based on empirical results. Europeans, he claimed, had too readily accepted the theory, without "a recurrence to those careful practical observations which ought to influence strongly the conclusions at which it is desirable to arrive." Years of testing and observing grafts—"accumulated experience," in his words— led the twenty-one-year-old Downing to a different conclusion, that there was nothing inevitable about the declining duration of fruit trees and that the phenomenon Knight and Van Mons described was the result of the improper grafting of unhealthy and healthy stock.[8]

Downing's horticultural efforts earned the respect of at least several prominent scientists. Asa Gray and John Torrey acknowledged Downing in their landmark work, *A Flora of North America* (1838–40), and Torrey later named a newly discovered genus of California plants in Downing's memory.[9] Downing addressed the Lyceum of Natural History in New York City, whose members were a powerful force in the professionalization of science, and entitled his talk "Remarks on the Natural Order Cycadaceae, with a description of the Ovula and Seeds of Cycas revoluta." The text was subsequently published in *Silliman's Journal* and excerpted in C. M. Hovey's *Magazine of Horticulture*.[10] He also contributed an essay arguing the superiority of native fruits that was published in the first volume of the *Transactions* of the Massachusetts Horticultural Society.[11]

The scientific accuracy of Downing's horticulture was not, of course, infallible. One notable instance in which he proved to be profoundly wrong was his assertion that, because of differences in soil and climate, foreign grapes would never become viable for winemaking in the United States. To be sure, Downing made this statement more than a decade before California became part of the United States and long before commercial winemaking became a significant part of the American economy. Moreover, he based his analysis largely on the published accounts of growers who had been unsuccessful in their attempts to naturalize European grapes. Even so, Downing's essay is, uncharacteristically, more indicative of patriotic sentiments and reformist impulse than of painstaking experimentation. He promoted the use of indigenous rather than imported vines in part because he believed that they would produce more abundantly and provide a better beverage. A thriving winemaking industry, he explained, would "lessen our heavy expenditures abroad, and . . . add another mighty link to our already extensive chain of agricultural resources." Downing also considered wine "an innocent and healthy drink" that promised an end to a major social problem: he praised the individuals who were developing American vineyards as benefactors who would save "thousands of our fellow creatures who go down to their graves victims to the intemperate use of distilled spirits."[12]

Downing's contributions to scientific horticulture have not been fully appreciated, perhaps because of a remark by Asa Gray that was published (without attribution) in Marshall P. Wilder's eulogy. Gray wrote of Downing, "Though not profoundly scientific, he was well grounded in vegetable physiology and the collateral branches of knowledge, and his quickness, tact, and practical good sense in applying his knowledge was quite remarkable."[13] Best remembered as a professor of natural history at Harvard and a staunch supporter of Charles Darwin, Gray studied under botanist John Torrey and in 1836–37 was curator of the Lyceum of Natural History in New York City. He and Downing collaborated on an American edition of John Lindley's *Theory of Horticulture* (1841), for which Downing contributed a preface and each provided annotative notes, individually signed.[14]

What Gray meant by the phrase "not profoundly scientific" has proven difficult to decipher. Gray knew firsthand Downing's horticultural writings, so his assessment may have referred to Downing's artistic rather than rigorously scientific bent. He may have been thinking of the contrast between Lindley's *Theory of Horticulture,* a landmark in scientific botany, and Downing's *Treatise,* in which the theory is aesthetic rather than scientific. It is possible that Gray thought of Downing as someone eager to test ideas and evaluate experiments but not as a pioneer, leading science in new directions or positing new theories. Gray's colleagues at the Lyceum of Natural History were overwhelmingly graduates of the most prestigious colleges, "incipient professionals," in historian Thomas Bender's words, whereas Downing's formal education had ended in his sixteenth year and his experimental horticulture was directed toward practical applications. The differences in their writings about similar subjects may well reflect each man's professional orientation. In his *Manual of the Botany of the Northeastern United States* (1848), for example, Gray's treatment of the oak is straightforwardly descriptive of its characteristics, while Downing's evokes Arcadian lore and ancient and modern writings in celebration of the genus. Where they describe the same tree, the difference in the tenor of their respective accounts is significant. For the overcup or burr oak (*Quercus macrocarpa*), Gray wrote, "*Leaves obovate,* deeply and lyrately sinuate-lobed, pale or *downy underneath,* the lobes obtusely toothed." By contrast, Downing praised the burr oak as a "noble tree" with "uncommonly fine" foliage.[15] Although each identified the location of the species and provided the appropriate technical information, one text was written in the language of science, the other in words accessible to the general reader, especially someone seeking information about trees suitable for placement in the garden. Ultimately, then, Gray's assessment of Downing may have been an unintended testament to the distance that increasingly separated their two worlds—one professional and scientific, the other artistic and humanistic—during the years since they had first met, and it should not detract from the significance of Downing's efforts to promote horticultural knowledge. Indeed, the words Downing used to describe Lindley's *Theory of Horticulture* are equally applicable to his own writing: "It is at once remarkably simple, and highly philosophical; free from superfluous technicalities, and at the same time truly scientific."[16]

Downing also attempted to advance horticultural science in his role as a founder of the Horticultural Association of the Valley of the Hudson (fig. 6). Prior to his involvement in the launching of this organization, Downing had praised horticultural and agricultural societies for their contributions to the "increase and dissemination of information."[17] The new association was not the first such group to promote horticultural improvement in New York, and, indeed, similar societies flourished in New England, particularly in Massa-

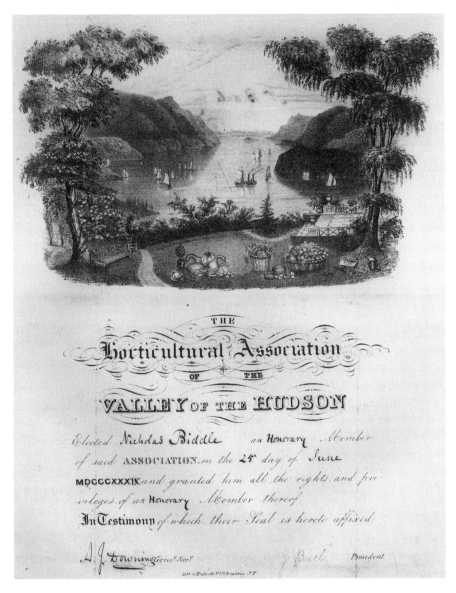

Figure 6. Certificate of Membership in the Horticultural Association of the Valley of the Hudson, presented to Nicholas Biddle as an honorary member and dated June 25, 1839. Downing's signature is at the lower left, Jesse Buel's at the lower right. The vignette appears to be a view from the southern gate of the Hudson Highlands. Bannerman's Island, between Storm King and Breakneck mountains, is in the distance. Courtesy of Franklin D. Roosevelt Library, Hyde Park, N.Y.

chusetts.[18] But existing horticultural societies were "too *local*" in orientation, explained the circular announcing the formation of the society, whereas the new association embraced "the whole of the river counties of the Hudson." This was an area diverse enough in climate and soil characteristics to provide the optimal conditions for comparative study, and it embraced numerous prosperous communities with commercial nurseries and the estates of wealthy individuals. The objects of the organization included "the promotion of Horticulture and the taste for rural improvements in general, by comparative exhibitions, at which medals and premiums shall be awarded, by procuring and disseminating choice fruits and plants; by experiments in culture through different sections of the territory embraced; [and] by lectures and essays on various subjects connected with the science and practice of Horticulture." Jesse Buel, a Whig judge and editor of the Albany *Cultivator,* who was nationally known for his efforts in horticultural and agricultural improvement, served as president, while John Torrey and a handful of other distinguished New Yorkers, including Philip S. Van Rensselaer, Edward Livingston, James Alexander Hamilton, and William Emerson, Ralph Waldo Emerson's older brother, were vice presidents. Downing, then in his twenty-third year, was corresponding secretary, a position that required him to communicate the affairs of the association to the periodical press.[19]

Downing's involvement in scientific horticulture was important for several reasons. Research and travel expanded his knowledge of plant materials and brought him into contact with leading American horticulturists, while his writings on the subject reached interested readers across the United States. Equally important, in the course of his visits to nurseries, country seats, and estates throughout the northeast, Downing met or learned of the work of a rising generation of architects and landscape gardeners. His quest for horticultural knowledge would prove to be enormously beneficial in the future.

✧ During the 1830s Downing also published several articles that addressed questions of landscape and architectural design, subjects that would become central to the *Treatise.* The first may well have been an 1832 essay entitled "Rural Embellishments," which advocated the "many advantages of the picturesque style." Signed "XYZ, Newburgh, N. Y.," the article praised the evidence of progress in horticulture but lamented that landscape gardening was "completely in its infancy" in the United States. Like some of Downing's signed articles of the mid-1830s, this essay castigated the overreliance on the axe that had been evident in earlier stages of settlement. The author observed approvingly, "[W]e begin to be as actively engaged in planting as our ancestors were in exterminating," though without, he added, adequate knowledge of the art of gardening. The most common practice was planting "a uniform row or cluster of trees immediately before the front of a mansion," a practice the author found deplorable in a country so well "adapted to the more picturesque method of grouping" trees and shrubs.[20] Whether or not he was the author of that essay, Downing sounded a similar note in 1834, when he expressed chagrin that "so little attention is paid to the planting of ornamental trees, with a view to the embellishment of our country residences." Although most of the later article was devoted to the description of trees, Downing once again noted that the destruction of forests which had accompanied the process of settlement was passing. It was time, he wrote, to "direct the attention of the [American] arboriculturist to our own trees."[21]

More indicative of Downing's developing concern for the interplay between horticulture and aesthetics was an essay on architecture that appeared in August 1836. Downing began by applauding "the rapid improvement in the taste for building," but the essay was hardly uncritical. Although he expressed appreciation for the "elegant proportions and chaste purity of style" of the Greek Revival, he denounced what he termed a "universal mania for the five orders." The Greek style was not only tiresome in its ubiquity, but its symmetry often proved antithetical to the "requirements of domestic life." Downing was also concerned that mock temples had been placed in settings that were highly inappropriate, especially locations that were "wilder, more romantic and picturesque." Downing was articulating two principles of design that would remain important in his later work, fitness and "harmony of expression with the landscape." Depending on the topography of the setting, he recommended Gothic, Italianate, or Swiss styles for domestic architecture.[22]

Even in its earliest stages Downing's crusade for more appropriate dwellings attempted to unite house and garden as a single composition. He urged readers to improve the "*situation* of the house" by locating it at a greater distance from the road and by creating grounds that exemplified "well cultivated and nicely discriminating taste." He also recommended the use of vases, especially for Greek Revival buildings, to give "additional charm" to highly finished lawns and gardens.[23]

Still other essays indicate Downing's interest in the history of horticulture and landscape design. In 1837, for example, he published a ten-page assessment of gardening in the United States that contained references extending back to antiquity. Most of Downing's article examined recent developments, particularly in the vicinity of Philadelphia, Boston, and the Hudson Valley, the commercial nurseries that supplied the wants of gardeners, and the ten American societies that promoted improvements in horticulture. He paid particular homage to the pioneering plantsman John Bartram, to whose horticultural discoveries he attributed the tradition of outstanding gardens in Philadelphia. "Filled with the love of nature and science," Downing wrote, "this naturalist explored, almost at the peril of his life, the swamps, the mountains, the borders of the lakes, and, in short, every part of North America, where he thought a beautiful plant or a new forest tree might be discovered." Although the overall tone of the essay celebrated the increasing prominence of horticulture, Downing expressed disappointment that none of the existing horticultural societies in the United States possessed "a single acre of land appropriated to the purposes of a public experimental garden!" He suggested the establishment of a public garden, supported by the federal government and modeled after the Jardin des Plantes in Paris, as the best means of overcoming this obstacle to horticultural progress.[24]

What is perhaps most surprising about Downing's writings on landscape and aesthetics in the 1830s is their paucity, especially when compared with the much larger number of essays he wrote on horticultural matters. This appears to corroborate evidence from surviving letters that document the evolution of Downing's *Treatise*, which began as a book on trees but became something quite different. It also suggests the importance of horticultural societies and journals to the emergence of landscape gardening in the United States.[25] Even while few in number, Downing's essays on taste introduced many of the themes that would be central to his later writings.

Collectively, the essays and notes Downing published during the 1830s demonstrate that he was carefully reading English and European books and journals devoted to horticulture and landscape design. They report on his extensive professional travel to examine horticultural discoveries—journeys that became a vehicle for the careful study of the best in American domestic architecture and garden design—as well as his immersion in the history of his chosen profession. Each of these themes, elaborated in the *Treatise* in far greater detail than was possible in brief essays, would contribute to the book's success.

✍ The state of landscape gardening in America had not improved dramatically since the late 1820s, when a committee of the New-York Horticultural Society described it as "yet in its infancy among us as an art."[26] To be sure, increasing wealth and taste were evident in the design of numerous homes, especially in the vicinity of cities, but the absence of a thoughtful, comprehensive book explicating the principles of landscape design and horticultural operations appropriate to American conditions was impeding similar progress in gardening. The need for such a book was "so frequently urged by persons desiring advice," Downing wrote in the preface to the *Treatise*, that he had "ventured to prepare the present volume in the hope of supplying, in some degree, the desideratum so much required."[27]

Downing opened the *Treatise* with three chapters, "Historical Sketches," "Beauties and Principles of the Art," and "On Wood," that together serve as a summary of the development of landscape gardening and an introduction to the author's philosophy of taste.[28] Downing defined landscape gardening as "an artistical combination of the beautiful in nature and art—an union of natural expression and harmonious cultivation." In succeeding pages he acknowledged two American antecedents of his own work: "The Pleasure, Or Flower-Garden" published in Bernard M'Mahon's *American Gardener's Calendar* (1806),[29] and the designs of the Belgian-born André Parmentier, a Brooklyn, New York, nurseryman best remembered as the landscape gardener for Hyde Park, David Hosack's Hudson River estate, whom Downing described as "the only practitioner of the art, of any note."[30]

Downing then traced the purposes and evolution of the garden from the ancient or geometric style to the modern or natural way of laying out grounds. Although the purpose of each style was beauty, the means of accomplishing this goal differed. The allées, parterres, and geometric elements of the ancient garden (fig. 7) resulted in a "studied and elegant regularity of design." Its beauties were "those of regularity, symmetry, and the display of labored art." Downing found a number of formal gardens praiseworthy: when good taste was appropriately combined with "highly decorated architecture," the effect could be "splendid and striking." But much of his account

Figure 7. The ancient or geometric style of landscape gardening, from Downing, *A Treatise on the Theory and Practice of Landscape Gardening,* 2d ed. (New York, 1844). Courtesy of Shadek-Fackenthal Library, Franklin & Marshall College.

of the formal garden was critical, especially descriptions of the French and Dutch gardens that, in his opinion, exhibited the "absurdities of the ancient style." Downing was particularly displeased with the formulaic approach of the geometric garden, in which beauty was too often "attained in a merely mechanical manner, and usually involved little or no theory."[31]

By contrast, the modern style attempted to "exhibit a highly graceful or picturesque epitome of natural beauty." Downing made no secret of his preference for the modern over the ancient style. Indeed, he posited a progression of taste from a formal, ordered garden to a naturalistic landscape. The geometric garden had been favored when eastern North America was still a "new country," in which primitive nature or wilderness predominated, because "the distinct exhibition of art would give more pleasure by contrast, than the elegant imitation of beautiful nature." Nevertheless, he felt that the settlers' reliance on the formal garden was evidence of "a meagre taste, and a lower state of the art, or a lower perception of beauty in the individual." Downing clearly hoped that the reader would follow his argument to its logical conclusion: that as the eastern United States had moved beyond the stage of a newly settled area, taste in landscape gardening should likewise evolve from the ancient or geometric to what he termed the "present more advanced state," the modern or natural style. His analysis of history, then, was more than an overview of changing taste in the landscape; it served as justification for the style of gardening he championed.[32]

As was true of the eighteenth- and early-nineteenth-century English writers whom he took as models, Downing divided taste in modern landscape gardening into two categories, the beautiful and the picturesque. What constituted beauty or picturesqueness in the landscape had been the subject of an intense debate in English artistic and philosophical circles for almost a century prior to the publication of Downing's *Treatise*. Edmund Burke's celebrated *Philosophical Enquiry into the Origin of Our Ideas of the Sublime and Beautiful* (1757) marked a clear break with Renaissance ideas of beauty, which he characterized as consisting of rationalist qualities such as proportion, and argued instead for the importance of what he termed an emotional response to works of art. Burke divided all objects into two classes, those that "cause love, or some passion similar to it," which he classified as beautiful, and those that "excite the ideas of pain, and danger," such as awe, terror, or astonishment, which he termed sublime. Although Burke did not address the picturesque as a separate category, by the last decades of the eighteenth century it had achieved prominence in its own right. William Gilpin, for example, identified a range of objects characterized by roughness of surface and irregularity of outline as possessing "picturesque beauty" and considered them a distinct category subsumed under Burke's beautiful. Sir Uvedale Price, by contrast, argued that objects that were rough, irregular, and characterized by "sudden variation" formed a distinct category in their own right, different from either the beautiful or the sublime, which he called the picturesque.[33]

This philosophical debate became an important part of the tradition in landscape gardening to which Downing's writings belong. Lancelot "Capability" Brown's landscapes of sweeping lawns, serpentine waters, and clumps or belts of trees epitomized the beautiful in landscape gardening and effectively banished the remnants of the ancient or formal garden from mid-eighteenth-century England; but with the rise of the picturesque, his work came under attack. Toward the end of the century Humphry Repton, Brown's most prominent successor, reintroduced the terrace and the use of formally designed gardens adjacent to the house. He also emphasized the importance of fitness, utility, and convenience in the garden as well as the relationship between landscape and architecture. Following Repton's death in 1818, John Claudius Loudon became the most prominent figure in nineteenth-century English garden design. A prolific writer, Loudon built upon Repton's legacy yet also took advantage of the new plants made available by the horticultural revolution of the early nineteenth century and emphasized individual trees and beds of exotic flowers, a style he termed "gardenesque."[34]

Downing clearly drew extensively upon the writings of English authors—the *Treatise* is punctuated with quotations from Alexander Pope, Thomas Whately, Thomas Hope, Price, Gilpin, and others—but it was to Repton and Loudon that he was most indebted. In the *Treatise*, Downing praised Repton's taste as "cultivated and elegant," while he acknowledged Loudon as "my valued correspondent." Although he described Loudon as someone who preferred "mere artistical beauty to that of expression"—a damning indictment, given that Downing considered expression the "master key to the heart"—and as a result found him "somewhat deficient as an artist, in imagination," Downing nevertheless praised Loudon as "the most distinguished gardening author of the age."[35] When John Lindley characterized Loudon as a "crotchetty man," Downing defended him as

> an ardent and unflinching advocate of the rights of the laboring classes. In all his works we see most strongly marked his desire to raise the British working man, so long degraded by the sway of caste, to his proper and natural position. To this end, he not only designed and published plans of cottages and grounds calculated to improve the social, physical and moral condition of the working class, but he held up to public censure those in high places, who forced their dependants to live in houses more comfortless than those of their domestic animals.[36]

Downing found in Loudon's voluminous writings information about new developments in gardening as well as a summary of the Reptonian principles of utility, fitness, and variety that Downing applied both to landscape and architectural design. From Repton's *Observations on the Theory and Practice of Landscape Gardening* (1803) and *Fragments on the Theory and Practice of Landscape Gardening* (1816) Downing clearly borrowed the title of the *Treatise,* while numerous references in the text indicate a careful reading of these and other of that author's writings. For example, he drew upon Repton to establish the eight "principal requisites" for roads in the "modern style."[37]

The *Treatise* was, in important respects, a derivative work. Especially in the first three chapters, Downing borrowed heavily from English authors to explain the history and principles of landscape gardening. Most of the remainder of the book is more original, especially the sections devoted to trees, shrubs, and other plants, the exception being the chapter entitled "Landscape or Rural Architecture," which again relies heavily on English precedents. For example, Downing informed Alexander Jackson Davis that he intended "to introduce two or three views of Lodges" similar to those published in Loudon's *Suburban Gardener.*[38] Downing readily acknowledged his dependence on earlier sources, but as English and American critics alike recognized, the value of the *Treatise* was the result of the author's ability to synthesize a vast amount of information, much of it abstract or philosophical, and to present it in a straightforward prose style that was at once scholarly and conversational in tone.

Following the lead of his English mentors, Downing described the beautiful and the picturesque as the cornerstones of the modern or natural style of landscape gardening and characterized them as "two species of beauty, of which the art is capable." The "graceful" style, the name Downing chose to describe the beautiful in the first two editions of the *Treatise,* was "nature or art obeying the universal laws of perfect existence (i.e., beauty), easily, freely, harmoniously, and without the *display* of power." It was an "idea of beauty calmly and harmoniously expressed," its forms, like those of a Repton landscape, "characterized by curved and flowing lines—lines expressive of infinity, of grace, and willing obedience." Downing's illustration of the graceful (fig. 8) captured precisely these qualities: the house is vaguely classical, with urns serving as a transition from building to landscape; the trees are round-headed, the lawn smooth and closely cropped, the drive and path follow a sweeping curve. Here was a serene, harmonious environment, a point made explicit by the figures of a woman and female child walking toward the house.[39]

The picturesque, by contrast, was "characterized by irregular and broken lines—lines expressive of violence, abrupt action, and partial disobedience, a struggling of the idea with the substance or the condition of its being." As a style of landscape gardening, it sought to achieve "the production of outlines of a certain spirited irregularity; surfaces comparatively abrupt and broken;

Figure 8. The graceful or beautiful in landscape gardening, from Downing, *A Treatise on the Theory and Practice of Landscape Gardening*, 2d ed. (New York, 1844). Courtesy of Shadek-Fackenthal Library, Franklin & Marshall College.

Figure 9. The picturesque in landscape gardening, from Downing, *A Treatise on the Theory and Practice of Landscape Gardening*, 2d ed. (New York, 1844). Courtesy of Shadek-Fackenthal Library, Franklin & Marshall College.

and growth, of a somewhat wild and bold character." The vignette of the picturesque (fig. 9) illustrated the different attributes of the style: the dwelling is a Rural Gothic cottage, the trees spiry-topped (conforming to the outlines of the mountains in the distance, which in the mid-nineteenth century served as symbols of masculinity), the lawn irregular in surface, and the rocky foreground overgrown with plants. The trees bear testament to nature's power, while a rustic shelter sits atop the hill to the right. This was a very different environment, a less ordered and controlled landscape, which Downing emphasized by placing the figure of a man with a dog walking down the path.[40]

Downing recommended both the graceful and the picturesque, though he clearly favored the roughness and variety of the latter.[41] The choice of style, he advised, had to be determined by the characteristics of the location, what Alexander Pope termed the "genius of the place": a relatively flat site would be more appropriate for development in the graceful style, while a rugged, hilly site would be more suitable for picturesque treatment. But, having chosen one or the other style, Downing cautioned, the improver must not attempt "to produce a fac-simile of nature." In the hands of a skillful improver landscape gardening could unite, "in the same scene, a richness and a variety never to be found in any one portion of nature." The landscape garden was not untouched nature but nature improved by art.[42]

To assist the reader in applying these concepts, Downing then articulated the principles of unity, harmony, and variety, which, he explained, were "universal and inherent beauties, common to all styles, and, indeed, to every composition in the fine arts." He described unity as "the *production of a whole*" and as a "leading principle of the highest importance" in every branch of art.

Figure 10. "View of a Country Residence, as frequently seen," from Downing, *A Treatise on the Theory and Practice of Landscape Gardening*, 2d ed. (New York, 1844). Courtesy of Shadek-Fackenthal Library, Franklin & Marshall College.

Unity necessitated some controlling idea, usually, in landscape gardening, determined by the physical characteristics of the site, as well as "some grand or leading features to which the others should be merely subordinate." The mixing of incongruous styles and other violations of unity, Downing wrote, "are always indicative of the absence of correct taste in art." Variety, which Downing described as "a fertile source of beauty," had to be kept subservient to the the whole. If unity required comprehension of the overall effect of the design, variety involved "details" that, when used properly, produced "intricacy" and "a thousand points of interest" in the landscape. Harmony was "the principle presiding over variety, and preventing it from becoming discordant." Because it restrained variety within the bounds of a unified composition, Downing considered harmony the most important of the three.[43]

Articulating these components of the theory of landscape gardening was central to Downing's effort to educate the public taste, but as the title of the *Treatise* indicates, practice was equally important. Thus, in the third chapter he provided examples of proper taste in landscape design. Two vignettes of the same country residence contrasted traditional building practice in rural areas and the superior attractions of the modern style, a technique Repton had used in his Red Books. The dwelling prior to improvement—"a portrait of a hundred familiar examples"—was "a plain unmeaning parallelogram"; a straight drive bordered by a regular belt of trees provided access from the road (fig. 10). In the companion view the "improved" house has become an "old English cottage," with its central gable, porch, and clustered chimneys strikingly similar to Design II in *Cottage Residences*; the plantings are less formal and the entrance drive has acquired a gentle sweep (fig. 11). "Effects like

Figure 11. "View of the same Residence, improved," from Downing, *A Treatise on the Theory and Practice of Landscape Gardening*, 2d ed. (New York, 1844). Courtesy of Shadek-Fackenthal Library, Franklin & Marshall College.

these," Downing advised, "are within the reach of very moderate means, and are peculiarly worth attention in this country, where so much has already been partially, and often badly executed."[44]

Other wood engravings illustrated ground plans for a country seat, a mansion residence, a suburban villa (Bishop Doane's Riverside, in Burlington, New Jersey, which was designed by architect John Notman), a *ferme ornée,* and a cottage. These ranged in size from very large to only a quarter of an acre. Downing advised that the plans were for illustrative purposes only and warned readers against attempting to copy them. In the modern style, he cautioned. it was "almost impossible that the same plan should exactly suit any other situation than that for which it was intended." The prospective improver should instead study nature and adapt the design of the property—of whatever size—to the specific conditions of the site.[45]

Downing's emphasis on the genius of the place extended from the proper style of landscape to the design of the house. In the preface to the *Treatise* he explained that the "lively interest of late manifested in Rural Architecture, and its close connexion with Landscape Gardening, have induced me to devote a portion of this work to the consideration of buildings in rural scenery." Downing insisted, first and foremost, that the style of architecture be appropriate to the setting. Indeed, he cautioned that the beauty of rural houses would be dependent upon whether they were "happily or unhappily combined with the adjacent scenery." To place a picturesque building in a graceful setting or a classical structure in rough, irregular terrain would be as inappropriate as erecting a five-story townhouse in the country.[46]

Following the lead of Repton and Loudon, Downing articulated three "leading principles" of rural architecture: fitness, expression of purpose, and expression of architectural style. Fitness involved both the selection of a proper site for the dwelling, preferably "middle grounds," neither too high to be exposed to the elements nor too low, where dampness might be injurious to health, and provision for the "comfort and convenience of the various members of the family." Expression of purpose, Downing wrote, is "that architectural character, or *ensemble,* which distinctly points out the particular use or destination for which the edifice is intended." The two elements that most directly announced the domestic purposes of a structure, especially in a rural setting, were chimney tops and porches. Chimney tops were "strongly indicative of human habitations," and the sight of smoke curling above a house suggested hearth and family. The porch, or veranda, functioned "both as a note of preparation, and an effectual shelter and protection to the entrance." Moreover, the porch served as a means of adapting English architectural ideas to the climate of the United States. Downing frequently noted that the porch not only sheltered the first floor rooms from extreme heat but provided a shaded seating area, a kind of American analogue to more formal paved terraces adjacent to English houses. So important was this feature to the expression of purpose, Downing wrote, that a house built without some entrance shelter was "as incomplete, to the correct eye, as a well-printed book without a title-page." The porch also served as a transition from house to garden, uniting the two in a single composition.[47]

For the average reader, architecture as "an art of taste" was undoubtedly more difficult to comprehend than the principles of fitness or expression of purpose. Downing therefore reviewed the origins of classic and romantic architecture, once again warning against the Greek Revival as unfit for American domestic life. The rigid symmetry of a Greek Revival dwelling (fig. 12) did not allow for rooms of different sizes to meet the various needs of a family, while it was almost impossible to build an addition to a "rectangular parallelogram" without destroying the very qualities that made the temple form attractive in the first place.[48] Although Roman architecture was "less perfect as a fine art" than the Greek, it was, in his opinion, a "more rich, varied, and, if we may use the term, *accommodating* style." But the style of architecture derived from classical principles for which Downing reserved greatest praise was the Italianate (fig. 13), which was "decidedly the most beautiful mode for domestic purposes, that has been the direct offspring of Grecian art." He es-

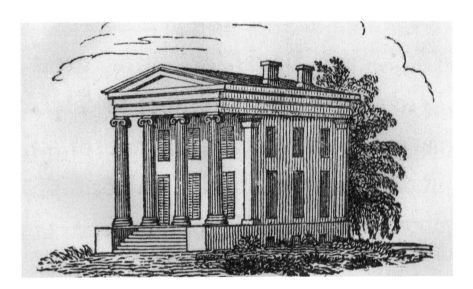

Figure 12. "Grecian Residence," from Downing, *A Treatise on the Theory and Practice of Landscape Gardening*, 2d ed. (New York, 1844), p. 353. Courtesy of Shadek-Fackenthal Library, Franklin & Marshall College.

Figure 13. "The New-Haven Suburban Villa," from Downing, *A Treatise on the Theory and Practice of Landscape Gardening*, 2d ed. (New York, 1844), p. 359. Courtesy of Shadek-Fackenthal Library, Franklin & Marshall College.

Figure 14. "The Swiss Cottage," from Downing, *A Treatise on the Theory and Practice of Landscape Gardening*, 2d ed. (New York, 1844), p. 363. Courtesy of Shadek-Fackenthal Library, Franklin & Marshall College.

pecially appreciated its "bold irregularity, and strong contrast of light and shadow" and recommended the Italianate as "admirably adapted to harmonize with general nature, and produce a pleasing and picturesque effect in fine landscapes." Downing also pointed out that even the most modest villa could achieve "elegant and expressive character" in the Italian style, while additions, instead of destroying symmetry, would enhance the building's picturesque appearance.[49] A variation on the Italianate was the Swiss style (fig. 14), which Downing described as "bold and spirited" as well as "highly picturesque and interesting." He found it an appropriate style of building for a "wild and mountainous region," where its broadly overhanging roof, supported by brackets, would be in keeping with the scenery.[50]

From the Swiss style Downing apparently derived the bracketed mode (fig. 15), which became one of his most important contributions to the American architectural vocabulary. The bracketed style was especially suited for smaller cottages and wood (preferably board-and-batten) construction, while its overhanging eaves were "entirely adapted" to the American climate. "We

Figure 15. "The Bracketed Mode," from Downing, *A Treatise on the Theory and Practice of Landscape Gardening*, 2d ed. (New York, 1844), p. 363. Courtesy of Shadek-Fackenthal Library, Franklin & Marshall College. This was the "cottage villa in the bracketed mode," Design V of *Cottage Residences*, as constructed of wood.

Figure 16. "The Castellated Mode," from Downing, *A Treatise on the Theory and Practice of Landscape Gardening*, 2d ed. (New York, 1844), p. 367. Courtesy of Shadek-Fackenthal Library, Franklin & Marshall College.

hope to see this Bracketed style becoming every day more common in the United States," Downing wrote in 1844, "and especially in our farm and country houses, when wood is the material employed in their construction."[51]

In much the way that all styles of classical architecture evolved from the Greek, Downing reasoned, so did the styles of romantic architecture descend from the Gothic. Just as he favored the picturesque over the graceful in landscape design, so did he consider the Gothic, which gave evidence of "much higher proofs of genius," superior to the Greek in architecture. Downing then reviewed the principal styles of Gothic architecture. The castellated (fig. 16) he considered "too ambitious and expensive . . . for a republic," whereas the Tudor afforded "the best example of the excellency of Gothic architecture for domestic purposes." The parapets or gables of the Tudor style (fig. 17) presented a striking outline against the sky, and its asymmetry provided flexibility in the arrangement of interior spaces. Hallmarks of this style included bay and oriel windows, which not only lighted the interior but provided views of the grounds surrounding the house, while the addition of a veranda adapted the English style to American climate. Although critics usually castigated Elizabethan architecture as barbaric, Downing praised the finest examples of this style for their "surprising degree of richness and picturesqueness" and recommended simple Elizabethan-inspired buildings for particularly rugged sites.[52]

The romantic style that Downing praised as best adapted to American needs was the English or Rural Gothic (fig. 18). This style differed from the Tudor "in that general *simplicity* which serves to distinguish a cottage or villa of moderate size from a mansion." Downing particularly favored such features of the Rural Gothic style as its gables, verge boards, chimney shafts, and porches, which were equally applicable to a large mansion or a humble cottage. Combining "so much of convenience and rural beauty," a dwelling in this style was especially desirable because it came "within the reach of all persons of moderate means."[53]

Figure 17. The Tudor Gothic residence of Joel Rathbone, near Albany, N.Y., designed by A. J. Davis, from Downing, *A Treatise on the Theory and Practice of Landscape Gardening*, 2d ed. (New York, 1844), facing p. 369. Courtesy of Shadek-Fackenthal Library, Franklin & Marshall College.

Figure 18. The English or Rural Gothic cottage of S. E. Lyon, White Plains, N.Y., from Downing, *A Treatise on the Theory and Practice of Landscape Gardening,* 2d ed. (New York, 1844), facing p. 371. Courtesy of Shadek-Fackenthal Library, Franklin & Marshall College.

Downing devoted so much space to the theory of architecture not only because of its relationship to landscape but because he considered the improvement of American houses a national priority. When handsome villas and cottages began to dot the American countryside, he suggested, they would "not only become sources of the purest enjoyment to the refined minds of the possessors," but would "exert an influence for the improvement in taste of every class in our community."[54]

To illustrate the theory of domestic architecture, and to add the dimension of practice promised in the title of the *Treatise,* Downing turned to architect Alexander Jackson Davis. Downing and Davis met in late 1838 or early 1839 through their mutual friend Robert Donaldson, whose Hudson River estate, Blithewood, Davis had designed. Davis had already published *Rural Residences* (issued in 1838), arguably the first American house pattern book, but its designs generally were for large, expensive dwellings (though Davis did include a design for a "Farmer's House," a modest board-and-batten cottage) and its hand-colored lithographs made it a very costly volume. As Downing would do in the *Treatise,* Davis had criticized most American houses as "bald and uninteresting" and had decried their lack of relationship to the site. In December 1838 Downing informed Davis that he was "at present busily engaged in preparing a work for the press on Landscape Gardening and Rural Residences with the view of improving if possible the taste in these matters in the United States." Downing's purpose in writing the book and his request of the architect's help "must have appealed strongly to Davis," according to Jane B. Davies, the foremost Davis scholar; for the next decade the two men were, in her words, "collaborators in the picturesque."[55]

The 1841 edition of the *Treatise* presented views of twelve houses, of which six were Davis's designs: Donaldson's Blithewood and its gate lodge; Henry Sheldon's cottage in Tarrytown, New York; Philip R. Paulding's Knoll (now known as Lyndhurst), also in Tarrytown; the Gothic cottage of Nathan R. Warren near Troy, New York (fig. 19), with its crow-stepped gables; the Tudor Gothic residence of Joel Rathbone, near Albany, New York (fig. 17, above);

Figure 19. The cottage of Nathan R. Warren, near Troy, N.Y., designed by A. J. Davis, from Downing, *A Treatise on the Theory and Practice of Landscape Gardening,* 2d ed. (New York, 1844), facing p. 380. Courtesy of Shadek-Fackenthal Library, Franklin & Marshall College.

and the engraver James Smillie's Italianate villa at Roundout, New York, to which Downing asked Davis to add "a kind of architectural terrace with *vases as ornament*" to illustrate the text's treatment of "the beauty of terraces & their decorations."[56] Davis also drew on wood blocks other illustrations for the *Treatise,* including Washington Irving's Sunnyside, in Irvington, New York; John Notman's plans for the Doane villa in Riverside, New Jersey; the cottage of Nathan Dunn; a Greek Revival villa in Brooklyn owned by Joseph W. Perry, which Downing wanted to include because of its "highly beautiful conservatory"; and the author's own residence in Newburgh. Davis may also have drawn William Denning's house on Presque Island, in Dutchess County, New York, which Downing considered a valuable example of the Roman style, and the vignette of the "New Haven Suburban Villa," but there is no record of these in Davis's papers. Save for the frontispiece, a steel engraving of Blithewood drawn by Davis and engraved by Henry Jordan (fig. 20), the *Treatise* is illustrated with woodcuts executed by Joseph A. Adams and Alexander Anderson.[57]

Figure 20. "View of the Grounds at Blithewood, Dutchess Co., N.Y., The Residence of Robert Donaldson," drawn by A. J. Davis and engraved by Henry Jordan, frontispiece of Downing, *A Treatise on the Theory and Practice of Landscape Gardening,* 2d ed. (New York, 1844). Courtesy of Shadek-Fackenthal Library, Franklin & Marshall College.

To the preparation of the *Treatise* Davis's most obvious contribution was the illustrations that accompanied Downing's prose. How much Davis influenced Downing's thinking about architecture, either through numerous conversations or through the example of buildings he designed, has proven impossible to determine. The reverse is also true: surviving documents do not suggest the degree to which Downing's ideas may have inspired Davis's efforts. What can be measured is Downing's gratitude toward Davis–in his mention of Davis at the end of the chapter devoted to rural architecture, in his acknowledgment of Davis in the preface (in both cases Downing also mentioned John Notman), and in the numerous occasions in which Downing recommended Davis to prospective clients. Clearly, the *Treatise* was a more successful book because of the handsome illustrations Davis provided.

◡ The publication of Downing's *Treatise,* exclaimed a writer in the *New York Review,* "may be considered a new epoch in the annals both of our literature and of our social history." *The United States Magazine and Democratic Review* concurred, calling the *Treatise* a landmark, "the first work of the kind, of any considerable pretensions, that has come from the American press."[58] Other early reviewers were equally laudatory. *Silliman's Journal* predicted that the *Treatise* would "at once take the rank of *the* standard work" on the subject; C. M. Hovey's *Magazine of Horticulture* praised it as "an excellent volume" and "a pioneer in the great art of landscape gardening"; the *North American Review* lauded Downing as a "practical artist," whose advice "is worth having"; and the *Cultivator* used the appearance of the *Treatise* to "date a new era in our rural architecture." Almost invariably these reviews praised the thoroughness with which Downing addressed the topic, the effectiveness of the author's prose, and the quality of the illustrations. They also encouraged readers to consult the *Treatise* prior to constructing a house or undertaking improvements to their grounds. A couple of the longer reviews adopted Downing's explication of the importance of well-designed homes and gardens as marks of civilization and urged citizens of an increasingly prosperous nation to begin planting trees and embellishing the landscape.[59] Similar praise came from England. J. C. Loudon described the *Treatise* as "a masterly work," while John Lindley conceded that he knew of no book that better explained the principles of landscape gardening: "No English landscape gardener has written so clearly, or with so much real intensity."[60] All in all, the author must have been extraordinarily pleased with the book's initial reception and the brisk sales it enjoyed.

Several of the reviews pointed to a profound reason for the work's appeal to at least part of Downing's generation. In the preface Downing acknowledged that a love of place, a "strong attachment to natal soil," was "a counterpoise to the great tendency towards constant change, and the restless spirit of emigration, which form part of our national character." After quoting Alexis de Tocqueville's famous remark that one consequence of American mobility was a relaxation or severing of intergenerational ties, Downing suggested that anything which fostered an individual's "love of home" strengthened that person's familial and civic responsibility. "Whatever, therefore, leads man to assemble the comforts and elegancies of life around his habitation," Downing wrote, "tends to increase local attachments, and render domestic life more delightful; thus not only augmenting his own enjoyment, but strengthening his patriotism, and making him a better citizen."[61]

Although Downing often professed an aversion to politics, the *Treatise* was about more than landscape gardening and rural architecture: as the preface makes explicit, and the text indicates at least implicitly, Downing was promoting an essentially conservative world view, a vision of a stable society, at a time of tremendous economic and social change. As Tocqueville had explained only a year earlier, "in the United States a man builds a house in which to spend his old age, and he sells it before the roof is on; he plants a garden and lets it just as the trees are coming into bearing; he brings a field into tillage and leaves other men to gather the crops; he embraces a profession and gives it up; he settles in a place, which he soon afterwards leaves to carry his changeable longings elsewhere."[62] The philosophy of the *Treatise*, as well as its plans for houses and their grounds, held out an alternative for America, a social order characterized by permanence, by love of place, and by a corresponding degree of civility in human interaction.

Downing developed this theme of home and garden as a conservative bastion of social stability at greater length in subsequent years, but even in its first formulation he struck a resonant chord with reviewers. The *North American Review*, for example, hoped that Downing's book would be especially appealing to younger readers, as it would not only "counteract the restlessness and disposition to change, which is characteristic of our people," but would also "check the passion for luxuries of all kinds, which is rapidly extending itself with the increase of our public hotels, and the facilities of transportation from place to place."[63] The *New Englander and Yale Review* concurred: the development of "rural embellishments," it predicted, would "surely subdue" the "restless inquietude of our landholding population."[64] Still another reviewer suggested that Downing's advice would "promote a genuine patriotism" and strengthen a citizen's sense of attachment to community.[65]

As was true of Downing's preface, each of these reviews posited a conservative nationalism in keeping with what historian Daniel Walker Howe has termed Whig political culture.[66] None of the critics noted, at least initially, that Downing provided few designs for modest houses and grounds that would address the needs of the very people most likely to migrate. Nor did they find it worth comment that there was a regional cast to the examples Downing chose to illustrate this ideas—virtually all of the houses and grounds were drawn from the Hudson Valley or New England—which might have raised doubt about his appeal for a national style of architectural and landscape design. Instead, the critics found most praiseworthy Downing's evocation of the reformist powers of the middle landscape—a domesticated landscape nestled, symbolically, between the frantic pace, squalid conditions, and sordid temptations of city life, on one hand, and the barbarism of the frontier on the other—which would help stabilize the nation's institutions, discipline a mobile population, refine and civilize all Americans. His vision of American society was, like Jefferson's, rooted in the soil, although for him the garden had joined and perhaps superseded the farm as the bedrock of the republic.

Publication of the *Treatise* established Downing as the preeminent American authority on landscape gardening and rural architecture. Critics hailed him as the American Loudon or as the "Sir Joshua Reynolds of our rural decorations."[67] Similar recognition arrived from Europe. "I have lately received a compliment from the other side of the Atlantic," Downing wrote John Jay Smith, "in the shape of a diploma of corresponding membership from the 'Royal Prussian Gardening Society,' Berlin and from the 'Royal Botanic Society,' London." With more than a touch of irony, he attributed these honors to the *Treatise,* which, he added, "though poorly enough executed, seems to have startled the Europeans, who can hardly believe that we have anything but log houses."[68]

The fame that accompanied authorship undoubtedly contributed to the increasing number of requests for Downing's professional services as a landscape gardener and may well have generated additional business for the family nursery. In November 1841 Downing informed Robert Donaldson that he had "scarcely been without a commission for laying out grounds" during the previous two months and concluded that "Landscape Gardening bids fair to become a *profession* in this country."[69] Because of the critical acclaim accorded his chapter on rural architecture, and because he recognized the need for smaller, less expensive examples of architectural excellence appropriate to the middle class, Downing began, almost immediately, the compilation of designs that became *Cottage Residences*, which would be published in 1842.[70]

3

Theory and Practice

My different works have indeed been most kindly received by
my countrymen—and I have in various parts of the country
had the satisfaction of seeing—what I believe but few authors
do see—my hints carried at once into execution.
                                        —Andrew Jackson Downing

🙰 Throughout the long period in which he was writing the *Treatise*, Downing continued to work with his brother Charles in managing the family business, Botanic Garden and Nurseries, in Newburgh, which was flourishing.
The nursery, he boasted in 1839, was "sending trees and plants to almost every
part of the Union."[1] Already deeply involved with business concerns, especially during the peak planting seasons, Downing was encouraged by the
brisk sales and flattering reviews of the *Treatise* that there was a substantial
audience for his ideas about the proper arrangement of houses and gardens.
Invitations to inspect properties and design grounds followed the publication of the *Treatise*, which surely meant additional orders for the nursery.
Downing explained that he wrote the *Treatise* in response to numerous requests he received from clients for advice on how to landscape their grounds,
and it seems reasonable to presume that he received more and more requests
for consultation as his reputation spread. The publication of the *Treatise* thus
launched Downing's career as a landscape gardener and provided his first important opportunities to translate theory into practice.[2] Through those efforts Downing would establish the foundations of the profession of landscape
architecture in the United States.[3]

   By the end of 1841 Downing was deeply engrossed in the preparation of a
second book, one devoted to cottages and their gardens: he had already
arranged with Alexander Anderson to prepare the wood blocks on which architect Alexander Jackson Davis would draw the illustrations for the volume,
and in December of that year he sent Davis the elevation and floor plan for
the first of the designs he had completed.[4] A month later Downing informed
Robert Donaldson that he was writing a book on architecture "partly *con
amore* and partly at the solicitation of a great many persons who want *plans*

having some degree of adaptation to our country; & which also come within the means of the middle class." He hoped that the book would prove to be "of some use in directing the public taste."[5] Undoubtedly because of its much reduced size, but perhaps also because of the author's experience and the publisher's certainty that there was a ready market for the book, *Cottage Residences* (1842), in contrast to the *Treatise,* was completed in a remarkably short time. Six months after sending Davis the first of the illustrations, Downing delivered the finished text to his New York publisher, Wiley and Putnam.[6]

Cottage Residences, Downing admitted in the preface, was "a slight and imperfect contribution," but one the author hoped would stimulate the preparation of "more varied and complete works from others, adapted to our peculiar wants and climate." Downing's apparent modesty, however, did not prevent him from claiming to have written "the first [book] yet published in this country devoted to Rural Architecture."[7] Whether *Cottage Residences* merited that distinction is a matter of debate. Alexander Jackson Davis, the architect who prepared most of the illustrations for *Cottage Residences* as well as for the *Treatise,* had issued the first two parts of his own book, *Rural Residences,* in 1838; but as Downing owned a copy of this, he clearly thought of his own effort as something different. Davis intended *Rural Residences* to be published in stages, with each of its six parts containing four plates, but because of the expense of production and the cost—$2.00 per part for the version with hand-colored plates, $1.50 for the black and white—he did not publish the remaining parts of the projected volume.[8] Thus, Downing may have been differentiating *Cottage Residences* from Davis's still incomplete work, or he may have believed that what he had written was so novel in other respects, both content and format, that it had no predecessors. What is certain is the degree to which Downing's second book differed from previous architectural publications.

Prior to the 1840s, most books about architecture were builders' guides. As the name indicates, these books specifically addressed the needs of the craftsman: they tended to be technical in language, large in format, and generally contained plates of the classical orders as well as structural details. Minard Lafevre, Asher Benjamin, and other authors of these handbooks sometimes presented elevations of buildings, almost invariably in the Roman or Greek Revival styles, and provided precise instructions that would enable a builder to replicate each design. Few, if any, provided guidance on the arrangement of domestic space or the proper treatment of the grounds, information that would be useful to the client.[9]

Davis's *Rural Residences* introduced several important new developments in architectural publishing in the United States. The illustrations were hand-colored lithographs rather than black-and-white engravings, as was usually the case in builders' guides; and the page opposite each design included a brief description of the building, as well as a paragraph describing the construction, that was clearly directed at a prospective client. Although Davis did not articulate the relationship between site and architectural style, as Downing would do in his books, in seven of the eight lithographs Davis presented the building in an appropriate landscape setting. Equally important, the designs included in *Rural Residences* were strikingly original and represented a new "romantic" aesthetic, "the American beginnings, or near-beginnings," according to Jane B. Davies, "of many of the forms and motifs that the next three decades would see repeated and developed in Davis's work."[10] Most prominent among these new designs were the Collegiate Gothic villa, the "rustic" cottage, and the simple board-and-batten farmer's house (fig. 21), all of which would have an enduring influence on American architectural development, not least on the designs Downing would include in his books. *Rural Residences* thus stands as an intermediate step between the older tradition of builders' guides and the next stage in architectural publishing represented by Downing's books.

House pattern books tended to be smaller in size than builders' guides, used wood engravings for illustrations, which were integrated with the text, were bound in cloth rather than leather, and took advantage of other innovations in publishing to be far less expensive.[11] Most of these books followed Davis's lead in shifting the audience from builder to client and the perception from detail or elevation to completed structure in a landscape setting. The texts of Downing's writings and many later house pattern books, however, paid far more attention to the philosophy of taste and appropriate styles of architecture than did *Rural Residences*.[12] They also provided floor plans, advice on the style of landscape appropriate to each type of dwelling, and ground plans and plant lists to help the reader create the optimal surroundings for the home. In addition to these new features, house pattern books appropriated an important element of the builders' guides by including details that explained the construction of unusual elements, such as porches, verge boards, window treatments, and chimneys. A reader could learn from Downing's advice, select a particular design, and then take it to a local craftsman, who generally would be more familiar with classical revival or vernacular traditions than with Gothic cottages or Italianate villas, but who could follow the instructions in *Cottage Residences* to erect the house in much the way the client expected.[13]

Downing decided to write *Cottage Residences*, he explained in the preface, because of his "HEARTY desire to contribute something to the improvement of the domestic architecture and the rural taste of our country." Al-

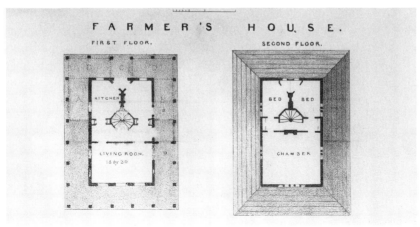

Figure 21. A. J. Davis, board-and-batten farmer's house, which the architect described as "simple, economical, and adapted to the American climate," hand-colored lithograph from Davis, *Rural Residences* (New York, 1837–38).

though he conceded that the book was only a brief introduction to the sub-ject, Downing was convinced that improving the design of American homes was central to the progress of the nation. To promote this cause he began *Cottage Residences* with the chapter "Architectural Suggestions," which reit-erated the principles of fitness, expression of purpose, and expression of architectural style that he had included in the *Treatise*. But whereas in his first book he had addressed each of these topics only to establish a general understanding of their importance, in *Cottage Residences* Downing adopted a conversational tone to explain the practical application of these principles in everyday terms. Fitness, or "beauty of utility," meant attention to the practical needs of comfort and convenience: the optimal location of rooms in relationship to climate, the arrangement of rooms to meet the requirements of a family's social life or habits, and the introduction of such new conveniences as "rising cupboards" (dumbwaiters), running water, and water closets. Fitness also involved the materials used in constructing the house, and Downing recommended brick or stone over wood, which was not only less durable but becoming more costly due to scarcity. Expression of purpose in domestic architecture, he explained, was the "beauty of propriety"; this was conveyed by such features as "the chimneys, the windows, and the porch, veranda, or piazza," which clearly identified a building as a residence. The absence of a clearly defined purpose was central to Downing's criticism of the Greek Revival style, which was used in so many building types that it was often difficult "to distinguish with accuracy between a church, a bank, and a hall of justice," not to mention a dwelling. Important too was color, and Downing denounced the ubiquitous use of white, which he considered "entirely unsuitable, and in bad taste" for a wood house. Instead he recommended that cottages be painted in "a cheerful, mellow hue harmonizing with the verdure of the country." To guide the reader in selecting the proper tones for exterior walls, he included a color chart, the only colored illustration in any of his writings about architecture and landscape design.[14]

Achieving fitness and expression of purpose in a dwelling, however, was not enough. These were utilitarian qualities, not the realization of architecture as a fine art, which necessarily involved the expression of style, or the "beauty of form and sentiment." Downing believed that it was no more expensive to build a well-designed house than an "awkward and unpleasing" dwelling, and that the family would enjoy superior comfort in the former. What was required to create a home that was both beautiful and practical was the introduction of "a spirit and a grace in forms otherwise only admirable for their usefulness," which Downing considered "the *ideal* of architecture as an art of taste." Downing admitted that he was "still more anxious to inspire in the minds of my readers and countrymen more lively perceptions of the BEAUTIFUL, in every thing that relates to our houses and grounds." A graceful, elegant, or picturesque house, he asserted, would "not only refine and elevate the mind, but pour into it new and infinite sources of delight." Significantly, he explained, these qualities could be found in "some humble nook-hidden cottage" as well as in the grandest of buildings.[15] In

Cottage Residences, as he had done in the pages of the *Treatise* and as he would continue to do throughout his career, Downing assumed the mantle of apostle of taste.

Downing's articulation of what constituted good taste in architecture paralleled the analysis of garden design he had presented in the *Treatise*. In much the way that he considered the geometric garden a reflection of the first stage in the evolution from barbarism to a higher level of civilization, so he regarded the uniformity of the square or rectangle, the basis of classical architecture, as the first principle of beauty most humans associated with architecture. Just as a natural garden marked an advance in taste over the formal, a dwelling in the modern style, with a "picturesque" balancing of parts that Downing termed "artistical irregularity," was superior to simple symmetry. He illustrated this point by contrasting a vernacular classical dwelling with a Gothic villa. While people unfamiliar with the true beauties of architecture might prefer the simpler, symmetrical design, he believed that "more cultivated minds" would find the former the more appealing style.[16]

Downing then turned to particular styles of architecture, cautioning however, that a dwelling must adapt the elements of any style to "the humbler requirements of the building and the more quiet purposes of domestic life." The appropriateness of any style would be determined by "the climate, the site, or situation, and the wants of the family" that was building the house. Once again he asserted that the popular temple form of Greek Revival buildings was unsuitable for residential use and recommended other styles— Roman, Italianate, Swiss, Flemish, and especially variations of the English Gothic—as more "characteristic of domestic life, and indicative of home comforts." Ultimately, he advised, the style of dwelling had to be appropriate to the setting: "A great deal of the charm of architectural style, in all cases, will arise from the happy union between the locality or site, and the style chosen." Whatever style a reader might select, and whether the building was a humble cottage or a mansion, he concluded, good taste was within the reach of every individual.[17]

Following this introduction to the theory of domestic architecture, Downing devoted each of the remaining ten chapters to a single design for a dwelling and its grounds. Unlike the *Treatise*, in which Downing's residence was the only building of his own design among the many illustrations of his ideas on architecture, *Cottage Residences* contained numerous applications of his theory to the design of homes and the arrangement of interior and exterior spaces. To present his designs in the best manner possible, he again relied on the skilled pencil of A. J. Davis, who, as Jane Davies has explained, once again contributed enormously to the success of Downing's effort. Davis generously shared with the author his own ideas and sketches, and at least

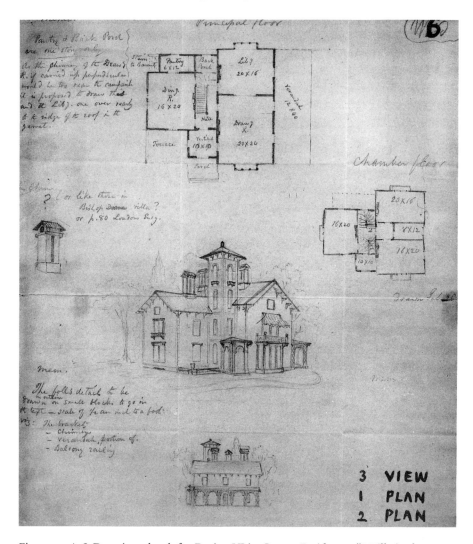

Figure 22. A. J. Downing, sketch for Design VI in *Cottage Residences,* "A Villa in the Italian Style, Bracketed." Courtesy of Metropolitan Museum of Art, Harris Brisbane Dick Fund (24.66.363), 1924, all rights reserved.

one of the designs in *Cottage Residences,* Design III, was a variation on one of the architect's finished commissions. Moreover, in the course of transferring Downing's sketches to wood blocks for engraving, Davis frequently revised the drawings, added the architectural details that would prove immensely useful to builders, and, for most of the sketches, provided the landscape setting so effective in conveying Downing's message that house and garden were a single composition.[18]

Of the ten designs in *Cottage Residence*, the ninth was an "Italian or Tuscan" cottage by John Notman, the tenth, Downing's "beau ideal" of a villa, was the Gothic residence of Joel Rathbone near Albany, New York, which had been designed by Davis (fig. 17, above). The other eight represent Downing's first effort to create the kinds of homes he thought appropriate for his readers, though the author's surviving letters and sketches testify to the collaborative role Davis played in articulating those ideas. Design VI, a bracketed Italianate villa, was the design Downing prepared first (fig. 22). "I send you today the plan and a hasty sketch of the exterior of a plan which I wish you to examine critically, correct any errors of detail or otherwise that your scientific knowledge may seize hold of, and then put it on the block without delay for Anderson," he wrote Davis. This was "one of the most irregular of my subjects," Downing admitted, "but I think it will be picturesque and comfortable."[19] He favored the Italianate because it permitted the expression of "a rich domestic character in its balconies, verandas, ornamental porches, terraces, etc." These same attributes, he believed, made the style appealing to "persons who have cultivated an architectural taste, and who relish the higher beauties of art growing out of variety." Davis redrew Downing's sketch (fig. 23), reducing the height of the tower and adding a landscape setting for the

Figure 23. A. J. Downing, "Villa in the Italian Style, Bracketed," from *Cottage Residences* (New York, 1842), facing p. 117.

house; he also provided a detail of the latticed veranda. If erected using board-and-batten construction, the house would cost an estimated $6,800.[20]

Surviving correspondence does not indicate whether Downing or Davis drew the ground plan of the "ornamental portion" of the 150-acre property accompanying Design VI (fig. 24), though surely the ideas were Downing's. Because the site was located on a plateau along a river, the veranda faced in that direction, and paths wound through the densely wooded lower ground along the riverbank. Nearer the house Downing recommended a closely cropped lawn, interspersed with a series of irregular beds of flowers, a feature popularized by J. C. Loudon. The overall effect of the improvements to the grounds, he asserted, respected the "character of dignity and simplicity arising from extensive prospect, large and lofty trees, and considerable

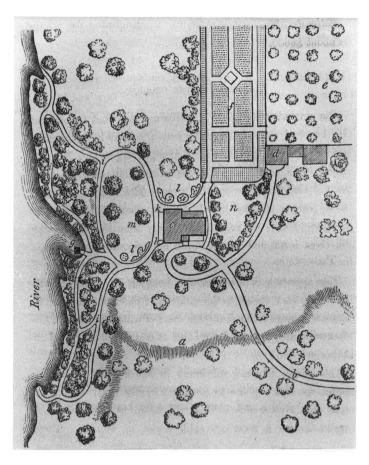

Figure 24. A. J. Downing, plan of the grounds of the villa in the Italian style, bracketed, from *Cottage Residences* (New York, 1842), p. 122.

Figure 25. A. J. Downing, "An Ornamental Farm-House," from *Cottage Residences* (New York, 1842), facing p. 81.

breadth of lawn." In addition Downing placed a kitchen garden adjacent to the house (but screened from view) and a large orchard and fruit garden nearby, to which he appended a list of varieties suitable for planting in the middle states.[21] Downing explained more completely the ideal of domestic environment as a total composition in an 1848 essay in the *Horticulturist*. Describing a modest but well-designed cottage he wrote, "[Y]ou felt, at a glance, that there was a prevailing taste and fitness, that gave a meaning to all, and brought all into harmony; the furniture with the house, the house with the grounds, and all with the life of its inmates."[22]

A sketch Downing sent Davis in January 1842, published as Design IV in *Cottage Residences,* was a simple but comfortable and pleasingly detailed farmhouse (figs. 25 and 26). The dwelling was a rectangular box with a central hallway, a familiar vernacular design, to which Downing added wash, dairy, and wood rooms behind the kitchen to accommodate the particular wants of a farm family. The building was simple, perhaps "too plain," he wrote Davis, "but it has some expression of style & if more be added I feel the farmers will think it too ornamental & will not touch it." Downing advised that the farmhouse be built of stone found on the property and estimated that

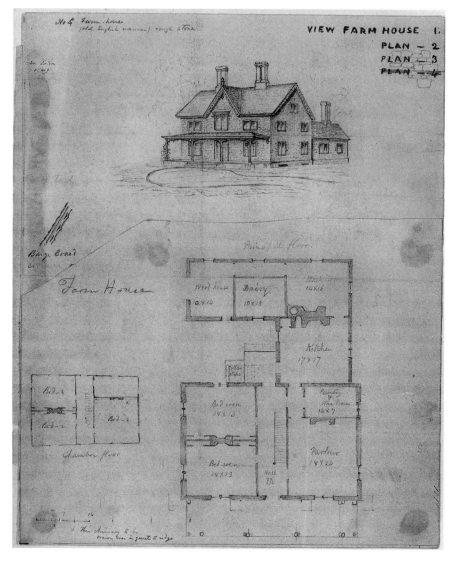

Figure 26. A. J. Downing, sketch for the ornamental farmhouse. Courtesy of Metropolitan Museum of Art, Harris Brisbane Dick Fund (24.66.363[b]), 1924, all rights reserved.

the cost would not exceed $1,700. He also added a plan for the ornamental part of the grounds (fig. 27), a sweeping lawn interspersed with deciduous trees planted singly and in clumps, rather than in a row, as the natural appearance would "evince a more cultivated taste in a farmer" and make the grounds appear more extensive than in fact they were. Hedges separated lawn

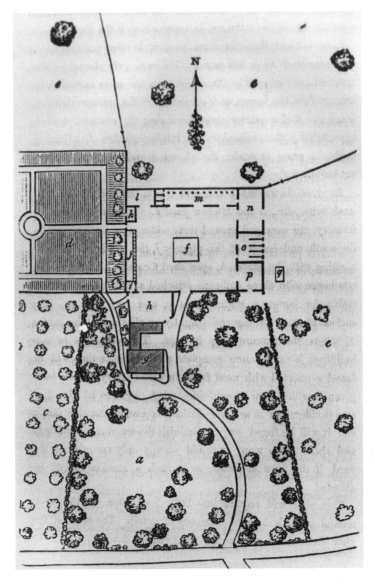

Figure 27. A. J. Downing, plan of the grounds of the ornamental farm-house from *Cottage Residences* (New York, 1842), p. 88.

from the orchards and fields to the east and west of the dwelling, while the kitchen garden and complex of farm buildings stood to the rear of the house.[23]

Perhaps the most widely copied of the designs in *Cottage Residences,* the English or Rural Gothic cottage published as Design II (fig. 28), incorporated several elements common to Davis's work, notably the central gable, second-story Gothic window, and clustered chimneys, each of which Davis illustrated in more detailed drawings for publication.[24] However, as Downing's sketch of the house (fig. 29) demonstrates, he integrated Davis's familiar forms in strikingly original ways, especially the tripartite treatment of the porch roof, which made possible the addition of a balcony accessible through the gable window (fig. 30).[25] Design II, Downing explained, illustrated "how the genius of pointed or Gothic architecture may be chastened or moulded into forms for domestic habitations." The house should be built of brick or stucco scored to resemble stone, he advised, and could be erected at a cost of approximately $4,500. On the lot (fig. 31), an area of an acre and a quarter, Downing devoted half the space to a kitchen garden, separated from the rest of the property by an irregular line of densely planted evergreens, which was "laid out as a lawn, shrubbery and flower-garden, in the picturesque manner."[26]

Of the remaining five designs, one was for a small suburban cottage (Design I), one a Tudor cottage (III), one a bracketed "cottage villa," illustrated both in stone and wood (V), one a vaguely Gothic cottage (VII), and one an

Figure 28. A. J. Downing, "A Cottage in the English or Rural Gothic Style," from *Cottage Residences* (New York, 1842), facing p. 42.

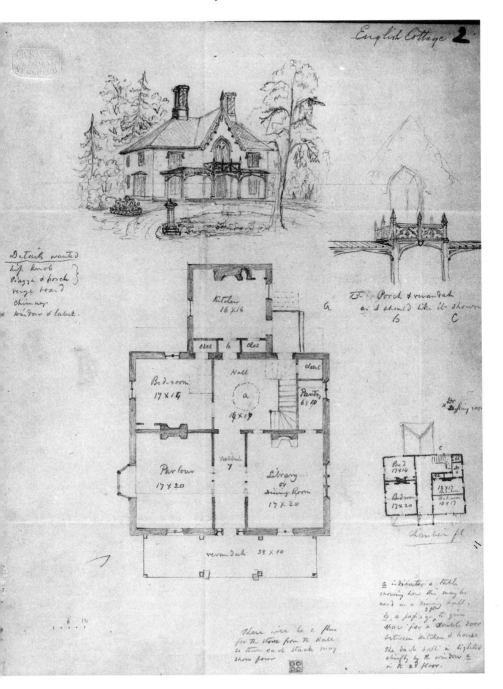

Figure 29. A. J. Downing, sketch for "A Cottage in the English or Rural Gothic Style." Courtesy of Metropolitan Museum of Art, Harris Brisbane Dick Fund (24.66[lot]), 1924, all rights reserved.

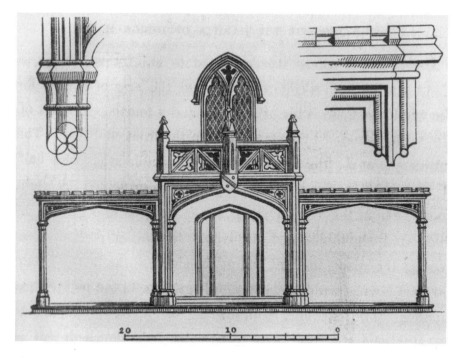

Figure 30. A. J. Downing, detail of porch and other Gothic elements for "A Cottage in the English or Rural Gothic Style," from *Cottage Residences* (New York, 1842), p. 48.

Italianate villa (VIII). As a group, Jane Davies has asserted, the designs represented "avant garde styles, styles that only the most adventurous architects and clients were yet undertaking in America."[27] *Cottage Residences* thus served to familiarize readers with these new styles and to promote their use in residential architecture, as well as to convey Downing's belief that the improvement of homes and their grounds was a matter of profound cultural significance.

As had been true of the *Treatise*, *Cottage Residences* proved to be an instant success, though it generated more criticism than the first book. The initial reviews, published in the horticultural press, were particularly flattering. *The Cultivator* praised Downing's second effort as "a fit companion for his Landscape Gardening" and predicted that it would have "a most salutary effect in correcting the great and acknowledged defects of our cottage architecture, and introducing a better style, more consonant to the wants of a prosperous people." Hovey's *Magazine of Horticulture* likewise admitted that the "cottage and villa architecture of this country is full of defects, and needs the aid of a reforming hand," which could be found in the author of *Cottage Residences*. *The American Review* welcomed the publication of Downing's

Figure 31. A. J. Downing, plan of the grounds for an English or Rural Gothic cottage, from *Cottage Residences*, p. 50.

second book, calling its author a "public benefactor" for his efforts: "he is causing our river-banks, our valleys, and here and there a farm, to appear with new beauties." But while these reviews heartily recommended the book to persons preparing to build or improve their homes, each also pointed to an important need Downing had not addressed. *The Cultivator* called for a similar book devoted to farm dwellings and other modest rural buildings, while the *Magazine of Horticulture* objected to the cost of the designs Downing had presented. A series of less expensive plans, it asserted, "would have served a better purpose, and have furnished more examples from which dwellings would have been erected." Three years later agricultural reformer Solon

Robinson echoed this critique: "Notwithstanding the high character and the adaptability of Mr. Downing's works to the 'upper ten thousand,' the wants of the lower *ten hundred thousand* are not satisfied."[28]

Other reviews similarly charged that the designs Downing published in *Cottage Residences* were too expensive for the vast majority of Americans. Equally important, a number criticized the architectural styles—the taste—the author was promoting. The *New Englander and Yale Review,* for example, criticized the new direction in architecture it associated with Downing and the National Academy of Design; and at least one New York journal accused the author of "corrupting the public taste, and infecting the parvenues with the mania for Gothic Castle-building," or for promoting the construction of such unseemly dwellings as a "gingerbread, crocketed, turreted cottage."[29] These criticisms appear to have had little impact on sales. Perhaps because the book was priced inexpensively ($2.50), perhaps because of its author's reputation, *Cottage Residences* found a welcome reception among the reading public. Wiley and Putnam issued a second edition—really a second printing—in 1844, a third edition, which added four new plans, in 1847, and a fourth edition, with a chapter devoted to "Further Hints on the Gardens and Grounds of Cottage Residences," in 1852. The fourth edition was reprinted in 1853, 1856, 1860, 1863, 1865, 1866, and 1868. In 1873 John Wiley issued still another edition of *Cottage Residences,* edited by architect George Harney, that included a more extensive treatment of horticulture and gardening, written by Henry Winthrop Sargent and Charles Downing. Sales between 1842 and 1853 totaled roughly 6,250 copies, an indication of popular enthusiasm for the author's ideas.[30]

✷ In providing designs for homes and their grounds that he considered suitable for the American public, Downing began the process of translating theory into practice. While reviews present only an imperfect measure of the popular reception of *Cottage Residences,* the frequency with which readers incorporated elements of its published plans in their houses and gardens provides a second dimension to Downing's influence. Author Catharine Sedgwick told Fredrika Bremer that Downing's books "are to be found every where, and nobody, whether he be rich or poor, builds a house or lays out a garden without consulting Downing's works. Every young couple who sets up housekeeping buys them."[31] Philadelphia diarist Sidney George Fisher concurred. "The influence of Downing's books is seen everywhere in buildings & grounds," Fisher wrote in 1847. "He has done a vast deal of good in reforming the style of country residences and suggesting new & beautiful embellishments."[32]

Numerous examples of buildings erected following the designs presented in *Cottage Residences* suggest that these assessments of Downing's influence were probably an accurate reflection of his appeal to the middle class. Shortly after its publication the author could write, "Some of my 'castles in the air' I have the satisfaction in knowing will soon be brought into palpable form by amateurs in different parts of the country." He added that Design II, the English or Rural Gothic cottage, was "an especial favorite."[33] Beginning in May 1843 the *American Agriculturist* used a variation of Design II, placed in a pastoral setting with farm animals and buildings, as its masthead (fig. 32). Versions of Design II, Downing noted in the fourth edition, had "been executed in various parts of the country," including Staten Island, New York.[34] Downing did not mention other examples, but he may have been referring to a brick house in Sydney, Ohio, and the Sedgwick House in Syracuse, New York, which were clearly copied from *Cottage Residences*. Downing may also have known of the federal-era house in Salem, Massachusetts, that was updated

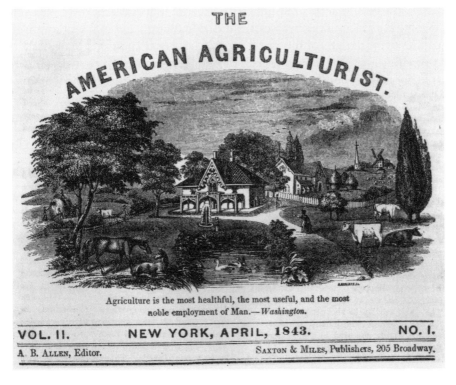

Figure 32. Downing's "Cottage in the English or Rural Gothic Style" adapted to a rural setting, on the masthead of the *American Agriculturist*. Courtesy of Special Collections, Morris Library, University of Delaware.

with the addition of a gable, porch, and Gothic details derived from Design II.

These and other examples of dwellings erected according to the plans Downing presented in *Cottage Residences* suggest that readers responded eagerly to his ideas. Whether they purchased the book or studied copies of Downing's plans in the periodical press—in addition to the *American Agriculturist*'s distribution of his designs, the *Cultivator* published Design IV, the ornamental farmhouse, complete with text, floor plan, architectural details, and landscape design, in its September 1842 issue—significant numbers of aspiring homeowners erected dwellings that conformed to his advice on style and comfort. An Oxbridge, Massachusetts, dwelling that Fredrika Bremer visited in November 1849 was probably also erected following a plan published in *Cottage Residences*. After months of thorough study, its owners, a newly married couple, "had built their house according to one of Mr. Downing's designs," Bremer wrote, "and laid out their garden also after his plan."[35]

Most of the houses patterned after designs in *Cottage Residences* appear to have been substantial dwellings, an indication that Downing's audience was prosperous. It seems reasonable to assume that readers who followed Downing's advice were either wealthy individuals attracted to the innovative qualities of his designs or the emerging middle class that aspired to the tasteful dwellings and the associations of home he promoted. If so, this would confirm the most pointed criticism of *Cottage Residences,* that it failed to provide inexpensive dwellings suitable for average Americans, most of whom were farmers or laborers. Perhaps as a result, Susan Fenimore Cooper, daughter of James Fenimore Cooper and author of *Rural Hours,* found to her dismay that the new taste in domestic architecture Downing was promoting had not progressed from the larger cities and towns to the more rural parts of the nation. Most dwellings in the vicinity of Cooperstown were log houses or "shallow-ornate" versions of the classical orders.[36] Downing attempted to redress this shortcoming of *Cottage Residences* in subsequent years through the publication of plans for modest houses in issues of the *Horticulturist* and in his 1850 book, *The Architecture of Country Houses.*

A second dimension of Downing's effort to apply his theories during these years was his emergence as a practicing landscape gardener. On June 1, 1842, the same month in which he completed the preface to *Cottage Residences,* Downing published an advertisement offering his services as a "professional" landscape gardener (fig. 33). Because of "numerous applications and inquiries" regarding his "professional terms in giving designs for laying out grounds, in forming new residences, or in embellishing or improving old ones in accordance with correct principles of taste," Downing established a list of charges for professional consultation. These included a $30 fee for designing the grounds of a cottage; $50 for preparing a plan for the landscape

ADVERTISEMENT.

PROFESSIONAL LANDSCAPE GARDENING.

The numerous applications and inquiries made of the undersigned respecting his professional terms in giving designs for laying out grounds, in forming new residences, or in embellishing or improving old ones in accordance with correct principles of taste, have induced him to publish his list of prices, as below. It is proper, also, to state, that when extensive improvements are required, in places at a distance, within a certain time, it is desirable to receive notice by letter, a week or two in advance, as, otherwise, previous engagements might give rise to disappointments.

For a design for the grounds of a villa residence, (the survey, or plan of the place, in its existing state, being furnished) . . . $50 00

For the same, with the working drawings, details of ornamental structures, &c. complete, and the principal outlines staked out on the ground, and lists of trees and shrubs furnished . . . 100 00

A design for the grounds of a cottage residence 30 00

For the same, with details, working drawings, lists of trees, &c., &c. 60 00

₊ The travelling expenses are to be added to the above, when the place to be visited is more than fifty miles from New York.

A design for a flower garden . . . . , ... 10 00

A sketch, with working drawings for any ornamental garden building of rustic work, a gate lodge, gardener's house, or green-house 15 00

When a professional visit is required at any place, to give an opinion, to suggest, superintend, or carry out any improvements in the buildings, garden, or grounds, the charge is $15 a day (of six hours,) while at the place, and travelling expenses.

A. J. DOWNING.

Botanic Garden and Nurseries, ⎰
Newburgh, N. Y., June 1, 1842. ⎱

Figure 33. Advertisement offering A. J. Downing's professional services as a landscape gardener, from Hovey's *Magazine of Horticulture* 8 (1842). Courtesy of Library of Congress.

surrounding a villa residence; $100 "[f]or the same, with the working drawings, details of ornamental structures, &c. complete, and the principal outlines staked out on the ground, and lists of trees and shrubs furnished"; $10 for the design of a flower garden; as well as fees for traveling expenses and a per diem charge of $15.[37]

Downing cast some light on several of these requests for his professional services in a November 1841 letter to John Jay Smith. "I have been employed to a very considerable extent this season in giving designs for laying out grounds both in the neighborhood of Boston and New York," he wrote, adding, "Landscape gardening bids fair to become a profession in this country." The most ambitious of the projects to which he referred was a plan for the Boston Public Garden, which, despite its name, was initially a private endeavor, organized in 1837 by a group of members of the Massachusetts Horticultural Society interested in creating a botanical garden. Downing, who proposed that the boundary be a scientifically arranged arboretum, "prepared a list of trees and indicated the precise places where they were to be planted on the plan."[38] He was eager that his design be carried out and must have been deeply disappointed when it was not. The proprietors lost title to the land in 1847, whereupon it reverted to public ownership. Not until 1859, seven years after Downing's death, was the Boston Public Garden created; and instead of being built following Downing's plans, the site was developed according to a design prepared by architect George F. Meacham. Other than Downing's letter to Smith and several published notices of the effort to create a garden on newly filled land next to the Common, no documents explaining the original design for the public garden apparently have survived.[39]

Downing's professional consultations continued in succeeding years. In October 1842, for example, he informed correspondents that he was "thoroughly driven with business matters—persons occupying my time here, or landscape journeys abroad, constantly." Among the commissions he had received were designs "for private places at Boston, Albany, New Haven, Long Island, Staten Island, two places in New Jersey, &c., so that you see my art is flourishing."[40] Although surviving documents do not reveal the identity of most of these clients, Jane Davies has determined that one of the "Boston" commissions was the "suburban cottage" of John Angier, a relative of Caroline Downing's, in Medford. Downing sketched a plan in preliminary form and, just as he had done with the illustrations for his books, transmitted it to A. J. Davis for completion of "working drawings, elevations and specifications."[41] The Angier cottage (fig. 34), with its gables, Gothic details, and trellised veranda, is remarkably similar to Design II of *Cottage Residences* and may well have been Downing's first architectural design other than his own house in Newburgh.

Although no documents dating from the early 1840s explain in detail how Downing practiced landscape gardening, entries in Sidney George Fisher's diary from the second half of the decade provide a useful glimpse of his work. In November 1847 Fisher noted that Downing had spent two days with his cousin, Joshua Francis Fisher, to "advise him about the house & grounds." During the same visit Downing also spent a day on Harry Ingersoll's property, Medary. Two years later Fisher recorded another of Downing's visits: on November 5, 1849, he wrote, "[D]rove out to dine at [Joshua] Fisher's to meet Downing, the landscape gardener, who was there for a few days to help him lay out the grounds of his place." Fisher, a notorious snob, described Downing as "a Yankee & not thoroughbred," and disdainfully observed, "Landscape gardening with him is a profession & not a liberal taste." Despite his personal feelings, Fisher must have been impressed with Downing's professional skill, for he secured Downing's services to advise his brother, Henry, who was choosing the site for his house, an Italianate villa designed by architect John Notman. "Downing goes in this way to give advice, professionally," Fisher concluded. "His charge is $20 per diem."[42]

Figure 34. John B. Angier cottage, High Street, Medford, Mass., designed by A. J. Downing and A. J. Davis. Photograph ca. 1880s. Courtesy of Medford Public Library and Medford Historical Society.

Fisher's account suggests that on his professional visits Downing transmitted specific details of his designs orally, perhaps, as his advertisement of services indicates, by staking the outlines of major elements—house site, drives and walks, flower beds, and the like—on the ground. He surely also prepared garden or estate plans based on a survey of the grounds provided by the client, a less expensive service he mentioned in his list of professional fees, but apparently no such plan has survived. One of these designs was for the grounds adjacent to the plantation home of Joel R. Poinsett, on the banks of the Peedee River, near Charleston, South Carolina. Although Downing never traveled to that part of the country, Bremer found on her visit there that adjacent to the house was "a park or garden, rich in the most beautiful trees, shrubs, and plants of the country, planted by Mr. Poinsett himself, according to Mr. Downing's advice." Poinsett, who told Bremer that the landscape gardener "has done much for this country," was particularly proud of "the beautiful *Lamarque* rose which Mr. Downing had given him." Bremer waxed poetic about Poinsett's garden, where the birds and tropical plants were "all splendid and strangers to me," but she described it in only vague terms, and any plans or correspondence that would cast light on Downing's design apparently have not survived.[43] Nor have any working drawings or details of ornamental structures for gardens Downing also advertised. Indeed, other than the illustrative plans published in his various books and in the *Horticulturist*, the only landscape design in Downing's hand that exists today is his plan for the public grounds, the area between the Capitol and the President's House, in Washington (1851). Two other designs that can be documented reasonably completely as Downing's are the gardens adjacent to his Newburgh home and those at Springside, Matthew Vassar's estate in Poughkeepsie, New York.

Perhaps the most important commission Downing received in the early 1840s was an invitation to design a landscape suitable for the grounds of the New York State Asylum at Utica.[44] In September 1842 the managers of the asylum wrote Downing to request "the benefits of [his] taste and skill" in making their property "as beautiful as the most cultivated and refined taste could desire."[45] Asylums for the insane were new institutions, created in the antebellum years largely as a result of Dorothea Dix's crusading zeal. Predicated at least in part on the belief that the relentless pace and stress of urban life precipitated a deterioration in mental capabilities, these institutions were located on large tracts of land outside cities, physically removed from the environment contemporaries considered the foremost cause of insanity. Downing must have been intrigued with the possibility of creating a landscape that would meet the psychological needs of the inmates. Six years later, in March 1848, he observed, "Many a fine intellect, overtasked and wrecked in the too ardent pursuit of power or wealth, is fondly courted back to reason, and more quiet joys, by the dusky, cool walks of the asylum, where peace and rural beauty do not refuse to dwell." Indeed, he considered the grounds of such asylums "a strong illustration of our general acknowledgment of the influence of the beautiful."[46] Although he was so busy with other professional commitments that he was unable to schedule an immediate journey to the site, he asked a member of the asylum's board of directors, C. A. Mann, to provide an accurate map of the grounds and promised that he would inspect the property if necessary. Shortly thereafter Downing did visit the "magnificent" new classical revival asylum and on October 26 completed and shipped a plan and list of trees suitable for the climate at Utica. The plan included two alternatives for the entrance drive, a curving path that, he predicted, would "look best in the ground for the next 10 years," and a "straight avenue" that would acquire "the most imposing and magnificent effect when the Elms are partially grown, say 18 years hence."[47] For reasons unexplained in surviving documents, the managers chose the straight avenue and began constructing the design. In 1855 they reported to the state legislature that the improvements to the grounds would be completed that year "in accordance with the original plan of Mr. Downing."[48] A view of the grounds from 1854 (fig. 35) reveals two important elements of Downing's design, an open lawn in front of the building and dense plantings on the perimeter to provide a visual enclosure to the property.[49]

Figure 35. New York State Lunatic Asylum, Utica, N.Y., 1854, from *Gleason's Magazine.* Courtesy of Kenneth B. Hawkins.

Several years later Downing had a second opportunity to create a landscape setting for an asylum. Horace A. Buttolph, who had been an assistant physician at the Utica institution when Downing planned the grounds there, had been named superintendent of the New Jersey State Lunatic Asylum at Trenton. The main building was a classical structure designed by John Notman, and Buttolph invited Downing to design the grounds in a way that would promote the therapeutic purposes of the institution. Although neither a plan nor correspondence have survived, Buttolph wrote in 1849 that the property was being laid out "according to a tasteful design by A. J. Downing, landscape gardener."[50] A contemporary engraving (fig. 36), made from a daguerreotype, illustrates several features of Downing's plan, including a curving drive, an undulating lawn, and masses of deciduous and evergreen trees. Here was a therapeutic landscape that would promote the recuperation of patients, an ordered, tranquil landscape that created the visual impression of boundlessness to counteract the confinement of institutionalization.[51]

✑ Even as he was actively building a professional practice, Downing continued to pursue longstanding horticultural interests. "I am now very much engaged on a work which has more or less occupied me for two years," he wrote J. J. Smith in August 1843, "a Treatise on Fruit trees with well digested descriptions of fruits." Previous works on the subject, he explained, were "full of errors." Downing anticipated transmitting the book to the publisher that fall, and a month later informed Smith that he was leaving for Boston "for the exhibition of pears which I must attend in order to complete my comparisons."[52] Finishing the research, writing, and preparation of the illustrations took far longer than Downing had anticipated; the *Cultivator* noted in December 1844 that *Fruits and Fruit Trees of America*, though "advertised to have appeared some time since, has been delayed" so that the author could "test additional varieties and settle . . . some doubtful points." The book was not published until 1845, by which time it had swollen to 594 pages.[53]

Part of the reason for the delay in completing *Fruits and Fruit Trees of America* was the time Downing devoted to preparing an ambitious new edition of the *Treatise on Landscape Gardening*. In November 1843 he informed Davis of this project and added, "I hope again to get some of your artistical aid in putting some of the vignettes tastefully on the block." What Downing envisioned was a series of views for the opening chapters, to illustrate the textual descriptions of theory and practice in much the way that Davis's drawings had supplemented the author's discussion of rural architecture in the earlier edition. The major difference, Downing explained, was that he wanted the new drawings to be more "landskippish." In sending the first two "rough

Figure 36. Principal building and grounds of the New Jersey State Lunatic Asylum, Trenton, engraving after daguerreotype, 1848, from *Annual Report of the New Jersey State Lunatic Asylum*. Courtesy of Kenneth B. Hawkins.

little sketches," he asked Davis to make drawings of a size similar to those of the Doane and Paulding villas in the 1841 *Treatise* but with the overall perspective modified by "removing the house more distant and *showing more trees and grounds*—than in those other cuts."[54]

New illustrative material added to the second edition of the *Treatise* included the classic vignettes of the graceful and the picturesque, several views and plans of grounds, and woodcuts of more than twenty houses. The textual additions were equally significant. "I am now so deep in the literary river," he wrote his friend Smith, "that I do not fairly see the shore."[55] Although the overall message remained the same, Downing rewrote large portions of the first three chapters, clarifying and elaborating the ideas he had presented in 1841. The *Cultivator* praised the new edition as "greatly improved" and attributed to Downing's writings "the great change of taste which has taken place" in the design of American homes and their grounds during the preceding three years.[56] The English authority John Lindley, who found "much error" in Downing's analysis of the historical evolution of gardening, nevertheless praised the second edition: "there is a vigor of thought and a homey strength of expression, combined with a correctness of taste, which would put to shame many a professing [English] landscape gardener of the present day."[57]

The publication of the new edition of the *Treatise* (and a near-simultaneous second printing of *Cottage Residences*) finally enabled Downing to devote his energies to completing the long-delayed work on American fruits. Fruit growing, he observed in the preface to that book, was "the most perfect union of the useful and the beautiful that the earth knows." *Fruits and Fruit Trees of America* had two purposes: to "increase the taste for the planting and cultivation of fruit-trees," and, for those readers with some knowledge of fruits, to provide a "work of reference to guide them in the operations of culture, and in the selection of varieties." The book was compendious both because of the different growing conditions throughout the country and the sheer number of fruits from which a reader might select, but Downing claimed to have tested all of the varieties he described and offered his "most impartial judgment" on each.[58]

Fruits began with several chapters devoted to the general subject of fruit culture, including such topics as the propagation of varieties (in which he again disputed the theories of J. B. Van Mons and T. A. Knight on the declining yield of fruit trees), pruning, training, and transplanting of trees, and prevention of infestation by insects. Chapters dedicated to specific fruits followed, beginning with general observations on the care of the tree or vine, advice on collecting and preserving the fruit, and uses of the fruit. Downing then identified each variety by its place of origin, provided a terse description of its appearance and properties, and in many cases included a line drawing to illustrate its correct form. The varieties he described included 190 apples, 16 apricots, 76 cherries, 35 foreign and 12 native grapes, 27 plums, and 75 peaches. There were similarly comprehensive treatments of numerous other fruits. To bring as much uniformity as possible to the work, he adopted the nomenclature of the Horticultural Society of London as the standard for identification.[59]

Unlike the *Treatise on Landscape Gardening,* which generated highly laudatory reviews, and *Cottage Residences,* which garnered generous praise but also calls for designs more appropriate to working Americans, *Fruits* provoked some controversy. This may have been due in part to existing books—notably William Coxe's *View of the Cultivation of Fruit Trees* (1817), William H. Prince's *Pomological Manual* (1831), William Kenrick's *New American Orchardist* (3rd ed., 1841), and Robert Manning's *New England Fruit Book* (2d ed., 1844)—which Downing challenged on numerous points.[60] In particular, Downing's debate with Van Mons and Knight drew the scorn of C. M. Hovey, Kenrick, and other horticulturists, especially from the Boston area, who had accepted Knight's work as standard and who may have interpreted Downing's strictures as threats to their own reputations as scientific horticulturists.[61] Several critics expressed disagreement with Downing's classifications, and particularly objected to the lack of precision in the comparisons he was making. One of the most forceful of this group, Henry Ward Beecher, then minister of a church in Indianapolis, conceded that the errors he detected in Downing's work were due to the enormity of the task and the difficulty of making precise comparisons, especially given the distance between nurseries and the rapid spoiling of fruit.[62]

The most critical notices appear to have resulted from several passages in *Fruits* that seemed, to those reviewers, to be blatant advertisements for Downing's nursery and attacks on their livelihoods. Particularly objectionable was Downing's description of coastal areas, *"where the climate is rude, and the soil rather sandy,* as upon Long Island, in New Jersey, near Hartford, and around Boston," and his association of those conditions with the enfeeblement and blight of certain apples and pears. Downing's comparison of the same varieties, when grown in "healthy interior districts to the sea-board,"[63] provoked the ire of Hovey, who claimed that his Boston nursery had raised 100,000 pear seedlings the previous year, and of Samuel B. Parsons, proprietor of a nursery in Flushing, Long Island. Hovey expressed "regret that Mr. Downing has allowed his work, so unexceptionable in most respects, to contain such an erroneous statement." "To show the excellence of the climate and soil on the Hudson River," he added, "it was not necessary to denounce the climate or soil of Boston and its vicinity." Parsons too defended his nursery by similarly chastizing Downing for having "adapted his theories to his own soil and climate." Downing's assertion of the inferiority of coastal nurseries, Parsons concluded, was a ruse to promote similar establishments farther from the coast, among which Downing's "Highland Botanic Garden holds a conspicuous place."[64]

Other reviewers jumped to Downing's defense. J. J. King, for example, pointed out that the most critical evaluations "have nearly all belonged to a class so evidently interested in disproving certain home truths . . . that their motives have been understood by the public at large." In particular King defended Downing against the charge of "heresy" for disputing the theories of Knight and cited a recent article by John Lindley to support Downing's position.[65] The book-buying public rushed to endorse Downing's labors: priced at $1.50, *Fruits* proved to be a remarkable commercial success, with five large printings within a year of its initial publication.[66] The *American Agriculturist* judged *Fruits* to be "the standard pomological work of this country," while the *Broadway Journal* found it to be the "most valuable of all the books which Mr. Downing has contributed to the higher departments of our rural literature."[67] An octavo edition, with color plates published in Paris, followed in

1847, as did numerous honors. Downing was elected a corresponding member of the horticultural societies of London, Berlin, and the Low Countries; Frederick William IV of Prussia bestowed upon Downing his country's Gold Medal of Science; and Anna Pavlova Romanova, Queen of Holland, sent him a garnet ring.[68] The response to the book proved overwhelming, as Downing wrote his friend J. J. Smith: "I received a letter from a gentleman in Germany near the Baltic last week, who has my work on Fruits—it has got as far as that—and he considers it so superior to all that he has seen that he wants to translate and publish it in German. It has been, on the whole, the most popular gardener's book ever written. I am now correcting for the eighth edition."[69] Downing continued to refine the work, and at the time of his death was contemplating a completely new and enlarged edition.[70] That task was carried out by his brother Charles, and *Fruits* remained the standard work on the subject for decades to come.

ᴥ During the first half of the 1840s Downing proved to be a prolific author whose ideas on taste in landscape and architectural design reached a wide audience. He also began a professional career as a landscape gardener, and in succeeding years continued to provide clients with his ideas on the proper design of their homes and gardens. In much the way that he attempted to unite house and garden as a single composition, Downing's theory and practice, his publications and professional consultations, were part of an overall crusade to improve American taste. During the second half of the decade, as editor of the *Horticulturist,* he found an even larger audience eager to hear his gospel of taste and refinement.

4

A Gospel of Taste

Mr. DOWNING was altogether AMERICAN. To his own land, in her young and luxuriant life, his feelings were truly devoted. He studied how to prune her wildness, direct her growth, and harmonize her chaotic elements. —Mary E. Monell

When Fredrika Bremer began her two-year tour of the United States in the autumn of 1849, the first home she visited was Downing's in Newburgh. This redoubtable Swedish champion of women's rights had come to the United States "to establish a new hope." Deeply saddened by the failed European revolutions of 1848, she traveled with an "inquiring and searching spirit," anticipating that a "distant land, where the people erected the banner of human freedom" and "declared the human right and ability to govern themselves" would rekindle her faith in a more democratic future.[1] Although she was ultimately disappointed by the condition of the slaves in the parts of the South she toured and by the limited advances in women's rights and education throughout the nation, Bremer was enchanted by Downing and the domestic environment he had created. She returned at the end of her travels to enjoy once again what she considered an ideal American home.

Bremer and Downing had corresponded for some time before her arrival, but those letters did not prepare her for her host's youth and personality. She expected to meet a middle-aged man of fair complexion, and was greatly surprised to find that Downing was thirty-three, tall, with dark eyes and long, gently curling dark hair. During her three-week stay, the Swedish visitor established a deeply affectionate relationship with her "American brother," as she called Downing, and with his wife. Bremer described Downing as handsome and quiet, almost melancholy, and gently solicitous, with an acute and discriminating mind, and her "dear friend" Caroline as a "true woman," charming and amiable, with "gentle, bright" eyes "as blue as our Swedish violets."[2]

The house Downing had designed and built struck Bremer as standing in the midst of a "park," surrounded by open lawn, with "shadowy pathways" in other parts of the garden. House, furnishings, and gardens alike were carefully designed in "the finest taste," she wrote, and bore "the stamp of a refined and earnest mind." As an example of this, she described the parlor, with its Gothic bookcases and busts of Linnaeus, Franklin, Newton, and other pioneers of scientific knowledge. There she spent her favorite hours, evenings when the Downings read the works of their favorite authors—William Cullen Bryant, James Russell Lowell, and Ralph Waldo Emerson—or discussed important topics of the day, such as Horace Mann's crusade for educational reform or the new experiment in socialist living, the North American Phalanx, then underway at Raritan Bay, New Jersey. Marcus Spring, the wealthy New York businessman who underwrote much of the cost of the Fourierist enterprise, visited Bremer at the Downings. So did the Massachusetts writer Catharine Sedgwick, whom Downing greatly admired and whose novels promoted the ideal of a republican social order. Downing's house impressed its Swedish visitor not because of outward luxury, though it was certainly comfortable, but because of its "inward richness"—the abundant flowers that brought brilliant color into every room, the evidence of good taste throughout, and the refined life of its inhabitants. "One sees in this habitation a decided and thorough individuality of character," Bremer wrote, "which has impressed itself on all that surrounds it. . . . One feels here Mr. Downing's motto, '*Il buono e el bello*,'" the good is the beautiful.[3]

During her stay her hosts took Bremer to places of natural beauty, such as Mount Beacon, across the Hudson from Newburgh, which Downing had described in his first published essay, as well as to the residences of numerous friends. The Downings, she wrote, "seem to live for the beautiful and the agreeable in life amid a select circle of friends, who for the most part reside on the lovely banks of the Hudson, and a cheerful and unembarrassed social intercourse seems to characterize the life of this circle." Among the homes she visited was Blithewood, the estate of Robert Donaldson near Annandale-on-Hudson, which had been designed by A. J. Davis and an illustration of which Downing used as the frontispiece of the *Treatise*. There the Swedish visitor was feted at a breakfast for sixty or seventy guests, strolled the handsome grounds, and was musically entertained by her hosts. She also attended the celebration of the ninetieth birthday of Caroline Downing's grandmother, at the DeWint house in Fishkill, where landscape painter Christopher Pearse Cranch regaled the audience with renditions of Italian arias that Bremer found exquisite. And she visited the family of James Alexander Hamilton in Westchester County, New York, where she enjoyed dinner with the noted American author Washington Irving. When it came time for her to depart, Downing gave Bremer letters of introduction to friends throughout the nation and helped her design an itinerary. Together the Downings escorted the Swedish visitor to the Astor House, a posh New York City hotel where they stayed for several days, during which time they visited the annual exhibition of the American Art-Union and met numerous other friends. As the Downings were leaving to return home, Bremer felt the pain of loss as well as deep gratitude for having spent "so richly intellectual and delightful a time" in their midst.[4]

The accounts of other friends and visitors corroborate many of Bremer's impressions and cast additional light on Downing's home and personal life. At the time George William Curtis first met Downing, in 1846, he had read the author's books and anticipated meeting "a kind of pastoral poet, . . . a simple, abstracted cultivator, gentle and silent." He too was surprised by Downing's "singularly hearty" yet reserved demeanor, his "easy elegance" and grace, and what Curtis interpreted as "a certain aristocratic *hauteur* in his manner." To this aspiring writer Downing's personality was almost dualistic, at once gracious and critical, a seemingly congenial conversationist who "watched you from behind that pleasant talk, like a sentinel." The sensitive Downing had erected a wall around his inner self that only a few ever penetrated, which led Curtis to speculate that his host might be "wrestling with demons," that he carried the psychological scars of a lonely, impoverished childhood.[5] Whether Curtis's reflections about Downing's personality are accurate is impossible to determine. He claimed to have based this interpretation on Downing's most intimate letters, those to his wife, which have not survived, and no other contemporary writing about Downing supports this analysis. One review of *Rural Essays,* while not specifically addressing Curtis's assessment of Downing's personality, dismissed as inaccurate the loneliness and poverty of Downing's youth that the author of the "Memoir" cited as the cause of his subject's psychological complexity.[6]

In other respects Curtis found Downing to be the generous, considerate host Bremer described. On a morning stroll, Curtis expressed delight with a magnolia blossom, and thereafter Downing always placed one at his guest's seat in the dining room. "This delicate thoughtfulness was universal with him," Curtis concluded, and was invariably extended to friends and guests. As a visitor, Curtis reveled in the gardens, where, sequestered and serene, he became "quite careless and incurious of the world beyond." Rambles through the countryside, visits to the homes of Downing's friends, and picnics filled other daylight hours. Evenings too were memorable, with music and dancing, games, especially charades, and "some slight violation of the Maine Law"— wines, which often were provided by Downing's friend Nicholas Longworth, who had a large vineyard near Cincinnati.[7] Caroline Downing's niece, Lenora Cranch Scott, recalled that, to her mother, the Downings' home was "a paradise where friends met congenial friends, and where the feast of reason and the flow of soul mingled with delicately seasoned meats, fruits and wine."[8]

Downing's home was also his place of work, yet visitors were invariably impressed by how little those responsibilities weighed upon their host. Fredrika Bremer noted that Downing wrote ten or twelve letters daily, but seemed to work as effortlessly "as the lilies in the field, which neither toil nor spin," so that he "had plenty of leisure and pleasantness for his friends." The eminent Massachusetts horticulturist Marshall P. Wilder similarly described his friend as "always the *master,* never the *slave*" of his professional obligations. Curtis too found that Downing "was producing results implying close application and labor, but without any apparent expense of time or means."[9] These published accounts all cast Downing's life in terms of a traditional ideal of gentility, which, as historian Richard Bushman has observed, required "an existence free of work, devoted to conversation, art, and the pursuit of pleasure."[10] Only over several visits did Curtis discover that behind the veil of gentility Downing worked long and hard to support his style of living. Awaking from his first night's sleep at the Downing home, he descended to breakfast, where he found his host, who "had the air of a man who has been broad awake and at work for several hours," in the library. After breakfast Downing returned to his study, where he spent most of the day and often the evenings as well. Curtis described how, several years later, he was reading in the library, long after everyone else appeared to have retired, only to be surprised when Downing emerged from a recently constructed office wing. Curtis recounted the event to explain Downing's ingenious solution to the problem of joining the addition to the house—through a door cut within the frame of one of the bookcases, so that the appearance of the library remained unaltered—but his words testify to the habits of a highly disciplined writer.[11]

The individual who emerges from these sketchy accounts was clearly an attractive man, proud of what he had accomplished though too considerate of others to be thought of as vain. Contemporaries described him as quiet, reserved, somewhat withdrawn, which perhaps explains why he so eagerly surrounded himself with gregarious friends, and as a devoted husband, "kind, generous, tender & considerate," in Caroline Downing's words.[12] In addition to these personal traits, Downing was a creative, intelligent individual, who read the most recently published journals and books and who enjoyed discussing ideas with friends. His was a genteel world where even work was a crusade for taste, not the pursuit of wealth. From these accounts, Downing impressed contemporaries as a remarkable individual, an esteemed friend, a man whose indisputable talent made him a paragon of the good life. What is equally striking in these biographical descriptions is how inseparable Downing's personality was from his house and gardens. These were extensions of the man, at the same time the product of his creative powers and an environment that defined him and projected his image of self to the world. There he existed, in a kind of seemless web of taste, amid a circle of like-minded friends who reinforced his ideal of a refined society.

Despite the apparent harmony of his domestic and professional lives, Downing experienced a period of acute financial distress between 1846 and 1849. Although it is impossible to reconstruct the circumstances precisely, Downing was "seriously embarrassed" when his father-in-law, John Peter DeWint, apparently charged that Downing was circulating fraudulent notes drawn on his account. Downing described this as a "storm of persecution"[13] and believed his situation so grave that in November 1846 he transferred ownership of his house and gardens to Frederick J. Betts and George Cornwall, who as assignees placed an advertisement in local newspapers requesting that "those having claims against him . . . present the same to the undersigned for settlement."[14] Six months later, perhaps to meet the claims of creditors, Betts and Cornwall sold the lot Downing and his brother Charles owned in common for $3,880.[15] A bitterly divisive lawsuit between Downing and his father-in-law ensued. It was settled in Downing's favor in April 1849, though not without considerable cost: one stipulation of the agreement involved a release of encumbrances on Downing's property and income, which surely had caused financial hardship; in another, DeWint promised "to effect a complete reconciliation between the families." Although Downing's attorneys were "almost certain of a large verdict" had the case gone to trial, he eagerly agreed to the settlement: "My greatest source of gratification," Downing wrote his publisher, Luther Tucker, "is for my wife's sake who is thus restored to her old associations and family ties, from which she has been so completely estranged for a long time."[16]

With the exception of Curtis, Downing's contemporary biographers failed to mention this period of financial and personal turmoil, and the passages of the "Memoir" that treated it drew a gentle rebuke from a reviewer in the *Horticulturist*. Save in letters to his closest friends Downing too seemed unwilling to divulge his problems. To visitors he remained outwardly tranquil and gave no evidence that the genteel world he had created was in danger of slipping from his grasp. For example, when he informed a client and friend of the sale of his nursery—which surviving documents suggest was a necessary step in meeting the claims of creditors—Downing made that event seem a welcome development. "I have sold out all my nursery interest, stock of trees, &c.," he wrote J. J. Smith, "and am rejoiced at the freedom from ten thousand details, and a very heavy business correspondence, of which I am relieved." Downing gave Smith the impression that the sale was a logical result of his evolving interests: "I now shall devote my time to literary pursuits altogether, and my home grounds, as the nursery stock is gradually withdrawn, to experimental purposes—including a dash more of your favorite arboretum planting."[17]

The reluctance of Downing and his friends to discuss his financial problems may have been a very human attempt to avoid unnecessary embarrassment. It may have reflected what he and his peers considered the propriety expected of a gentleman. Recounting her distaste at meeting an individual who spoke of wealth, Fredrika Bremer noted that the "best people" despised such conversation. Discussions of money, she added, "would never defile the lips of . . . Mr. Downing" or other refined Americans whom she admired. It is also possible that Downing was attempting to maintain a public image. Although the impermanence of wealth in the United States was widely assumed—Downing's friends the Donaldsons insisted that their son learn a skilled trade, so that he would be able to earn a livelihood should the family lose its fortune[18]—Downing's position, as an exemplar of the primacy of taste over wealth, was particularly delicate. He frequently emphasized that fitness meant owning a house that honestly reflected the individual's means and livelihood, "that the simplest expression of beauty which grows out of a man's life, ranks higher for him than the most elaborate one borrowed from another life or circumstances."[19] Had his financial difficulties been widely publicized, Downing might have feared that the situation would be interpreted as proof that his style of living violated those very precepts.

Downing's friends, who "rallied to the rescue" and "assured to him his house and grounds," were surely motivated by loyalty to the individual.[20] But so closely was Downing identified with the domestic environment he had created—a landmark easily visible from the Hudson River, prominently illustrated in the *Treatise,* and a mecca for his followers—that intentionally or not they were also protecting the cause of taste and the cultural authority he represented.

ↂDowning's position as tastemaker was enhanced in July 1846, when he began editing the *Horticulturist.* As its subtitle indicates, this was a monthly journal devoted to "Rural Art and Rural Taste," and from the inaugural issue until his death Downing used the pages of the *Horticulturist* to expand his broadly reformist program of improving American taste. As he had done in the *Treatise,* Downing argued that as the United States moved beyond the stages of a pioneer society, its citizens should pour the "same zeal and spirit" once devoted to clearing the wilderness into "the refinements and enjoyments which belong to a country life, and a country home." According to the *Home Journal,* the *Horticulturist* was "the very best publication of its class in the country."[21] Years later Ulysses Prentiss Hedrick, a prominent agricultural historian, concluded that under Downing's aegis the monthly became "America's most notable contribution to periodical horticultural literature."[22]

In addition to editing the contents and selecting the illustrations for each issue, Downing contributed a leader that touched upon any number of subjects: horticulture, agriculture, landscape gardening, rural architecture (including such diverse buildings as rustic arbors, ice houses, simple rural cottages, country schoolhouses, and elegant villas), the need for improving country villages, and the establishment of public parks in cities. But whatever the issue he addressed, Downing made the leader a vehicle for the new gospel of refinement and gentility he preached, just as he had done through the design of his home and the books he published. In June 1849, for example, his essay began with the lament of a reader who had recently moved to a rural village in which every building was an eyesore, including the "absolutely hideous" church with its "huge pepper-box" of a spire, and where not a single tree graced the streets. "Is there no way of instilling some rudiments of taste into the minds of dwellers in remote country places?" the reader inquired. Downing responded by encouraging the reader to become an "APOSTLE OF TASTE," a mission he defined as promoting "some ideas of beauty and fitness" by providing examples of excellence in design worthy of imitation by the correspondent's less refined townspeople.[23] In this and other essays, Downing described the individual who built a beautiful house and garden as a "benefactor to the cause of morality, good order, and the improvement of society,"[24] words, significantly, that defined his own role as well.

Downing attributed the lack of taste in the nation largely to ignorance, or what he termed "a poverty of ideas, and a dormant sense of the enjoyment to be derived from orderly, tasteful and agreeable dwellings and streets." Nevertheless, he was certain that the "spirit of rural improvement" was "fairly awake across this broad continent," and redemption was at hand as the number of apostles increased and converted others to the gospel of good taste. The examples of their houses and gardens would overcome the opposition of the "ignorant and prejudiced," he believed, because of two principles that were fundamental elements of the American national character. These were the "principle of imitation," which, Downing explained, "will never allow a Yankee to be outdone by his neighbors," and the "principle of progress," which would "not allow him to stand still when he discovers that his neighbor has really made an improvement." People who were otherwise content to live in poorly designed houses, and who might at first even sneer at someone building a more tasteful dwelling, would be influenced by the "gradual but certain effect" of better examples of domestic architecture. In a year or so, new houses would incorporate some of the ideas first presented in the dwelling of an apostle—"good proportions, pleasing form, and fitness for the use intended." Gradually, other homes would be improved in the same way, transformed, perhaps, from a "plain unmeaning parallelogram" to a tasteful cottage, just as he had illustrated in the 1844 edition of the *Treatise,* or the "bare and bald" house altered by the addition of a projecting roof, eaves, gable, and veranda that Downing included in the first issue of the *Horticulturist* (fig. 37). Ultimately, a single example of good taste would transform a "graceless village" into a handsome community with "avenues of fine foliage, and streets of neat and taseful homes."[25]

Downing was not alone in his belief in progress through imitation. He approvingly quoted Timothy Dwight, a conservative social critic and former president of Yale College, who wrote: "Uncouth, mean, ragged, dirty houses constituting the body of any town will regularly be accompanied by coarse, groveling manners. The dress, the furniture, the mode of living, and the manners will all correspond with the appearance of the buildings and will universally be in every such case of a vulgar and debased nature." In contrast, residents of "good houses" would be awakened to superior impulses of beauty, surround themselves with tasteful possessions, and comport themselves with grace. The initial perception of beauty, the development of refined taste, was the key to the improvement of a "coarse society."[26] The communitarian reformer Arthur Brisbane similarly pointed to the spread of architectural taste as an essential step toward the realization of his ideal of a socialistic society: "if we can, with a knowledge of true architectural principles, build one house rightly, conveniently and elegantly, we can, by taking it for a model and building others like it, make a perfect and beautiful city."[27] Susan Fenimore Cooper found the American penchant for imitation in domestic architecture "amusing": "there is generally some one original genius in every neighborhood who strikes out a new variation" in domestic design, she wrote in *Rural Hours,* "and whether the novelty be an improvement, or an unsightly oddity, he is pretty sure of being closely followed by all who build about the same time."[28] The role of Downing's readers, his apostles, was to provide the proper examples, not the oddities.

In describing the operation of the principle of imitation Downing made it clear that taste was not restricted to a single class in society, the wealthy, or to the traditional conception of gentility, with its requisite devotion to the study of art, but was accessible to all. This was one important consequence of what Alexis de Tocqueville termed a "greater equality of condition" in the United States. Much as the astute French commentator emphasized the need to "educate democracy" to ensure the survival of republican political and social institutions, Downing was promoting what one contemporary termed "the education of the public taste."[29] Instruction was the key, as taste was not

FIG. 2. VIEW OF A COMMON COUNTRY HOUSE.

FIG. 3. VIEW OF THE SAME, IMPROVED.

Figure 37. A "bare and bald" vernacular classical house and the same house improved with the addition of Gothic details similar to those Downing had incorporated in Design II of *Cottage Residences,* from *Horticulturist* 1 (July 1846). Courtesy of Special Collections, Morris Library, University of Delaware.

a "natural gift" but something that had to be acquired, just as an individual could learn proper manners or obtain stylish clothes by consulting the right etiquette book or patronizing a skilled tailor.[30] Downing had taken one route, a self-directed course of rigorous study, but others could follow a different path. One simple way was by copying a well-designed dwelling; another was by following the plans Downing presented in *Cottage Residences* or the *Horticulturist*; still another was to employ an architect to design a tasteful residence.

Intentionally or not, Downing's crusade to make taste available to all citizens rather than keeping it the exclusive property of the elite contributed to the commodification of culture. Writing in the midst of a revolution in the availability of consumer goods, as well as in the production and distribution of books,[31] he linked the two developments: books could supply the advice that would help the individual acquire the emblems of taste—a suitably designed house, appropriate gardens, furnishings that complemented the style of the dwelling, even the right carpets and draperies. As was true of many of his contemporaries, Downing distinguished between taste, which was enduring, and fashion, which was transitory.[32] Yet in making taste accessible to readers without requiring a thorough understanding of its principles, he was at least potentially creating ready targets for the whims of fashion. In much the way that different etiquette books offered conflicting advice about proper behavior, so might architectural pattern books or manuals devoted to landscape design prove confusing to readers. Ironically, the very democratization of consumer goods and the availability of books made reliance on experts that much more essential, for only a tastemaker with the mantle of cultural authority—an individual such as Downing, who by cultivation or professional study had acquired a comprehensive knowledge of the subject—could guide the client or reader through the shifting sands of fashion to the grail of good taste.

Downing articulated his belief that the public needed proper guidance in matters of taste in a review criticizing J. J. Smith and Thomas U. Walter's *Two Hundred Designs for Cottages and Villas* (Philadelphia, 1846) for not adequately explaining their plans. Such a text was essential to the education of the prospective home builder or owner; in not providing appropriate advice, Smith and Walter were "asking from the architecturally uneducated person, who turns over a variety of designs, a good deal of the highest inventive powers of the best architect."[33] The same concern was evident in his review of the English-educated architect Gervase Wheeler's *Rural Homes* (1851). Downing had published at least one of Wheeler's designs in the *Horticulturist* and the same plan as well as another by Wheeler in *The Architecture of Country Houses*, but *Rural Homes* forced him to reevaluate the suitability of the author's prescriptions for American domestic architecture. What Downing found particularly objectionable in evaluating the book was Wheeler's assertion that his designs were suitable for "American Country Life." Downing dismissed the frontispiece as "one of the worst examples of that *bastard* style of Elizabethan, which all true architects have pronounced the most debased of all styles." The only truly American feature was a veranda, but that was so incongruously added to the building that Downing termed it an afterthought. Other designs were equally inept: the veranda of a country house that Downing dismissed as "poor and meagre in its cornice and supports," a story-and-a-half cottage he judged simply inappropriate to American climate, a summer house that he characterized in terms of its "poverty of detail and composition." Poor as these designs were for an American public that needed the "right *direction*" in taste, even worse were the assumptions of a rigid class system Downing found in Wheeler's text. Thus, he directed his most critical remarks at Wheeler's evocation of a "model *American* village," with a single church, tiny working men's homes, larger dwellings for entrepreneurs and professionals, and the "great house" of the town's wealthiest resident. Alas, to Downing, Wheeler was portraying an English village, with an "Established Church, a rural peasantry, and a nobleman's seat," not the "republican features of one of our prettiest country villages." These he described in terms of its "numerous places of worship, its broad avenues of Elms, overshadowing no single great man's house, but many homes, marked by that general diffusion of comfort, independence, and growing taste, which is the characteristic feature of our model villages in this country."[34]

Despite his rejection of Wheeler's evocation of a hierarchical society, the relationship of taste and wealth proved more vexing than Downing admitted. Although as a republic the United States had eliminated hereditary distinctions of rank and probed what historian John Higham has termed the "limits of ascribed status," the question of class remained to haunt Downing and his contemporaries. Downing's response, on one hand, was to deny any relationship between class and taste. He took Fredrika Bremer to two houses on the east bank of the Hudson River, a "lovely villa" owned by a modest brickmaker and a "beautiful little house, a frame house, with green veranda and garden" that was the property of a cart driver. Downing pointed to these dwellings as proof of the superiority of the New World over the Old, for in the United States a laborer could acquire the "refined pleasures of life, a beautiful home, and the advantages of education for his family" much more readily than in Europe.[35] In the *Treatise* he had argued that even the smallest cottage, affordable by an individual of "very moderate means," could be tastefully designed,[36] and in succeeding years he would provide plans for simple rural cottages, laborer's dwellings, and other modest homes.

On the other hand, Downing clearly identified important elements of taste with specific classes, or at least to what contemporaries described as stations in life. This was a key to what he termed the propriety of a dwelling. In presenting a design for a "Working Man's Cottage" in the September 1846 *Horticulturist,* for example, he urged readers to avoid the temptation to overdecorate simple houses through the introduction of "flimsy verge boards, and unmeaning gables," which invariably resulted in "exhibitions of bad taste." Downing then explained that there were "several classes" of dwellings, each appropriate to different circumstances. The architectural character of a mansion should be far different from the dwelling of an "industrious workingman, who is just able to furnish a comfortable home for his family." Whereas the mansion could be ornate, a cottage should be "simple and pleasing," not designed to resemble a more substantial house on a smaller scale: "architecturally," he wrote, "it is not fitting that the humble cottage should wear the decorations of a superior dwelling, any more than that the plain workingman should wear the same diamonds that represent the superfluous wealth of his neighbor."[37]

Figure 38. A "working man's cottage," a simple board-and-batten dwelling with projecting roof supported by brackets, from *Horticulturist* 1 (Sept. 1846). This became Design I in *The Architecture of Country Houses.* Courtesy of Shadek-Fackenthal Library, Franklin & Marshall College.

Propriety did not mean that the simplest dwelling should be devoid of taste, but that the taste it exhibited should honestly reflect the circumstances of the owner. "We wish to see him eschew all ornaments that are inappropriate and unbecoming," Downing wrote, "and give it a simple and pleasing character by the use of truthful means." Instead of unnecessary or inappropriate decoration that stretched the resources of the family, he advised that if possible the house have a veranda, a feature he described as affording the "greatest comfort" to residents. Otherwise, good proportion, a projecting roof supported by extensions of the rafters, simple eaves over the door and windows, chimneys, and board-and-batten siding would provide "character enough for the simplest class of cottages." The inexpensive buildings (at an estimated cost of $200 to $500) he used to illustrate this point (figs. 38 and 39) may have been little more than rectangular boxes that employed structural elements as ornament, but they met a family's real needs—comfort and economy—and were, in Downing's estimation, "not without some tasteful character."[38]

Figure 39. Another "working man's cottage," a larger board-and-batten dwelling with similar features, from *Horticulturist* 1 (Sept. 1846). Downing offered these examples of tasteful yet simple dwellings as alternatives to the "mania . . . for a kind of *spurious* rural gothic cottage." This became Design V in *The Architecture of Country Houses*. Courtesy of Shadek-Fackenthal Library, Franklin & Marshall College.

A month later, in the October 1846 *Horticulturist,* Downing explained the importance of propriety in the design of a simple farmhouse: "Now the life and habits of our farming population are in the main dignified and free, yet plain and simple." These attributes, he wrote, should likewise be reflected in their homes, which should be "simple in character, and unambitious in style." The house Downing chose to illustrate this idea, drawn by Alexander Jackson Davis, was a simple board-and-batten structure, forty feet square, with a projecting roof and veranda (fig. 40). Here was a dwelling that aptly expressed Downing's view of propriety, a farmhouse free of "useless and unmeaning ornaments" that made no pretentions to architectural style yet was

Figure 40. A. J. Davis, "Design for a Simple Country House," from *Horticulturist* 1 (Oct. 1846). Downing published a variation on this design as "Small Southern Country House" in *The Architecture of Country Houses* (New York, 1850), p. 312. Courtesy of Shadek-Fackenthal Library, Franklin & Marshall College.

tasteful as well as economical. "Such houses will always be found satisfactory," Downing assured his readers, "and the neat and quiet grounds, which they demand as accessories, are within the reach of almost every landholder in America."[39] Several months later a contributor to the *Horticulturist* suggested that Downing's design was "a very pleasing and satisfactory style for all country buildings, of a middle class."[40]

Downing's essays and the designs he published in the *Horticulturist* during the late 1840s thus anticipated some of the distinctions in house types that he would present in his final book, *The Architecture of Country Houses* (1850). Cottages were small dwellings suitable for "industrious and intelligent mechanics and working men, the bone and sinew of the land, who own the ground upon which they stand, build them for their own use, and arrange them to satisfy their own particular wants and gratify their own tastes." Although a cottage could be designed in any number of shapes and styles, its predominant characteristics should be simplicity and comfort. These same qualities were attributes of the farmhouse, which, he advised, should "show an absence of all pretension" and instead reflect the "virtues" cultivated in a farmer by the agrarian life—"simplicity, honesty of purpose, frankness, a hearty, genuine spirit of good-will, and a homey and modest, though manly and independent, bearing in his outward deportment." By contrast, the villa was a suitable dwelling for a "person of competence or wealth sufficient to build and maintain it with some taste and elegance." In addition to the convenience and comfort common to all residential architecture, a villa could aspire to much more architectural pretension. In the hands of a skilled designer or person of taste, Downing wrote, the villa could be "the most tasteful or beautiful of dwellings."[41]

What is striking is the degree to which Downing generally avoided using the word *class* in reference to economic or social groups and instead employed it to designate types of dwellings: he was positing not a hierarchical society but a hierarchy of house types. Although he appeared to follow Tocqueville's formulation of the middle class as the pervasive group in the United States, in his writings about domestic architecture Downing could not escape the implications of class.[42] A cottage, for example, was a smaller house, "intended for the occupation of a family, either wholly managing the household cares itself, or, at the most, with the assistance of one or two servants," whereas the more substantial villa required the help of at least three domestic employees.[43] Downing also insisted that the house was an outward expression of the owner's personal qualities, including means of livelihood, so an individual following this advice would in fact present his or her standing in society to the world through the design of the home and its grounds. The distinctions in house type were not a reflection of the value of certain occupations, for Downing considered all labor honorable, nor were they deterministic. In the United States, he believed, an "industrious, prudent, and intelligent day-laborer" could "certainly rise to a more independent position."[44] Because of the fluidity of American society, an individual who began life in a cottage (or even a log house) could acquire the taste and material comfort to enjoy a more refined existence, at which time a villa would be a more appropriate dwelling. In the same way, an individual such as Robert Donaldson's son, who began life amid elegant surroundings, had to be prepared for the possibility that in later years he would need to earn his own livelihood and reside in a humble dwelling. Nevertheless, while Downing argued that taste was universal, that its diffusion among all persons, no matter what the means, was one hallmark of republican social institutions, the hierarchy of dwelling types he advocated was in reality a reflection of a stratified society.

കൗ Another important manifestation of taste was its relationship to gender. The vignettes Downing employed in the *Treatise* to illustrate the principal types of landscape gardening had suggested that the beautiful or graceful, with its smooth lines, gently undulating lawns, and high degree of finish, was essentially feminine in character, while the roughness and irregularity of the picturesque were qualities more commonly associated with men. Although the text did not explicitly analyze different types of landscapes as separate spheres for women and men, Downing was part of a tradition, perhaps first clearly expressed in Edmund Burke's *Philosophical Enquiry into the Origin of Our Ideas of the Sublime and Beautiful* (1757), that associated characteristics of beauty with the feminine, more rugged scenery with the masculine. Contemporary American painting and literature similarly engendered specific kinds of natural settings: the contrasting landscapes of Edgar Allan Poe's "Landor's Cottage" and "The Domain of Arnheim" are strikingly similar to the characteristics of beauty and sublimity, which the author clearly associated with female and male spheres, while historian Angela Miller has demonstrated how in the 1850s American artists appealed to a feminine aesthetic in turning from "the strenuous masculine associations of the romantic mountain sublime to an interest in space as a container of colored air."[45] In subsequent writings Downing would likewise explore the relationship between gender and the domestic environment.

Downing recognized that women were natural allies in his crusade to improve American taste: "in all countries, it is the taste of the mother, the wife, the daughter, which educates and approves, and fixes, the tastes and habits of the people."[46] Moreover, the topics he considered so important—questions of art and taste, the proper design of homes and their gardens—were of special concern to American women. Catharine E. Beecher had made this explicit in her *Treatise on Domestic Economy* (1841), which argued women's primacy in all matters involving the household. Subsequent editions of Beecher's *Treatise* included house plans (designed by Daniel Wadsworth), information on the installation of labor saving devices, and such topics as ventilation, because women were responsible for the properly ordered home as well as the health and welfare of all members of the family.[47] Sarah J. Hale, the editor of *Godey's Lady's Book,* noted that a "fashion for building elegant cottages" was spreading throughout the nation. In 1846 she began publishing plans for model cottages, "to lend our assistance towards diffusing a taste for beautiful architecture." Hale expected that the designs she included in *Godey's* would prove useful in "educating young persons in architecture as an *art of taste,*" but she too directed her advice principally at female readers who aspired to make their homes the optimal setting for domesticity. To ensure that her suggestions for model cottages were as accessible as possible to "the female sex," Hale promised that the writing would be free from any technical terms. She considered the domestic environment so important that she also published appropriate designs for furniture along with the latest fashions in women's clothing.[48]

The writings of Beecher and Hale appealed to what *Godey's* termed women's "natural love of home and its duties" and sanctified the home as "a glorious temple," in Beecher's words, or as a "noble sphere."[49] This was Downing's mission as well: the plans for houses he published emphasized not only the tasteful arrangement of architectural elements but the efficient management of the household, which he considered an important factor in the improvement of women's lives. He also believed that women were by nature "mistresses of the art of embellishment." "All that is most graceful and charming" in decoration, he wrote, "owes its existence to female hands."[50]

Despite the similarities in their messages, it seems reasonable to presume that Downing's audience differed from that of the *Treatise on Domestic Economy* or *Godey's* in that many if not most of his readers were men.[51] Although his essays celebrated the refined home or the simple cottage in terms that were less specific to gender than were Beecher's or Hale's, Downing's writings complemented the crusade for domesticity that they championed. His own domestic life, however, did not conform to the separation of workplace and residence that was so important in their formulation of women's sphere: although he clearly associated the feminine with accomplishments in refined culture and accepted the masculine realm as the world of business, his place of employment was the nursery adjacent to his dwelling, and, after 1847, the desk at which he wrote or the table at which he prepared designs for homes and their gardens.

Downing did not usually address his audience in gender-specific terms, hoping instead to lead all readers to a greater understanding of the principles of appropriate design. He nevertheless clearly associated the smaller flower garden and the graceful landscape with feminine taste. Moreover, his prescriptions for interiors and furnishings clearly appealed to contemporary attitudes toward gender. As was true of many of his contemporaries, Downing attributed decorative traits to women: "the drapery of cottage windows comes more especially within the province of feminine taste," he wrote, "than within that of the architect," who presumably was male. The illustrations he chose for interiors similarly hinted at the differentiation of domestic space by gender. A view of a drawing room (fig. 41), for example, includes the figures of a woman sitting at a table reading and a man, standing behind her, who seems very much out of place, a temporary presence in what was nor-

Figure 41. A. J. Downing, "Drawing Room at Kenwood, Gothic Style," from *The Architecture of Country Houses* (New York, 1850), facing p. 384. Courtesy of Special Collections, Morris Library, University of Delaware.

mally a female realm; by contrast, the sketch of the library (fig. 42) depicts two men, one at a table reading, the other browsing the bookshelves of what clearly was a male preserve. Significantly, while the activity was the same, the illustrations presented women and men reading in different domestic settings. Downing's descriptions of furnishings also conformed to the codes of gender. In a drawing room, for example, he advised that the furnishings be "richer and more delicate in design," the colors "decidedly light," and the boudoir "essentially delicate and feminine in its general effect," whereas library chairs should be "rather heavy and solid, compared with those of the drawing-room or dining-room." The vignette he chose to illustrate an Elizabethan-style library, based on a room in Henry Winthrop Sargent's home, Wodenethe, in Fishkill, New York, included a "richly-carved bookcase, sofa, and table, executed in dark oak," and produced an effect Downing termed "very rich and striking."[52] Although Downing's descriptions of the properties of each room and its furnishings were less overtly specific to male and female realms than were the writings of Beecher or Hale, the words he chose—*light,*

Figure 42. A. J. Downing, "Library in the Elizabethan Style," from *The Architecture of Country Houses* (New York, 1850), facing p. 398. Courtesy of Special Collections, Morris Library, University of Delaware.

delicate, fancy, versus *heavy, dark, richly carved*—delineated female and male spheres.

As his writings on the home indicate, Downing was committed to promoting the welfare of women. Fredrika Bremer found him to be deeply interested in the "intellectual development of woman in America" and recorded the "great pleasure" he took in the publication of Susan Fenimore Cooper's *Rural Hours,* a lengthy journal of observation and description of natural life in the vicinity of Cooperstown, New York.[53] Downing was enthusiastic about *Rural Hours,* at least in part because it was a welcome exception to a longstanding concern of his, that American women did not enjoy and partake in the healthful pleasures of gardening.[54] In 1843 he had edited an American edition of Mrs. Jane Loudon's *Gardening for Ladies* and expressed hope that its publication would "increase, among our own fair country-women, the taste for these delightful occupations in the open air, which are so conducive to their own health, and to the beauty and interest of our homes."[55] Four years later, in reviewing Mrs. Loudon's books on ornamental perennials and annuals, Downing again urged the importance of gardening to the health and well-being of women. He called for a "successful war against perpetual *stitchery,*" a reference to the popularity of needlework, and expressed hope that needles and crochet hooks would no longer be considered "the only befitting implements of occupation." American women should enjoy the "pure, wholesome, and refreshing taste" of gardening, not be confined to parlors and enslaved to their sewing tables.[56] *Rural Hours,* he hoped, would provide women with "some objects of interest beyond their ordinary household cares and joys" and contribute to "an intelligent, genuine, feminine fondness for nature and rural life."[57]

This was especially important, Downing asserted, because American women had acquired a limited appreciation of the garden. They enjoyed the flowers they arranged with such skill, as well as the appearance of well-kept beds when viewed from the garden path, but they had not developed a true love of gardening. Indeed, he believed that many mistakenly felt that garden tasks were "rustic, unfeminine and unrefined." Downing explained that he was not proposing that women take up the "rough toil" of digging beds or transplanting trees and shrubs, but rather that they develop an understanding of garden operations and a knowledge of plants that would increase their enjoyment of the outdoors. Ultimately, however, Downing insisted that American women needed to become more involved in gardening as a source of fresh air and exercise, "so little a matter of habit and education" in the United States. Should women devote time each day to planting and pruning their gardens as well as picking flowers, the greatest bloom of all would be their improved health.[58]

↝ As an apostle of taste Downing projected a specific vision of American society. This was a middle-class republic, a society in which every individual had the potential to better his or her condition. While he did not believe in a universal equality—he recognized that each individual was endowed with certain talents and never challenged disparities in income based upon the type of employment—Downing did insist that taste was within the reach of all citizens, regardless of their economic circumstances. Convinced that there was an intimate connection between taste and social order, Downing believed that well-designed homes and gardens were the outward mark of civilization and a measure of the nation's cultural as well as material progress. His self-appointed role, and the responsibility he assigned to his readers, was to spread the gospel of taste by providing examples of residential architecture worthy of imitation by others.

The Massachusetts Horticultural Society honored Downing at its annual banquet in 1848. The interior of historic Faneuil Hall was richly decorated with garlands of flowers, a profusion of exotic plants, and a veritable cornu-

Figure 43. Horticultural Festival, Faneuil Hall, Boston, 1848. Among the placards hung at the gallery level of the hall, displaying the names of prominent horticulturists, Downing's is to the extreme right. From *Horticulturist* 3 (Nov. 1848). Courtesy of Special Collections, Morris Library, University of Delaware.

copia of fruits. Between the columns on the balcony were placards containing the names of prominent horticulturists, Downing's among them (see fig. 43). Marshall P. Wilder, president of the society, paid tribute to what he considered the republican orientation of Downing's mission, noting that whereas in Europe princes presented Downing with gold medals, in the United States the "sovereign people" honored him "in many a lowly but tasteful cottage" and "amid the quiet beauty of many a lovely landscape"—fitting testimony to the labors of an apostle of taste.[59]

5

Reforming Rural Life

He was the man best fitted to mould the architectural and rural
taste of the country to a correct model, to guide public sentiment to whatever is highest in Nature and purest in Art, and to
aid in making America what Heaven designed it should be, the
garden of the whole earth.   —Luther Tucker

On August 26, 1846, the Buffalo Horticultural Society expressed "great
satisfaction" with the first two issues of the *Horticulturist* and anticipated the
journal's "most useful and honorable career, in reforming, as well as improving, the rural taste of our land." At the same meeting members unani-
mously adopted "the authority of Mr. Downing in his 'Fruits and Fruit Trees
of America' as their standard in the classification and nomenclature of their
fruits" and directed the president to send the society's reports to Downing
for publication in the *Horticulturist*.[1] The resolution of the Buffalo Horticultural Society testified to two important developments in Downing's career:
the authority he had earned as a leader in scientific pomology and, as editor of
the *Horticulturist*, the role he would play in publishing information and transmitting ideas of central importance to the crusade to reform rural life.

In the inaugural issue of the journal, Downing promised to publish articles of significance and interest to "those whose feelings are firmly rooted in
the soil, and its kindred occupations." The essay, however, specifically addressed devotees of Flora and Pomona, the goddesses of flowers and fruits,
rather than those whose livelihood derived from agriculture. The following
pages presented articles on fruits, ornamental trees and shrubs, climbing
roses, and the use of guano as manure, as well as advice on improving "an
ordinary country house." Regular features included reviews of notable books
(in the first issue Downing praised John Lindley's *Vegetable Kingdom* and Asa
Gray's *Genera of the United States* but denounced Michael Floy's American
edition of George Lindley's *Guide to the Orchard and Fruit Garden* for its failure to include accurate information on improvements in fruit growing that
had occurred in the thirteen years since the book's initial publication), and
excerpts from books or articles, correspondence, announcements, and the

like collected as foreign and domestic notices, and the proceedings of the Massachusetts and Pennsylvania horticultural societies. Downing clearly envisioned an audience that shared his appreciation of the "refinements and enjoyments which belong to a country life, and a country home," but he apparently presumed that readers either already subscribed to one of the many agricultural periodicals then published in the United States or were not engaged in farming.[2] Subsequent issues similarly presented numerous articles on fruits and flowers, gardening operations, the design of houses and other buildings, assessments of the progress of the "rural arts" in various parts of the country, and related topics. One of the earliest architectural designs Downing published in his journal was a plan for a simple board-and-batten farmhouse with a broad veranda (see fig. 40, above).[3]

Downing's belief in the importance of taste, even in the humblest dwelling, quickly led him to address larger issues of concern to the rural population. From a beginning that accurately reflected its title, Downing made the *Horticulturist* into a journal that construed "rural art and rural taste" so broadly that it became an important vehicle for reforming rural life and a steadfast supporter of the cause of agricultural education in the United States. In 1850 the *Ohio Cultivator* judged the *Horticulturist* "the most popular and useful work" of its kind in the nation and attributed to it a "vast amount of good in diffusing correct taste and valuable knowledge." Fifty years later landscape architect Wilhelm Miller pointed out that through his writings Downing had "affected country life in its every aspect."[4]

The reaction of readers to Downing's monthly fare was enthusiastic. Within two months of its appearance Luther Tucker, the publisher, claimed that the *Horticulturist* had a paid circulation of two thousand,[5] and it seems likely that subscriptions increased in succeeding years: in 1849 Tucker noted that the journal's circulation was "equal to that of any similar magazine in Europe, and far beyond any of its class hitherto attempted in America."[6] The numerous articles and queries submitted by correspondents from all parts of the United States appear to confirm Downing's 1851 assertion that the journal circulated "in every state of the union."[7]

Perhaps because of the author's gentle prose and his gracious replies to letters, perhaps because of a shared interest in the topics addressed by the *Horticulturist*, readers established a cordial relationship with the journal and its editor. A subscriber from Peoria, Illinois, was delighted with the first issues he received and found that reading Downing's journal broke down the isolation of prairie life. The *Horticulturist* brought him into "the midst of highly gifted and refined minds, sensibly alive to the best interests of our common country."[8] From all points in the nation came letters seeking advice about the proper design of houses or gardens, or posing queries about the best remedy for some horticultural problem, from soil nutrients to insect infestation to blight that had afflicted the orchard; others asked for an autograph or a portrait; still others contained essays or random bits of information the writer thought might be valuable to other readers of the *Horticulturist*. Whether the letter was from an old friend or a stranger, a national expert on the topic or a beginner trying to select the best fruits to plant, Downing answered each patiently and cordially. Clarence Cook observed that Downing's correspondence "partook more of the nature of affectionate interchanges of friendship, than of the cold civilities which usually pass on business matters."[9] Readers traveling in the vicinity often stopped at Downing's to inspect the house and gardens and to meet the author whose writings they so greatly admired. Together, these readers, correspondents, and visitors became the "apostles" who spread his gospel of taste. Most undoubtedly shared Downing's concerns for improving the American countryside as well.

୬Given his longstanding interest in horticulture, and especially fruits, Downing's first effort to reform rural life focused on pomology. By the mid-1840s horticulture had become big business: the value of the national produce of gardens, orchards, and nurseries for 1847 was $459,577,533.[10] During the antebellum years horticulture emerged in the Northeast as an important response to the mechanization of agriculture and the transportation revolution, which brought grains and other traditional crops from the interior to eastern markets. The "farmer of the Hudson or the Genesee," wrote Downing, "finds that along side of his crops in the great market places, stand also the crops of the west, of as good quality and asking for buyers at lower prices."[11] Unable to "compete with the fertile soils of the west," eastern farmers turned to growing fruits and vegetables for the rapidly increasing urban population.[12] Downing obviously was interested in promoting horticulture as a commercial activity by establishing standards of nomenclature and quality, but he considered it more than a business: it was an essentially conservative pursuit that promoted an attachment to place, which itself was a powerful antidote to the "spirit of unrest" Downing attributed to many of his contemporaries. In July 1847 he argued, "Horticulture and its kindred arts, tend strongly to fix the habits, and elevate the character of our whole rural population."[13] While he knew from personal experience that most prominent horticulturists were men of considerable wealth, Downing was equally interested in spreading the benefits of the fruit garden and orchard among people of modest means. He cited the travails of an individual who was "anxious to plant only a few of the best and most valuable sorts" of a fruit such as the pear, and who faced the daunting task of choosing from among more than two hundred varieties. The sheer abundance of selections, together with the absence of a standard nomenclature as well as information about the suitability of each of the varieties for different climates and types of soil, left all but experts at the mercy of nurserymen. The result was a kind of "pomological lottery" in which the novice was more likely to choose an inferior variety or one inappropriate to the conditions of his orchard than to select the best choice.[14] Undoubtedly the brisk sales of Downing's *Fruits and Fruit Trees of America* was due at least in part to its effort to standardize the names of the many varieties of fruit, to describe growing conditions, and to assess their quality.

Because of the immensity of the task, Downing recognized that *Fruits and Fruit Trees* was but a first step in systematizing pomological knowledge. He surveyed notable fruit growers in the Boston area for their opinions of the best varieties of pears,[15] and published their recommendations in the *Horticulturist,* but the results did not cover enough of a geographical expanse and lacked the thorough grounding in scientific experimentation to be more than suggestive. In November 1847, recognizing the need for a coherent system of classification and evaluation, several prominent horticultural societies adopted a set of rules for American pomology, written by Downing, that were "calculated to stamp a character of scientific precision and accuracy on the nomenclature and description of fruits." Unsurprisingly, the committees that approved the "rules" adopted Downing's *Fruits* as the standard American authority on the subject.[16]

The following year, the Massachusetts and Pennsylvania horticultural societies and the American Institute organized what they anticipated would be the first national pomological convention, and Downing served as a member of the business committee that organized the event. The *Horticulturist* described this meeting, held in New York City in October 1848, as "by far the most important assemblage of horticulturists ever convened in the United States." Participants spent the first day comparing and analyzing hundreds of fruits, and so valuable were the results that they decided to form a permanent organization, the National Convention of Fruit Growers, which would hold annual meetings. Marshall P. Wilder was elected president and Downing named chair of its most important committee, the General Fruit Committee, which was responsible for developing select lists of highly recommended fruits as well as identifying those varieties that were inferior.[17]

The more than two hundred participants at the New York meeting hoped to establish national standards for the naming and evaluation of fruits. However, a month before their inaugural meeting a second group convened in Buffalo for much the same purpose. Hastily organized by the Buffalo Horticultural Society and attended largely by fruit growers from western New York and from Ohio, the Buffalo group took the name North American Pomological Convention. The appearance of this second society seemed, to at least some of those who organized and attended the New York meeting, to represent the divergence of eastern and western fruit growers. The Buffalo convention may have been a local event, but its title and its existence as a separate pomological society threatened the principal goal of the New York organization, the compilation of systematic knowledge through national comparisons and standards.[18] Perhaps the only thing worse than no national organization was the existence of two such groups that adopted divergent rules.

Downing was alarmed by the fractiousness and jealousy that surfaced between the two organizations. A correspondent from Buffalo argued in favor of two groups, one representing the seaboard, the other the inland states, because "the two sections of the country differ so widely in diversity of climate and soil." Another, from Wisconsin, lamented the existence of two societies that were at "sword's point" and called for their merger into "one harmonious whole."[19] Although he was one of the promoters of the New York organization, Downing worked to bring the two societies together. In September 1849, writing under his favorite pseudonym, "An Old Digger," Downing rejected the supposed divergence of eastern and western interests. "Exactly what you want in convention," he argued "is to bring all sorts of different experiences together." It was only through "conversation, and comparing notes, and sifting opinions" that true progress in horticultural knowledge would occur. To be successful this would have to take place on a national rather than a local scale.[20] Two months later delegates from the western organization attended the New York convention and, Downing reported, agreed, "with the largest spirit of good will and fraternity," to a merger of the two groups. The newly united society took the name American Pomological Congress and, undoubtedly in deference to the sensitivities of westerners, agreed to hold its first meeting in Cincinnati, in September 1850.[21]

Downing played an important role in the creation of a single national pomological society. At the 1849 meeting of the New York group he urged "the propriety and necessity of harmony among pomologists,"[22] and as editor of the *Horticulturist* he publicly supported the merger. Equally productive was the behind-the-scenes work he undertook, gently prodding friends in each group to realize the advantages of unification. In 1852, Marshall P. Wilder, the president of the American Pomological Congress, praised Downing's "prompt and energetic action in our endeavors to advance the worthy objects of this association, in the origin and progress of which his agency was so conspicuous."[23] Downing anticipated that the national congress, together with local societies, would assemble "a gradual record and accumulation of facts," which would "tend vastly to the progress of the art all over the Union."[24] He especially hoped that the congress would promote the cultivation of the "BEST *native* varieties of the finer fruits"—ones appropriate for the amateur with a small orchard as well as for market gardeners—rather than reward experimentation in exotics.[25] At the second convention of the congress, held in Philadelphia a month and a half after Downing's death, the organization lamented the loss of horticulture's "brightest ornament" and one of the nation's "most efficient benefactors." Marshall P. Wilder added, "His seat in this Congress is vacant! Another will make the report which was expected of him!" Just as Downing had intended, that report, from the General Fruit Committee, presented a select list in three categories: fruits worthy of general cultivation, new varieties that were promising, and rejected fruits—precisely the educational mission he had hoped the national organization would perform.[26]

꒰ Downing's efforts to create a single pomological organization, with the ability to establish national standards in nomenclature and evaluation for all fruit growers, was a logical extension of longstanding personal and professional interests. But even as he was laboring to establish that group, Downing's other writings in the *Horticulturist* represented a broadening of his commitment to reforming rural life. This was, at least in part, a measure of the importance of agriculture to the American economy. The vast majority of Americans were farmers, and the annual value of agricultural products was more than double that of all other occupations combined.[27] Although their contents would never be confused with that of an agricultural journal, the pages of the *Horticulturist* frequently included information on new plows and other agricultural implements as well as material of general interest to residents of rural America. Yet, even as he cited statistics about prosperity, Downing was aware that the social and economic condition of farmers varied greatly in different parts of the United States, as did the circumstances of daily life.

Downing was particularly concerned because there was no guarantee that farmers would translate material well-being into evidence of refinement and culture. Agricultural reformer Solon Robinson was surprised by the backward condition of long-settled areas located near major cities, such as Fairfield County, Connecticut, and Westchester County, New York, in the middle of the nineteenth century. He described the area between the New York State border and New Haven as "covered with bushes, or miserable little half-starved patches of cultivation, or with shanties that are a degree, at least, below the western log cabin." Farmers there were hidebound to traditional practices and seemed to be totally unaware that they were living in "the age of agricultural improvement." Farther to the east he found numerous other farms that testified to the "'American system' of skin, shave, and waste the soil."[28] Robinson characterized the farms he visited in Westchester County as having a "behind-the-age appearance." Ancient gambrel-roofed houses, "old barns and out-buildings, covered with an old mossy coat," wells, ice spring houses, even fields and stone walls—everything he saw testified to age and a state of disrepair. "Close as this county is to the city," Robinson wrote, "the majority of the inhabitants have not yet caught the infecting spirit of improvement."[29]

As Robinson and other commentators pointed out, conditions generally associated with the pioneer's life—the drudgery of work, the absence of communal amenities, and the total neglect of anything resembling beauty—were true of well-established farmsteads throughout much of the Northeast. A writer in the *Atlantic Monthly* characterized the typical New England farm dwelling as a "square brown house; a chimney coming out of the middle of a roof; not a tree nearer than the orchard, and not a flower at the door." Farmhouses were "unloved and unlovable things," places of unremitting toil, and devoid of taste and refinement, which accounted for the flight of children raised on farms to urban centers.[30] The problem, as the English commentator James Johnston observed in 1851, was that even in long-settled areas there was "scarcely any such thing as local attachment—the love of a place,"[31] one of the principal themes Downing had elaborated in the *Treatise* and continued to promote in later writings.

Downing crusaded to reform the American countryside by improving the condition of rural homes and villages. His plans for farmhouses and other modest dwellings attempted to provide for the tasteful accommodation of families amid the simple pleasures of life, gardens and orchards.[32] Although critics such as Solon Robinson and an anonymous husbandman from Clinton, New York, thought Downing's designs too expensive for most farmers, others disputed his strictures on fitness and insisted that farmhouses could aspire to something more pretentious than a sturdy simplicity.[33] Lewis F. Allen, for example, asserted that the location of a dwelling on a farm rather than its architectural style or other physical characteristic was what denoted a farmhouse. "We have an idea that the farmer, or the planter, according to his means and requirements," Allen wrote in 1852, "should be as well housed and accommodated, and in as agreeable style, too, as any other class of [the] community."[34]

Figure 44. Thomas H. Hyatt and Merwin Austin, plan of Elm-Wood Cottage, Mount Hope, New York, from *Cultivator*, n.s. 3 (Jan. 1846), p. 24. Courtesy of Special Collections, Morris Library, University of Delaware.

As the debate over the appropriate design for farmhouses continued, Downing's *Cottage Residences* and plans for modest dwellings published in the *Horticulturist* proved highly influential. In 1844, for example, Thomas H. Hyatt described how he was designing his new farmhouse, a cottage in the Rural Gothic style. This devotee from Monroe County, New York, had read and reread Downing's *Treatise on Landscape Gardening* and *Cottage Residences* "with so much interest and delight, and I trust with no little profit also." Inspired by these works, Hyatt sketched the design of a home for his family and had finished drawings prepared by architect Merwin Austin. The woodcut of the resulting dwelling (fig. 44) clearly indicates how much Hyatt relied upon Design II in *Cottage Residences*, yet he also personalized the home, adding to its general outlines in ways that met his individual and familial needs.[35] When Mrs. Matilda W. Howard prepared a design of a farmhouse to enter in a competition sponsored by the New York State Agricultural Society, she too turned to Downing's works for inspiration. The overall design of the exterior (fig. 45) clearly borrowed freely, and without acknowledgment, from Design V of *Cottage Residences* (fig. 46), though Mrs. Howard reorganized the interior to meet the needs of a farm family and added an extension to provide essential work space.[36] Whether or not he approved of these examples, Downing found evidence of improvement in the domestic architecture of rural America in many recently constructed dwellings. Nevertheless, he continued to exhort

Figure 45. Mrs. Matilda S. Howard, plan of a farm cottage, from New York State Agricultural Society, *Transactions* 7 (1848). Courtesy of Special Collections, Morris Library, University of Delaware.

Figure 46. A. J. Downing, "A Cottage Villa in the Bracketed Mode," Design V of *Cottage Residences* (New York, 1842).

Figure 47. A vernacular farmhouse with "Grecian portico copied from a great house of the neighboring town or village." Downing criticized the portico as having "nothing whatever to do with a true farm-house." From A. J. Downing, "Hints on the Construction of Farm-Houses," New York State Agricultural Society, *Transactions* 5 (1846): 235. Courtesy of Special Collections, Morris Library, University of Delaware.

Figure 48. A similar vernacular farmhouse "employing the more comfortable and more characteristic verandah." From A. J. Downing, "Hints on the Construction of Farm-Houses," New York State Agricultural Society, *Transactions* 5 (1846): 236. Courtesy of Special Collections, Morris Library, University of Delaware.

readers on the principles of propriety and fitness. A farmhouse should not be "a suburban villa, set down in the midst of a plain farm," or a mock temple with a useless portico (fig. 47), but "should be *unmistakably a farmhouse*"[37] (fig. 48).

Just as he believed that Americans were "deficient in the knowledge, and the opportunity of knowing how beautiful human habitations are made by a little taste, time, and means,"[38] so did Downing's efforts to improve community life in rural areas begin with education—instructing readers about the benefits of planting trees. Too many streets in rural towns across the nation he declared to be little more than "dirty lanes and shadeless roadsides" that not only contributed to the tawdry appearance of "miserable, shabby-looking towns and villages" but undoubtedly had a negative effect on the lives of residents.[39] Americans had so little attachment to place because most places had little to retain their affections.

Downing attempted to persuade his countrymen of the philosophical and practical need to plant trees. Philosophically, tree planting was a measure of civilization, a reflection of the nation's progress from an essentially pioneer state. "If our ancestors found it wise and necessary to cut down vast forests," he wrote, "it is all the more needful that their descendants should plant trees."[40] Practically, he insisted that streets lined with trees would provide cool shade and be an effective barrier to the spread of fire. Moreover, handsome trees would improve "graceless villages" and soften the appearance of even the most deformed house.[41] What was at stake involved more than aesthetics: "the tasteful appearance which we long for in our country towns," Downing wrote in 1850, "we seek as the outward mark of education, moral sentiment, love of home, and refined cultivation."[42]

Downing invariably pointed to older New England towns and villages to illustrate his ideal of a handsome community. He characterized the rural landscape of Massachusetts in terms of its "flourishing villages, with broad streets lined with maples and elms, behind which are goodly rows of neat and substantial dwellings, full of evidences of order, comfort, and taste." In explaining why this region was different from the rest of the nation, Downing noted that residents there were "better educated" than other Americans about the benefits of trees. Attempting to persuade his readers that they too could transform their towns into graceful communities, he pointed to the example of James Hillhouse, whose efforts a generation earlier had made New Haven the "City of Elms," as well as those of an anonymous individual in western New York, who paid fellow residents a bounty for each tree they planted. These men served as models for the ways in which readers—apostles of taste—could have a similar influence in towns and villages across the nation. Even more effective were citizens acting in concert: Downing celebrated the organization of the Ornamental Tree Society, in Northampton, Massachusetts, "whose business and pleasure it is to turn dusty lanes and bald highways into alleys and avenues of coolness and verdure"; and he applauded the Rockingham Farmers' Club of Exeter, New Hampshire, for its attempt "to rouse the public mind to the importance of embellishing the streets of towns and villages, and to induce everybody to plant trees in front of his premises."[43]

Not every tree was worthy of prominence in the landscape of rural America. In much the way that he had promoted native varieties of fruits, Downing also endorsed the use of American trees. He denounced the ailanthus, for example, not only because of its pungent odor and aggressive competition with other plants, but also on "patriotic" grounds, because it was an imported exotic, a "miserable pigtail of an Indiaman" that had no place on America's streets or in its gardens. The fashion for imported species had become so great that Downing made a word play on Sidney Smith's famous remark,

"Who reads an American book?," asking "Who plants an American tree—in America?" Instead of spending money on inappropriate plants from other lands, he advised, "[s]elect the finest indigenous tree or trees, such as the soil and climate of the place will bring to the highest perfection." Among the American trees he recommended most highly were elms, maples, oaks, tulip poplars, and magnolias, majestic trees that would add beauty to streets and private grounds and shade the sidewalks from the relentless rays of the summer sun.[44]

Improvements in the design of rural houses and the planting of trees were important steps, but they were not enough. Still another mark of the poor state of civilization throughout the American countryside was the prevalence of allowing "pigs and poultry" to range free, a practice Downing termed a remnant of "a low condition of civilization." Laws requiring the fencing of animals were on the books in every community, but with the exception of Massachusetts and Downing's own town of Newburgh they were rarely enforced. Where animals enjoyed the "freedom" to roam, they invariably contributed to the "*brutal* aspect of the streets" throughout the nation. Downing attributed the public's tolerance of this nuisance to two causes, public ignorance or indifference, and demagogic politicians who catered to the basest elements within the community, in particular "our hard-working emigrants from the Emerald Isle, [who] cling to their ancient fraternity of porkers." In the years since Newburgh had eliminated this "barbarism," Downing reported, "such an air of neatness and rural beauty has sprung up, that the place has almost changed its character." The same would be true in every town and village once residents were educated to cherish order and neatness rather than tolerate slovenliness.[45]

Downing strove to maintain the countryside as the bastion of the nation's strength and morality. His efforts to improve the design of rural homes and villages and to promote an attachment to place attempted to slow the decline of the rural population. In an influential essay published in 1905, landscape architect Warren H. Manning pointed to Downing's work as an important precursor to the village improvement movement of the late nineteenth and early twentieth centuries.[46]

❧In much the way that Downing worked to improve the appearance of rural America, so did he attempt to strengthen the economy and society of the countryside by promoting scientific farming and agricultural education. He firmly supported any efforts to "raise the character, and elevate the intelligence of the agricultural class,"[47] but particularly education. Agricultural education was a subject of enormous consequence to farmers, and one that agricultural reformers had been discussing for decades. In 1823, for example, the estimable Jesse Buel, then a member of the New York State Legislature, called for a publicly supported agricultural college, and nine years later the state agricultural society similarly advocated the establishment of an agricultural school and experimental farm. Throughout the 1830s and 1840s the legislature received hundreds of petitions calling for the establishment of such a school, but in every case it failed to enact a bill that addressed the educational needs of farmers.[48] Unfortunately, Downing pointed out, farmers had not developed a "just appreciation" of their rights and duties. As a result, despite the overwhelming preponderance of rural voters, governmental officials were not attentive enough to their needs, particularly with regard to the benefits of an agricultural college.[49]

During the late 1840s Downing made the *Horticulturist* a powerful voice in support of agricultural education. At first he used its pages to report the efforts of others to establish a modern agricultural college. In reviewing R. L. Allen's *Brief Compend of American Agriculture*, for example, Downing added his own call for state legislatures to "effect something more tangible for the education and advancement of farmers." He also excerpted Allen's plea for an institution dedicated to the "professional education of farmers." Although in subsequent years Downing differentiated his efforts from Allen's by emphasizing that instruction in practical farming should be coequal with the scientific curriculum, in 1846 he approvingly published the author's advocacy of a college and experimental farm that more closely resembled a research institution than a school for farmers. "These institutions," Allen wrote, "should be schools for the teachers equally with the taught, and their liberally appointed laboratories and collections should contain every available means for the discovery of what is yet hidden, as well as for the further discovery of what is already partially known."[50] Similarly, when he published David Tomlinson's essay on vegetable physiology, which ended with a plea for agricultural education, Downing again endorsed the proposal. An "AGRICULTURAL SCHOOL, endowed *on a basis liberal and broad enough to command the best practical and theoretical talent* to be found, would be of incalculable benefit to this great state," he asserted, but he cautioned that it must be an institution of "high character" or else it would fail.[51] To the remarks of Professor C. U. Shepard of Amherst College calling for agricultural education Downing added that the subject was of "vital importance" to farmers. A successful agricultural college, he insisted, needed not only to be well endowed financially but to embrace "the soundest practical and scientific ability in the country."[52]

In each of these instances Downing remained a peripheral figure in the campaign for agricultural education—a vocal supporter, but not a working farmer or an originator of ideas. In the spring of 1849, however, Governor Hamilton Fish appointed Downing one of eight commissioners charged to "mature a plan for an Agricultural College and experimental farm," which would be presented to the state legislature at the beginning of the 1850 session.[53] Each of the commissioners represented one of the judicial districts in the state, but beyond his place of residence, the reason why Downing was named a commissioner was not explained. Perhaps his appointment was in recognition of the increasing importance of horticulture to the agricultural economy of New York State; perhaps it resulted from his support for agricultural education, and particularly his emphasis on the practical as well as the theoretical needs of farmers. Whatever the reason he was named to the commission, Downing characteristically threw his energies into the project. By 1851 he could begin an address to the state agricultural society with the remark, "the interests of the farmer are very dear to me."[54]

Any records of discussions held by the commissioners apparently have not survived, but in December 1849—a month before the state legislature was to meet—Downing devoted the lead essay in the *Horticulturist* to the subject of agricultural education. He began by reiterating a familiar theme, that farmers were "the last to demand of government a share of those benefits which are continually heaped upon less important, but more sagacious and more clamorous branches of the body politic." The "giant that tills the soil" was "gradually wakening into conscious activity," Downing reported, and was becoming more aware of the importance of agriculture as the bedrock of the republic. This would inevitably result in the establishment of an agricultural school in New York, he predicted, one that would become the model for similar schools in every state in the nation.[55]

The deliberations of the commissioners must have revealed that many farmers were hostile to the idea of "book learning." As Solon Robinson pointed out, farmers were among the most conservative of humans and sometimes resisted innovation simply because it led to departures from the way their fathers and grandfathers had tilled the soil. Too often the farmer "delves on in the same beaten routine," the report of the commissioners added.[56] More worrisome was the appearance of significant disagreement over the purposes of an agricultural college, especially the divergence between practical and scientific education. Downing, however, was certain that farming was "both a science and an art," and believed that the "well educated agriculturist should combine in himself both the science and the art which he professes." His conception of education involved not simply the accumulation of knowledge, which could be either theoretical or practical, but the development of wisdom, which he defined as "knowledge put in action." In words remarkably similar to Emerson's prescriptions for the protean American Scholar, Downing called for the union of the head and the hand, theory and practice: "What the agricultural school, which this age and country now demands, must do to satisfy us, is to teach—not alone the knowledge of the books—not alone the practice of the fields, but that *agricultural wisdom* which involves both, and which can never be attained without a large development of the powers of the pupil in both directions." Thus, it was essential that the college attract the best, most talented faculty rather than entrust the next generation of farmers to the hands of "quack chemists and quack physiologists in the lecture halls, or those of chimerical farmers or dull teamsters in the fields."[57]

The report submitted to the state legislature on January 2, 1850, was signed by all eight commissioners, so it is difficult to determine the precise extent to which Downing's ideas shaped their recommendations. The report began by conceding that farming had not progressed to the same degree as other human endeavors, notably industry and transportation. New York's husbandmen, it argued, were just beginning to understand the practical benefits of scientific investigation and "perceive that success in agricultural pursuits depends upon the judicious application of knowledge." After reviewing the structure and curriculum of agricultural schools in Europe, as well as the few institutions in the United States that offered instruction in farming, the commissioners concluded that none possessed a framework that would provide the kind of education New York farmers needed. They called for an institution with a faculty of at least six professors, who would teach chemistry, natural history, mineralogy, mathematics, engineering, surveying, botany and horticulture, history, law, general science, "veterinary art," and anatomy. Other employees the commissioners believed essential to the success of the school included a skilled farmer, a gardener, a carpenter, and a blacksmith, who together would provide "practical knowledge of [the] arts so essential in the management of a farm."[58]

Governor Fish's charge requested that the commissioners investigate every aspect of the proposed school, so the remainder of the report discussed steps necessary to implement the plan. The commissioners called for an initial state appropriation to acquire the property and construct buildings, as well as an annual sum of $10,000 until the college was self-sufficient (through fees charged students and the sale of produce raised). Students would be expected to work on the farm three or four hours a day, learning the most advanced agricultural practices, and to spend the rest of their time in "study, lectures and recitations."[59]

The existence of such a school would benefit the state in numerous ways, the commissioners predicted. Most obviously, the work of faculty and students would advance scientific knowledge and replace the "heterogeneous and often discordant mass of materials collected in agricultural journals." The school would also function as a kind of agricultural extension program, analyzing the soil in different parts of the state and instructing farmers in the "most successful and proper plan of increasing and preserving their fertility." And, as graduates returned to their homes, they would "excite a spirit of emulation, both by precept and example," that would contribute to improved farming practices throughout the state.[60] Ultimately, then, in creating an agricultural college, the state would be investing in its own future, ensuring the prosperity of the largest and most valuable component of New York's economy.

Downing's contributions to the report most likely included its recommendation of a professorship in botany and horticulture as well as the employment of a gardener. "'Woodman, spare that tree,'" as he wrote in 1847, quoting George P. Morris's well-known poem, was "the choral sentiment that should be instilled and taught at the agricultural schools, and re-echoed by all the agricultural and horticultural societies in the land."[61] Given his decade of efforts to improve rural life, Downing was probably also the commissioner who argued most forcefully for the ultimate result of such a school: "Taste and skill, manifesting their existence among the farmers in every quarter," the report concluded, "would impart new beauty to our rural scenery, and make each neighborhood an object of attachment to those familiar with its local attractions and reared under their influence."[62]

The report called for a bill establishing an agricultural college, to be administered by eight commissioners, who would determine the location of the institution and have the authority to "purchase the farm, and proceed forthwith to erect the necessary edifices, fixtures and appurtenances" required for its successful operation. The principal structure, which would contain a large lecture hall to accommodate five hundred persons, classrooms, a library, and a chemical laboratory, was to be 100 by 60 feet.[63] As the work of the commissioners was nearing completion, Downing prepared a design for the college buildings. Surviving evidence does not indicate whether Downing was simply illustrating what the building might look like or whether he expected to receive the commission to design it, but the latter appears to have been the case. What he wrote of the overall operations of the college—that its plan ought to be entrusted only to persons "whose competence to the task is beyond the shadow of a doubt"—surely applied to the physical environment of the institution as well as its curriculum and finances.[64] Based on conversations with the commissioners, Downing made preliminary sketches for several college buildings in December 1849 and January 1850. He then solicited Alexander Jackson Davis's assistance in compiling a portfolio of finished drawings. The design for the principal building (figs. 49 and 50) was a vaguely classical structure, with a projecting central pavilion containing a broad entrance flanked by niches, presumably for statues, and a boldly projecting roof supported by brackets.[65]

Downing's correspondence with Davis, the principal source of information on this design, does not reveal why he considered this building particularly well suited to agricultural education. Downing had conceded that the classical styles were appropriate for public buildings, but the choice is somewhat surprising because Davis had designed several important collegiate structures in the Gothic Revival style. Surviving documents also do not indicate how Downing expected that the design of the building would promote the cause of taste among students who studied in its halls.

Downing was deeply disappointed that the bill authorizing establishment of the agricultural college failed to pass the state legislature. As did a number of other commentators, he attributed the outcome to the very people who would have profited most from the school, farmers, who remained divided about the benefits such an institution might confer. When publishing in the *Horticulturist* an article by E. W. Leavenworth explaining the fate of the bill, Downing added that the "lukewarmness, apathy, or indifference of the farmers themselves, more than any other cause," was responsible for the result.[66]

Downing remained committed to agricultural education. He continued his efforts to educate farmers about the value of a state-supported college and urged supporters to lobby their legislators in behalf of the bill. By 1851 he had become one of the most articulate and influential proponents of agricultural education in the nation: in his address to the state agricultural society that year, Downing offered a compelling analysis of the economic and social contributions such a college would make. Traditional farming practices were inherently inefficient, he declared, and resulted in the extraction of essential nutrients from the soil: "[the] productive power of nearly all the land in the United States which has been ten years in cultivation is fearfully lessening every season, from the devastating effects of a ruinous system of husbandry." As a result, farms along the Hudson that once produced thirty to forty bushels of wheat per acre were yielding only twelve to fourteen. The loss of prosperity was bad enough, but Downing was equally alarmed by the social consequences of profligate farming. Young men left eastern states to practice the same inefficiencies on virgin soil in the west, or gave up farming altogether and sought better opportunities in the city. The proverbial elderly

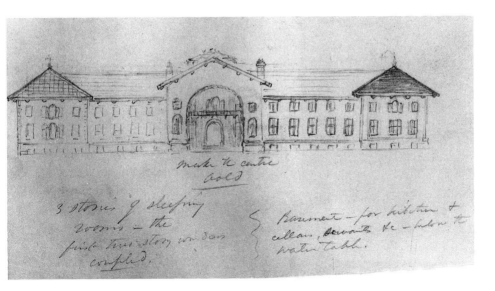

Figure 49. A. J. Downing, sketch for an agricultural college, 1850. Courtesy of Metropolitan Museum of Art, New York City, Harris Brisbane Dick Fund (24.66.1411[6r]), 1924, all rights reserved.

Figure 50. A. J. Davis, design for an agricultural college, 1850. Courtesy of Metropolitan Museum of Art, New York City, Harris Brisbane Dick Fund (24.66.1411[35v]), 1924, all rights reserved.

farmer found his sons "turning their backs upon civilization and the comforts of home because they must have either a new *way* [of life] or a new *soil.*"[67] Only comprehensively educated farmers, trained both in theory and practice, Downing insisted, could halt the decline of rural America and maintain the new world's primacy as the "garden of the whole earth."[68]

The agricultural college Downing envisioned would have eliminated both the economic and the social failings of traditional farming. Scientific instruction in botany and horticulture would have extended Downing's efforts in promoting improvements in pomology, while teaching students how to design plans and specifications for farm buildings would have contributed to the aesthetic improvement of rural life. A curriculum of the breadth he outlined would thus have ensured that graduates of the agricultural college would become educated farmers and citizens whose example and instruction would carry forward Downing's goal of reforming rural life.

6

Toward an American Architecture

Rome was not built in a day, and whoever would see a national architecture, must be patient till it has time to rise out of the old materials, under the influences of a new climate, our novel institutions and modified habits.

—Andrew Jackson Downing

In the October 1846 issue of the *Horticulturist,* Downing printed an excerpt of a letter he had received from a correspondent in Boston. The writer praised the plans for simple rural cottages Downing had published the previous month and expressed "hope that we may, by and by, have a style of building of our own, founded on just and sound principles, which shall be to us what the original ideas involved in the classical and pointed styles were to the ancients." Downing's response did not address the writer's broader concern, the development of a national style of architecture, but instead focused on a more modest goal, meeting the need for tastefully designed farmhouses. Nevertheless, he explained that rural architecture had to be "significant," which, he added, required that it "express the life and habits of our rural people."[1] This statement looked back to the themes he had articulated in *Cottage Residences,* especially fitness and propriety as the most important attributes of a properly designed dwelling, yet it also contained the germ of an idea Downing would develop in succeeding years, that a distinctive American architecture had to evolve from and reflect the nation's social, economic, and political institutions.

Downing's first two books had included the subtitle, "Adapted to North America," an acknowledgment that he was gleaning ideas from similar European books and journals but also an assertion that he modified plans for buildings and their grounds to conform to the climate and republican social structure of the United States. So successful was the author in this effort that a reviewer praised the 1844 edition of the *Treatise* as "strictly American in its character and adaptation."[2] By contrast, the designs for "model cottages" that Sarah J. Hale published in *Godey's Lady's Book* between 1846 and 1859 were almost entirely direct copies of plans published in English books, especially J. C. Loudon's *Encyclopaedia of Cottage, Farm and Villa Architecture*.[3] To be sure, the text occasionally included "analytical and critical remarks," but these were comments about style rather than an explanation of ways to alter the design to meet American conditions.[4] Downing must have been as displeased with *Godey's* choices as he was with Gervase Wheeler's unsuccessful attempt to graft English forms onto American homes.[5] Although Hale and Wheeler were undoubtedly influenced by the popularity of Downing's writings, and although Hale followed Downing's lead in the various styles of dwellings she chose to illustrate and the emphasis she placed on the importance of a design that embraced both building and grounds, the difference in their approaches was significant: whereas Downing attempted to develop an architectural aesthetic in keeping with what he considered the nation's social and cultural aspirations, the taste Wheeler and *Godey's* promoted was decidedly English.

Downing realized that the emergence of an American aesthetic in architecture would take years if not centuries. As citizens of a young nation, faced with the daunting task of domesticating a vast continent, the American people were "mainly occupied with the practical wants of life" and chose to devote little time to the fine arts. Save for "our Yankee clap-board house," he observed in 1850, the United States did not have a national architecture any more than it could boast of a national tradition in music. Nevertheless, Downing found evidence of the progress of taste in two developments: the shift away from the Greek Revival, which had been the near-universal choice for domestic architecture, though he conceded that "fashion" still needed the discipline of "right *direction*"; and the incorporation of "modern improvements" in each new generation of dwellings, which contributed to greater comfort and efficiency.[6]

Americans seemed, to Downing, to be of two minds about the progress of architecture. On one extreme were critics of every recently introduced style, who perceived anything but a "solid square block" as "barbarous." At the opposite pole were those so insistent on an American expression in the arts that they dismissed everything foreign—Gothic, Italianate, and Swiss, as well as Greek or Roman styles in architecture. These "hypercritical" commentators called for "an entirely new 'order,' " and had little patience for Downing and other tastemakers whose designs were "modifications of such foreign styles." Their insistence on an immediate and profoundly American style of architecture was a mistake, Downing replied, for a national expression in building did not immediately spring from the soil, "like the after-growth in our forests," or from the experiences of the American public, most of whom were of European descent. Americans, he noted, had not yet developed a national language or religion, and continued to follow Parisian fashion. It was equally logical that their architecture should be derived from European civilizations.[7]

No style of architecture, Downing explained, had simply been invented. Each developed through the process of modifying previous styles and modes of building, much as Roman architecture was built upon the lessons of the Greek. Each was the product of particular circumstances—"the climate, habits of the people, and genius of the architects, *acting upon each other through a long series of years*." Downing was confident that an American style of architecture would eventually take shape, because of the distinctive geography, society, and institutions of the nation. But while he was certain that architecture would some day reflect the destinies of a republic in which almost every citizen was a landowner, he cautioned that "the development of the finer and more intellectual traits of character are slower in a nation than they are in a man, and only time can develope [sic] them healthily in either case."[8]

The parallel Downing drew for the slow evolution of an American style of architecture was the development of a national character. In 1849 he enumerated the forces that were fostering the emergence of a distinctive national identity in the United States, including physical separation from Europe and the republican system of government. So powerfully did these forces operate, individually and collectively, that the nation annually "swallows hundreds of thousands of foreigners, and *digests* them all."[9] At a time of record high levels of emigration from Ireland and Germany and of powerful nativist yearnings in American political discourse, Downing was convinced that the nation would absorb these newcomers. In words strikingly similar to Crevecoeur's formulation of the immigrant as archetypal American,[10] he wrote: "no one can look reflectingly on all this, and not see that there is a national type, which will prevail over all the complexity, which various origin, foreign manners, and different religions bring to our shores." Pointing toward the English, a people similarly forged from many ethnic strands, Downing explained that a hundred years hence the United States would be "quite as distinct and quite as developed, in our national character."[11]

An American style of architecture would evolve as naturally as would a distinctive national identity. In the meantime, while the United States was "in the midst of what may be called the experimental stage of architectural taste," Downing preached patience. Exasperating though it might be to critics, as an aggregate of passionately independent people Americans "seem determined to *try everything*," in architecture as in other areas of human endeavor. Downing's list of architectural anomalies included a battlemented castle on the banks of the Hudson, built "after the fashion of the old robber strong-holds on the Rhine"; P. T. Barnum's Iranistan, near Bridgeport, Connecticut, which resembled "the minareted and domed residence of a Persian *Shah*"; Thomas

U. Walter's Greek Revival Girard College, in Philadelphia, a school for poor orphans in the shape of a temple to Jupiter; and James Renwick, Jr.'s Smithsonian Institution, which Downing described as having been designed "in the style of a Norman monastery—with a relish of the dark ages in it, the better to contrast with its avowed purpose of diffusing light" and knowledge. The degree of experimentation was so great that throughout the Northeast citizens were erecting houses "in all known styles supposed to be in any way suitable to the purposes of civilized habitations." Whereas critics might be appalled by these excesses, Downing celebrated them as indicative of a lively popular interest in architecture. Comparing the exuberance of various styles to the initial stages of winemaking, he predicted, the "froth of foreign affectations will work off, and the impurities of vulgar taste settle down, leaving us the pure spirit of a better national taste at last."[12]

The key to taming the excess of fashion, Downing believed, was an education in the virtue of simplicity. This was especially important in domestic architecture, because excellence in design could easily be compromised by "private *fancies,* and personal vanities." Throughout *Cottage Residences* and the pages of the *Horticulturist,* Downing insisted that "truthful simplicity" was better than "borrowed decorations." In building simple, honest dwellings, beautiful in their own right, Americans would avoid the mistakes of ill-fitting ornament—"carpenter's gothic," in his term—and plant the seeds that would mature into a style of architecture befitting their republican society.[13]

✑ Throughout the second half of the 1840s Downing promoted simplicity and taste in domestic architecture through his writings. In 1847, for example, he persuaded his New York publishers, Wiley and Putnam, to bring out an American edition of George Wightwick's *Hints to Young Architects,* which, he predicted, would prove to be of "real and practical assistance to the progress of Domestic Architecture in this country." In preparing a new introduction for American readers, however, Downing subtly but strikingly transformed the nature of the book. Wightwick envisioned his audience as architects and artisans, and his text and illustrations were "calculated to facilitate their practical operations." Downing particularly valued the architectural details and construction specifications Wightwick had included, which he judged "some of the most valuable suggestions that have yet come under our notice." Nevertheless, he realized that American readers needed to understand more basic architectural issues in order to benefit from the Englishman's advice. Thus, he appended a series of notes that attempted to "adapt" Wightwick's practical suggestions to American construction practices and a thirty-three-page primer on domestic architecture, "Hints to Persons About Building in the Country," that clearly addressed the prospective client.[14]

Downing devoted his "hints" to "matters of the greatest consequence" that even the most practical books too often ignored—where, what, and how to build. There was, he conceded, a widespread ignorance of these matters, proof of which was visible everywhere in dwellings that were poorly located, poorly designed, or failed to meet the functional needs and financial abilities of the owners. Although Downing admitted that the surest way to avoid such "evils" was to employ an experienced architect, he wrote for the much larger audience of persons who intended to build their own houses or employ a carpenter to do so.[15]

The selection of an appropriate location for a residence was most basic. Too many inexperienced homebuilders chose elevated sites, because of the extensive views they offered; but Downing advised against such places because of exposure to the elements, difficulty of access, and dryness of soil. Also popular were valleys, and while Downing conceded that these often proved to be excellent places for a dwelling, especially when adjacent to a large body of water, he warned the prospective builder to beware of narrow valleys and shallow, sluggish streams, which were potential sources of malaria as well as other illnesses and which, in winter, experienced premature frost and greater severity of cold. The best, most practical setting for a residence, Downing advised, was a moderate location, with good, well-drained soil, in a healthful neighborhood. Where the prospective builder could choose its aspect, Downing recommended that it face the "fair weather quarter," which in most of the United States was the southwest.[16]

Deciding what to build involved more than individual taste, Downing insisted, and should be predicated on the "philosophical principles . . . of _fitness_ and _propriety_." He reiterated several of his longstanding concerns: that any style of architecture be adapted to American conditions; that dwellings reflect the resources and livelihood of owners; that the type of architecture be in keeping with the scenery; and that stone, brick, or stucco were superior to wood as building materials.[17]

Downing's advice on how to build a house took the form of a familiar story. A man had determined that he would not only erect his own dwelling, but that it would be a better one than any he had seen before. After he had studied plans and determined an overall design, construction commenced, as did the problems—belated recognition of the need for an additional room, closets, "wholly overlooked" in the plan, that had to be added, a back stairway that the owner decided was of "incomparable value"—with the result that much of what had already been built had to be changed, at enormous cost.

Moreover, the man, functioning as his own contractor, had no experience in judging materials, so much of what he bought proved faulty, which became evident as cracks and shrinking disfigured the wood and plaster. Because of the numerous changes, the house turned out to be far more expensive, and far less satisfactory, than it would have been if he had hired an experienced architect in the first place. For those persons intending to build a house without engaging an architect, Downing suggested first deciding what they wanted in a residence, perhaps with the aid, it is tempting to think, of one of his books. He then advised employing a "master-workman, whose integrity and abilities are known," and provided a series of specifications and sample contracts to guide the prospective homeowner.[18]

Useful as Wightwick's *Hints* was for practical advice on location and construction, Americans still needed instruction in the proper design of houses, which Downing provided through the *Horticulturist*. Between July 1846, when he published in the inaugural issue a design for improving a common country house, and June 1850, the eve of his journey to Europe, Downing devoted the frontispiece and an article to architecture in thirty-three of the forty-eight monthly numbers of that journal.[19] Sometimes only a few paragraphs described the design; on other occasions several pages of text explicated the principles of taste or provided details of construction. Many of the views were accompanied by floor plans, and a few included specifications and details of cost. Among the thirty-three articles, two were on Gothic churches, two were devoted to rustic arbors, one described the design and construction of ice houses, and one presented a pair of schoolhouses first published in Henry Barnard's *School Architecture*.[20]

The remaining twenty-seven designs were for residences. Ten were cottages, three were cottage villas, one was a farmhouse, four were country houses, eight were villas, and one was a Gothic mansion—Philip St. George Cocke's Belmead, forty miles from Richmond, Virginia.[21] Classifying the buildings by type, style, and location is difficult, because Downing did not always identify them clearly and consistently. For example, his terminology usually equated a country house with a villa, though the former was less pretentious; but at least one design for a country house was included in the section devoted to farmhouses in *The Architecture of Country Houses,* while the farmhouse design presented in the *Horticulturist* became a small villa for the southern climate in Downing's 1850 book.[22] Based on the description or the appearance of the engraving, eighteen of the designs were for a rural location, three for a suburban site, three for small cities (A. J. Davis's designs for Lewis B. Brown's bracketed villa in Rahway, N.J., and the Rotch House in New Bedford, Mass., and Gervase Wheeler's English cottage in Brunswick, Me.),[23] and three were not identifiably designed for a specific location. Stylistically, eleven were Gothic (most the Rural Gothic Downing favored for cottages and smaller villas, though three were larger Tudor Gothic dwellings), four were Italianate, two were Swiss, and at least eight were "bracketed." Most of the bracketed buildings employed the board-and-batten construction Downing favored for wood structures.

Eleven of the designs published in the first four volumes of the *Horticulturist* were Downing's own. These included six cottages, a cottage villa, two country houses, and two villas. Stylistically, six of Downing's designs were bracketed, three were Rural Gothic, and two were Italianate.[24] A. J. Davis was, after Downing, the largest contributor to the designs published in the *Horticulturist*. In addition to the plans for the Brown and Rotch houses, he also supplied designs for a "simple country house," a "cottage villa" on Staten Island, and the illustration of Belmead.[25] As he had done for both the *Treatise* and *Cottage Residences,* Davis transformed many of Downing's rough sketches into finished drawings ready for wood engraving.[26] Other designs Downing published included those for a Swiss cottage, by "A Young Architect, of New-York"; the Swiss cottage of E. P. Prentice, at Mount Hope, near Albany, New York, by G. J. Penchard; an octagonal villa designed by Henry A. Page, of Boston; and a Gothic country house by "an amateur."[27] Four of the plans were republished from English sources, and two were by English-born architect Gervase Wheeler.[28]

Collectively, the designs Downing presented in the first four volumes of the *Horticulturist* are significant for several reasons. First, a number of them were very inexpensive and represented his effort to extend taste to even the simplest "working man's cottage." These plans attempted to meet the needs of an audience different from the one Downing had addressed in *Cottage Residences.*[29] Second, the architectural designs that Downing considered appropriate to readers of the *Horticulturist* were overwhelmingly rural; only three were for suburban houses, and the three located in small cities, already constructed according to designs by Davis or Wheeler, were spacious houses with ample ground for gardens. Downing's choice of these designs was not simply a concession to his readers, however: the plans he published reflected his belief in the superiority of rural life over that in cities. Third, although Downing appreciated the Swiss and Italianate styles, and believed them particularly appropriate for specific types of scenery, he clearly favored the Rural Gothic over other historical styles as best adapted to American life, and he championed the bracketed style as a significant step in the evolution of an American architectural idiom. In 1850 he described the bracketed style as a "most pleasing manner of building rural edifices of an economical character." It was the American style, Downing asserted, because it was well adapted to "our climate and the cheapness of wood as a building material."[30]

In presenting these twenty-seven designs in the *Horticulturist,* Downing was developing many of the ideas he articulated in his final book. Indeed, ten of the thirty-three designs included in *The Architecture of Country Houses* first appeared in the monthly, while three additional plates from the *Horticulturist* illustrated other designs.[31] The preponderance of cottages included in the first two volumes, and of villas in the third and fourth, is undoubtedly indicative of Downing's progress in writing his final book.

ᴗ During the summer of 1847 Downing began formulating plans for a new "volume on Cottage & villa architecture with some *interiors*" and requested Davis's cooperation.[32] The following January he outlined his intent at greater length: "In the 'Cottage Residences' frequent complaint was made that there were no *cheap* designs—for very small cottages—for a few hundred dollars each. In order to cover this difficulty I mean in the new volume to begin at the smallest cottages & go up to the best villas."[33] Downing reiterated this concern a year later, when he noted, "Our new work on *Country Houses . . .* will include designs for cottages of very moderate cost."[34] The first "very slight & feeble sketches" he sent Davis were for cottages "as small & plain as I know how to make them," and while Downing wanted to keep ornament to a minimum he also insisted that the designs exhibit "*character* and good proportions."[35]

The sketches were indeed far less polished than those he had sent Davis while working on *Cottage Residences,* an indication that over almost a decade of collaboration Downing had come to rely not only on the architect's "capital pencil" but on his ability to understand intent and translate rough ideas onto blocks ready for the wood engraver. "You have so complete and perfect an eye," Downing wrote in transmitting a drawing of an Italianate villa, "that I have only *suggested* in the sketches, leaving you to fill up."[36] He also counted on Davis to check the proofs that engraver Alexander Anderson made of the designs.[37] But Downing's proposal that Davis accept the benefits of publicity for his architectural talents and a percentage of royalties from the book in lieu of payment for each drawing—perhaps, given the timing of the offer, a measure of the degree of Downing's financial difficulties—was not accepted.[38]

As had been true of the *Treatise* and *Fruits and Fruit Trees of America,* writing and assembling illustrations for *The Architecture of Country Houses* took far longer than Downing had anticipated. He publicly noted that his book on country houses was in preparation in January 1849.[39] The following November he conceded that the work had "been extended beyond our original plan" and would "require a few weeks longer before it is out of press."[40] In

March 1850 Downing lamented that he had "never sat so unceasingly at my writing-table as for the past three months."[41] Sketches and letters continued to travel between "Attica," Downing's term for Davis's New York office, and Newburgh, until April 1850, at which time the book must have been just about ready for typesetting.[42] Published by D. Appleton and Company in July 1850, *The Architecture of Country Houses* ran to 428 pages and included 320 illustrations.

In the preface to *The Architecture of Country Houses,* Downing proposed "three excellent reasons why my countrymen should have good houses." First, the home was a "powerful means of civilization," a visible measure of the nation's progress from barbarism to a more advanced state of society. "So long as men are forced to dwell in log huts and follow a hunter's life," he wrote, "we must not be surprised at lynch law and the use of the bowie knife. But, when smiling lawns and tasteful cottages begin to embellish a country, we know that order and culture are established." Second, Downing asserted that the "*individual home* has a great social value for a people." Because nurture within the family shaped a person's character and personality, the design of the house, the physical frame in which child rearing took place, was critically important to the future of American society. Third, he argued, there was a "moral influence in a country home," a stabilizing counterweight to the "feverish unrest and want of balance between desire and the fulfillment of life" so characteristic of the United States. Thus, he concluded, the reform of domestic architecture should be a national priority: "the condition of the family home—in this country where every man may have a home—should be raised, till it shall symbolize the best character and pursuits, and the dearest affections and enjoyments of social life."[43]

Downing's intent in writing *The Architecture of Country Houses* was not to present a "scientific work on art" but to educate and persuade. As in the *Treatise* and *Cottage Residences,* he adopted a familiar prose style, a conversational tone he believed would be accessible to "all classes of readers." In much the way that those earlier books asserted that "correct taste" had to be learned and was "only the result of education," Downing again observed that the appreciation of the "beauty of expression, in architecture, as in other arts, and even in nature, required educated feeling." Punctuating the text with observations or advice for "a person uneducated in domestic architecture," or the "uninitiated reader," or the novice, he offered *The Architecture of Country Houses* with the modest hope that it might prove to be "of some little assistance to the popular taste."[44]

Because his purpose was educational, Downing entitled the first chapter "On the Real Meaning of Architecture." He again distinguished between the useful, a building that met the requirements of shelter in the most durable, economical, and convenient way, which he described as the practical "framework or skeleton on which Architecture grows and wakens into life," and the beautiful, which "appeals to a wholly different part of our nature." In *Cottage Residences* Downing had raised architecture above mere utility in building, but eight years later, undoubtedly influenced by the writings of John Ruskin, he presented a fuller and more sophisticated analysis of beauty. It was, he wrote, "a higher attribute of matter," an "original instinct of the sentiment of our nature." He compared the human reaction to beauty to "a worship, by the heart, of a higher perfection manifested in material forms."[45]

Ruskin's contribution to the evolution of Downing's ideas was important. Caroline Downing described Ruskin as someone who "handles so artistically & with such originality the various great subjects connected with nature & art" and considered the English critic one of her husband's favorite authors. Downing may well have read "The Poetry of Architecture," which Ruskin had published in J. C. Loudon's *Architectural Magazine,* and Downing's explication of absolute and relative beauty was indebted to *Modern Painters,* as was his understanding of symmetry, variety, and unity. Downing surely also obtained a copy of *The Seven Lamps of Architecture,* which Wiley and Putnam issued in 1849, shortly after its appearance in a London edition. Downing's assertion that architecture "appeals so powerfully to the whole nature of man—to his senses, his heart, and his understanding," marked a shift away from the associationist theory of Archibald Alison and toward what historian Roger B. Stein has termed a "romantic state of mind," which he associates with Ruskin. According to Stein, in following Ruskin's lead Downing was presenting aesthetic categories as "visual embodiments of moral and metaphysical abstractions."[46] Certainly Downing's statement that the beautiful in architecture was "an embodiment in which the idea triumphs over the material and brings it into perfect subjection" owed much to Ruskin, as did his assertion that the purpose of the fine arts was to elevate objects by giving them "a moral significance."[47]

Nevertheless, in the same way that Downing adapted European architectural plans to American conditions, so did he choose selectively from Ruskin as it served his purposes. Downing's own home, of stucco scored in imitation of stone, obviously violated one of Ruskin's cardinal principles of architecture—truth to materials. His use of an inferior material to resemble a more expensive one might be attributed to youthful enthusiasm or pretension, and certainly in *The Architecture of Country Houses* he echoed Ruskin's insistence that "the material should *appear* to be what it is"—that stone used in a building ought to look like stone.[48] Downing's advocacy of the bracketed style was due in part to its expression of the material, wood, in the design. Yet even after he had read *Seven Lamps,* Downing continued to prescribe the use of techniques that violated Ruskinian principles, such as the staining of cheaper wood in imitation of oak.[49] Nor did he object to nonstructural ceiling ribs in Gothic Revival interiors, which rested on brackets "so as to convey the idea of vertical support," or to the use of wallpapers that imitated frescoes, which, he wrote, could "produce a tasteful, satisfactory, and agreeable effect."[50] Valuable though he found Ruskin's writings, Downing was more interested in educating American taste than he was in positing architectural verities.

Perhaps the most important "truths" Downing preached in *The Architecture of Country Houses* had less to do with materials than with expression of purpose—that a rural dwelling ought to look like a rural dwelling—and with the relationship between the physical structure of the home and the life of its inhabitants. The various architectural anomalies he described, such as educational institutions in the shape of Greek temples or dwellings that resembled battlemented castles and minareted villas, he found inappropriate because the design of the structure bore no relationship to the experience of residents, let alone the republican society and institutions of the nation. As he had done in *Cottage Residences* and in the *Horticulturist,* Downing again insisted that a dwelling embody "truthfulness of character," that a home was "only perfect when . . . composed so as to express the utmost beauty and truth in the life of the individual."[51]

Downing divided *The Architecture of Country Houses* into two parts and thirteen sections or chapters. Part 1 included the opening chapter on meaning in architecture as well as seven additional chapters devoted to cottages, farmhouses, and other farm buildings. Once again he emphasized the importance of simplicity in modest dwellings, cautioning readers against the "frippery and 'gingerbread' look which degrades, rather than elevates, the beauty of the cottage." Because cost was so often a factor to persons who intended to build a cottage, Downing urged the use of board-and-batten construction, which clearly expressed "strength and truthfulness," instead of decoration that was not intrinsic to the structure. Indeed, as a preface to the thirteen plans for cottages, he wrote, "[W]e have aimed rather at producing beauty by means of form and proportion, than by ornament." This was especially true of the "designs for *cheap cottages*" (see, for example, fig. 51), dwellings suitable for working class families "desirous to have their home of three rooms tasteful and expressive."[52]

Nine of the thirteen designs for cottages in Downing's final book were original to that volume. Ranging from the simple box to modest bracketed and Rural Gothic cottages to an elaborate Swiss-style tenant's dwelling, the

Figure 51. A. J. Downing, "Small Bracketed Cottage," Design II of *The Architecture of Country Houses* (New York, 1850). Courtesy of Special Collections, Morris Library, University of Delaware.

thirteen plans varied in material from wood to brick and stucco to stone. True to his intent in providing designs for inexpensive houses, the estimated cost for the cheapest dwelling (see fig. 38, above) was about $400 if erected in the Hudson Valley, 15 to 20 percent less elsewhere in the country, based on the price of materials and labor. For each design, Downing provided plans for the principal and chamber floors; and in cases where the design called for elements that might be unfamiliar to some builders, such as the porch and overhanging chamber room in Design III, he included construction details as well (figs. 52 and 53).

The level of decoration Downing thought appropriate varied with the cost and pretentiousness of the house: whereas for the simplest dwelling, projecting rafters, vertical boarding, and door and window hoods were adequate, for more elaborate cottages he included ornamental trellises, verge boards, and clustered chimneys in the plans. For two designs, Downing included an

Figure 52. A. J. Downing, "Symmetrical Bracketed Cottage," Design III of *The Architecture of Country Houses* (New York, 1850). Courtesy of Special Collections, Morris Library, University of Delaware.

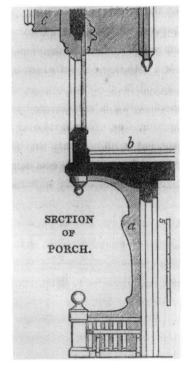

Figure 53. Detail showing section of entrance porch and projecting second-story overhang of the symmetrical bracketed cottage, from *The Architecture of Country Houses* (New York, 1850), p. 88. Courtesy of Special Collections, Morris Library, University of Delaware.

Figure 54. A. J. Downing, "Regular Bracketed Cottage" with "arbor-veranda," Design VIII of *The Architecture of Country Houses* (New York, 1850). Courtesy of Special Collections, Morris Library, University of Delaware.

"arbor-veranda," which consisted of trellises, supported by posts, that extended on three sides of the house (fig. 54). While far less expensive than a veranda, it would provide shade and "much beauty." What best characterized the designs for cottages was simplicity. The words Downing chose to describe Design VII, an Italianate suburban cottage (fig. 55), are applicable to all of the plans he published for this "class" of house: it occupied, he wrote, a middle ground between "entire baldness" and "the frippery of ornament" that characterized too many smaller dwellings.[53]

Downing devoted sections 5, 6, and 8 to farmhouses and miscellaneous farm structures. Farmhouses were by far the most numerous dwellings in the United States, and he found most of them to be of a "common-place and meager character." Downing attributed this to two causes, the lack of attention to this type of residence by architects, and farmers themselves, who "seldom consider what the beauty of a farm-house consists in." The problem was not the degree of embellishment, for agricultural journals frequently published designs for model farmhouses that adopted "the style or decorations of

Figure 55. A. J. Downing, "Suburban Cottage," Design VII of *The Architecture of Country Houses* (New York, 1850). Courtesy of Special Collections, Morris Library, University of Delaware.

the ornamental cottage or villa," but rather the absence of "truth," which was replacing fitness in Downing's architectural vocabulary. Most published plans were "not intrinsically farm-houses" because they did not "express the life and character of the farmer." Downing insisted that a "farm-house must, first of all, look like a farm-house" and express "that beauty . . . which lies in a farmer's life"—simplicity, honesty, frankness, and similar attributes. Farm dwellings should be characterized by breadth rather than height, to provide ample space for "all the in-door occupations of agricultural life," as well as "a certain rustic plainness" and solid construction. Above all, a farmhouse should be characterized by simplicity and an "absence of all pretension."[54]

The six designs for farmhouses Downing published in *The Architecture of Country Houses* were a diverse lot: a simple symmetrical stone dwelling, two board-and-batten houses, modifications of the English rural and Swiss styles, a farmhouse for a large northern farm, and a bracketed villa farmhouse. Materials ranged from wood to rough-cast to stone, and the cost varied from $1200 to more than $4000. The text accompanying each plan contained com-

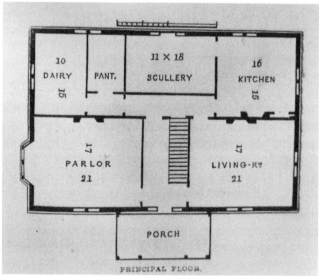

Figure 56. A. J. Downing, "Bracketed Farm House of Wood," Design XV of *The Architecture of Country Houses* (New York, 1850). Downing had published this design as a "country house" in the March 1850 issue of the *Horticulturist*. Courtesy of Special Collections, Morris Library, University of Delaware.

mon-sense advice on the disposition of interior spaces and construction, but invariably Downing returned to the gospel of simplicity. He described Design XV, a bracketed farmhouse (fig. 56), as "a roomy, substantial, comfortable, and sensible house," which demonstrated "neither ambition nor ostentation," while Design XVI, a dwelling in the rural English style (fig. 57), had "an unmistakable look of having been born and bred in the country" rather than "any cockneyisms copied from streets." These were homes befitting the honorable calling of the husbandman.[55]

Part 2 of *The Architecture of Country Houses* contained chapters devoted to villas, interiors and furnishings, and warming and ventilation. A villa, Downing wrote, was "the country house of a person of competence or wealth sufficient to build and maintain it with some taste and elegance." A suitable home for the "most leisurely and educated class of citizens," the scale was

Figure 57. A. J. Downing, "Farm House in the English Rural Style," Design XVI of *The Architecture of Country Houses* (New York, 1850). Courtesy of Special Collections, Morris Library, University of Delaware.

such that it required at least three servants to operate. As he did with cottages and farmhouses, Downing advised that a villa be convenient and "truthful or significant" in expressing its purpose. But unlike those smaller or less pretentious houses, a villa should aspire to being "the most tasteful or beautiful of dwellings" and the repository of "moral culture." Thus, Downing advised readers to erect houses that exemplified domestic life and that expressed the individuality and character of its residents rather than battlemented castles or other inappropriate dwellings: *unless there is something of the castle in the man,* it is very likely, if it be like a real castle, to dwarf him to the stature of a mouse."[56]

As he had done in the pages of the *Horticulturist,* Downing defended the use of foreign architectural styles so long as they were adapted to American conditions rather than slavish imitations of buildings appropriate to other cultures. Mere replication of the architecture or the social habits of other lands violated "republican tastes and manners," he argued, and too many architects who had been trained abroad did "great harm by building expensive and unmeaning copies of foreign houses." Downing reiterated his call for the development of an American style: "Our own soil is the right platform upon which a genuine national architecture must grow, though it will be aided in its growth by all foreign thoughts that mingle harmoniously with its simple and free spirit." The successful architect was one who studied the buildings of other countries but then worked "freshly from the inspiration of his own country—its manners, institutions, and climate."[57]

With an increasing number of substantial dwellings being erected in the United States, Downing felt it necessary to caution against building mansions of great size and cost. Such houses required an abundance of domestic help, which was not only expensive but increased the responsibilities of the owner. Moreover, in a nation without primogeniture and other forms of hereditary distinction, such houses were "contrary to the spirit of republican institutions" and stood "wholly in contradiction to the spirit of our time and people." Following the death of the proprietor, large estates were almost always divided by the children and the mansion sold, as one person's aspirations for home became another's property. Building such a house was sheer folly, Downing concluded, because "our institutions" would "finally grind it to powder." Instead of the castles and palaces of the Old World, Downing presented designs for homes in keeping with the contours of American society. These were republican dwellings suitable for "the virtuous citizen, rather than the mighty owner of houses and lands."[58]

Downing offered fourteen designs for villas; seven of them were his own (four of which had been refined by Davis), three were by Davis, two by

Wheeler, one by W. Russell West, a Cincinnati architect, and one by Richard Upjohn of New York City.[59] Five of these dwellings were in the familiar bracketed style, two others were Rural Gothic.[60] Downing also provided plans for two Italianate villas, a style he favored because of its projecting roofs, arcades, and asymmetrical appearance. Upjohn's King Villa (fig. 58), in Newport, Rhode Island, was especially noteworthy because of its careful balancing of irregular parts, which produced an overall harmony Downing considered superior to simple symmetry: "the satisfaction derived from harmony growing out of variety is as much greater than that arising from uniformity and simplicity, in architecture, as in music, where the first may be illustrated by one of Beethoven's symphonies, and the last by the simple melody of a ballad."[61] One design was in the Norman style (fig. 59), which Downing praised for its "very striking and spirited effect," three others were Pointed Gothic (fig. 60), which were more pretentious buildings than those in the Rural Gothic mode and which drew inspiration from the perpendicular phase of that style's evolution, and one was Romanesque (fig. 61).[62] Cost of construction ranged

Figure 58. Richard Upjohn, the Italianate villa of Edward King, Newport, R.I., 1845, Design XXVII of *The Architecture of Country Houses* (New York, 1850). Courtesy of Special Collections, Morris Library, University of Delaware.

from $2300 to $14,000, reflecting the scale of the building, level of decoration, expense of labor, and materials employed.

Because he believed that "the province of the architect does not cease with designing the general plan and exterior of any building," Downing devoted the next chapters to interiors and furnishings. His premise was twofold: that the design of a dwelling "should carry out the same spirit or style in all

Figure 59. W. Russell West, "Villa in the Norman Style," Design XX of *The Architecture of Country Houses* (New York, 1850). Courtesy of Special Collections, Morris Library, University of Delaware.

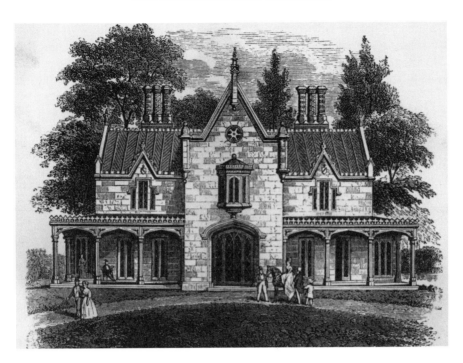

Figure 60. A. J. Davis, "Villa in the Pointed Style," Design XXX of *The Architecture of Country Houses* (New York, 1850). Courtesy of Special Collections, Morris Library, University of Delaware.

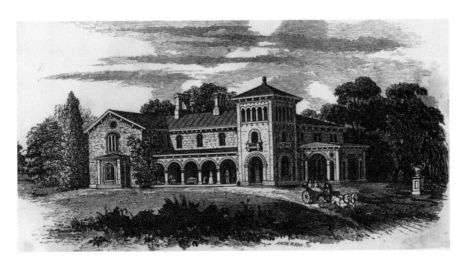

Figure 61. A. J. Downing, "Southern Villa—Romanesque Style," Design XXXII of *The Architecture of Country Houses* (New York, 1850). Courtesy of Special Collections, Morris Library, University of Delaware.

parts" and that the rules of proportion and tasteful expression should characterize interior spaces just as they did the exterior of a dwelling. Downing provided advice on decorating the simplest cottages, including treatment of woodwork, the most durable and economical methods of painting walls, types of wallpaper best suited to small dwellings, even the kinds of prints that should hang on the walls and the curtains that would add grace to the home.[63]

As the exterior of a villa was more elaborate than that of a cottage, so was the interior. The added space, as well as the greater means of the owner, permitted the use of different styles, though Downing cautioned that "unity of design" was the paramount consideration. He provided descriptions of each

Figure 62. A. J. Downing, "Interior in a simple Gothic Style," from *The Architecture of Country Houses* (New York, 1850), p. 383. Courtesy of Special Collections, Morris Library, University of Delaware.

Figure 63. A. J. Downing, "Interior in the Bracketed Style," from *The Architecture of Country Houses* (New York, 1850), facing p. 393. Courtesy of Special Collections, Morris Library, University of Delaware.

of the widely employed styles of interior decor—Grecian, Italian, Gothic, Romanesque, Elizabethan or Renaissance, and bracketed—and illustrated the text with woodcuts drawn by Davis (figs. 62 and 63). The floor plans depicted several strategies for the disposition of space to meet the needs of families with different interests and included new technologies, such as the water closet and bathing rooms, that Downing particularly recommended.[64]

Downing's advice on furniture similarly emphasized appropriateness. Furnishings should, he informed readers, conform harmoniously to the overall design of the house, "be essentially *country-like*," and combine "taste, comfort, and durability in the greatest degree." Although attention to furnishings was a logical extension of his longstanding concern for the home as a total environment, preparing a chapter on this topic marked a new venture for Downing; and for many of his ideas he turned to furniture makers and retailers in New York City and Boston, such as Alexander Roux, George Platt, and Edward Hennessey, as well as to two books, J. C. Loudon's *Encyclopaedia of Cottage, Farm, and Villa Architecture* and Thomas Webster's *Encyclopedia of Domestic Economy*. Most of the furnishings Downing illustrated were new styles (fig. 64 and 65), popular in metropolitan centers, which was unsurprising given the sources upon which he relied for information.

The chapters on interiors and furnishings are especially important because there are very few photographs of interiors from 1850 or earlier, so *The Architecture of Country Houses* provides a rare insight on upper- and middle-class taste in domestic design, especially in the newer fashions (though not, as Kenneth L. Ames has pointed out, in the traditional forms, such as

Figure 64. Alexander Roux, New York, design for sideboard and dining room chair in the Gothic Revival style, from *The Architecture of Country Houses* (New York, 1850), p. 448. Courtesy of Special Collections, Morris Library, University of Delaware.

Figure 65. Edward Hennessey, Boston, designs for cottage chamber furniture, from *The Architecture of Country Houses* (New York, 1850), p. 417. Courtesy of Special Collections, Morris Library, University of Delaware.

Windsor chairs, or vernacular furniture). In addition, they represent the author's increasingly ambitious role as tastemaker to middle-class America.[65]

Other sections of *The Architecture of Country Houses* covered miscellaneous details—the proper construction of fireplaces and chimneys, the use of ornamental shingles on roofs, techniques for staining wood and painting walls, and other steps to ensure economy and durability in construction—as well as advice on the best ways of warming and ventilating homes. In much the way other parts of the book educated readers on matters of style and arrangement of space, these sections instructed individuals who were building their own homes in matters essential to a comfortable dwelling.

The *Architecture of Country Houses* contained numerous references to the types of scenery appropriate for different styles of dwelling, but surprisingly, no advice on landscape gardening. Perhaps Downing considered that subject amply covered in the *Treatise*, a new edition of which had appeared in 1849; perhaps including the garden would have made an already large book too expensive and unwieldy.

Critics greeted the publication of *The Architecture of Country Houses* enthusiastically. *Harper's Monthly*, for example, described Downing as someone who brought "the refinements of true culture and the suggestions of a vigilant common-sense to the improvement of Rural Architecture." Praising both the taste of the author and his practical advice on construction, it asserted, "[N]o one who proposes to erect a house in the country can fail to derive great advantage from consulting his well-written and interesting pages."[66] George P. Morris and N. P. Willis's *Home Journal* similarly commended the author's taste and described Downing as "a man to whom his countrymen owe much, and to whom they feel happy to acknowledge their obligations."[67] The *Cultivator* described *The Architecture of Country Houses* as "*exactly* [the book] now wanted by the country at large" and as "decidedly the most widely useful work yet from the pen of its popular author."[68]

At least two reviewers compared Downing's book with John Ruskin's *Seven Lamps of Architecture*. Whereas the *Methodist Quarterly Review* had expressed an "inability to sympathize with the enthusiasm" of Ruskin, it praised Downing's prose as "intelligible to the uninitiated, and divested, as far as may be, of technical phraseology."[69] The *Home Journal* described *Seven Lamps* as a "splendid work of genius" but conceded that it was so complicated that a generation would pass before it was "fully appreciated." Downing's *Architecture of Country Houses*, by contrast, it called a "simple, practical work" that would have immediate influence because its conversational prose style was accessible to the general reader. "Like all Mr. Downing's writings," the *Home Journal* concluded, "it is characterized by a wonderful combination of common sense with great enthusiasm, and a thorough appreciation of the beautiful in nature, art and science."[70]

The *Literary World,* an avowedly nationalistic journal, predictably raised the issue of an American architecture, though in a somewhat ambivalent manner. Pointing out that many of the designs Downing had included in *The Architecture of Country Houses* were "modifications of European styles," it called for "our own American style of country architecture, something in harmony with our country modes of life." As Downing had done, the *Literary World* nevertheless conceded that architecture was still in its "educational period" in the United States and that the full maturation of a distinctive national style would have to wait for some distant future. Until that time it was probably wise to follow the example of foreign designs, but, the reviewer cautioned, books such as Downing's were "the means, not the end," and predicted, "[H]owever beautiful these means, the end will be far more beautiful."[71]

"Mr. Downing's designs are adapted to all tastes, and, what is more important, all purses," the *Literary World* noted, and so was the book itself. The division of *The Architecture of Country Houses* into two parts, one devoted to cottages and farmhouses, the other to villas and interiors, enabled Downing to reach an audience interested in building simple but tasteful dwellings, because D. Appleton and Company published, in 1851, a separate edition of Part 1 under the title *Downing's Cheap Cottages and Farm Houses* (fig. 66). Sold at the price of $2.00, half the cost of the entire volume, the shorter book was advertised as "especially adapted to the wants of the American people, who wish to build convenient, comfortable, and tasteful homes, at a very moderate expense."[72] The inexpensive edition of *The Architecture of Country Houses,* the *Ohio Cultivator* noted, was "emphatically a BOOK FOR THE MILLION."[73]

As was true of Downing's previous books, *The Architecture of Country Houses* proved an instant success. By 1853 it had sold approximately 3,500 copies, a figure that apparently did not include the cheaper version. A year later D. Appleton noted that the fourth reprinting brought the total number of copies to 13,000, and four additional printings, the last in 1866, kept *The Architecture of Country Houses* before the American public until after the Civil War.[74] According to Calvert Vaux, the book was "much read," and "influenced the public taste particularly by the great variety of plans and the varied arrangement for convenience and comfort" Downing provided in its designs. *The Architecture of Country Houses* dealt "a severe blow" to the "previously almost universal plan" of American dwellings, the central hall flanked by two rooms on each side, and promoted instead what Vaux termed "the advantages of a studied irregularity and broadly conceived picturesqueness in arranging country houses."[75]

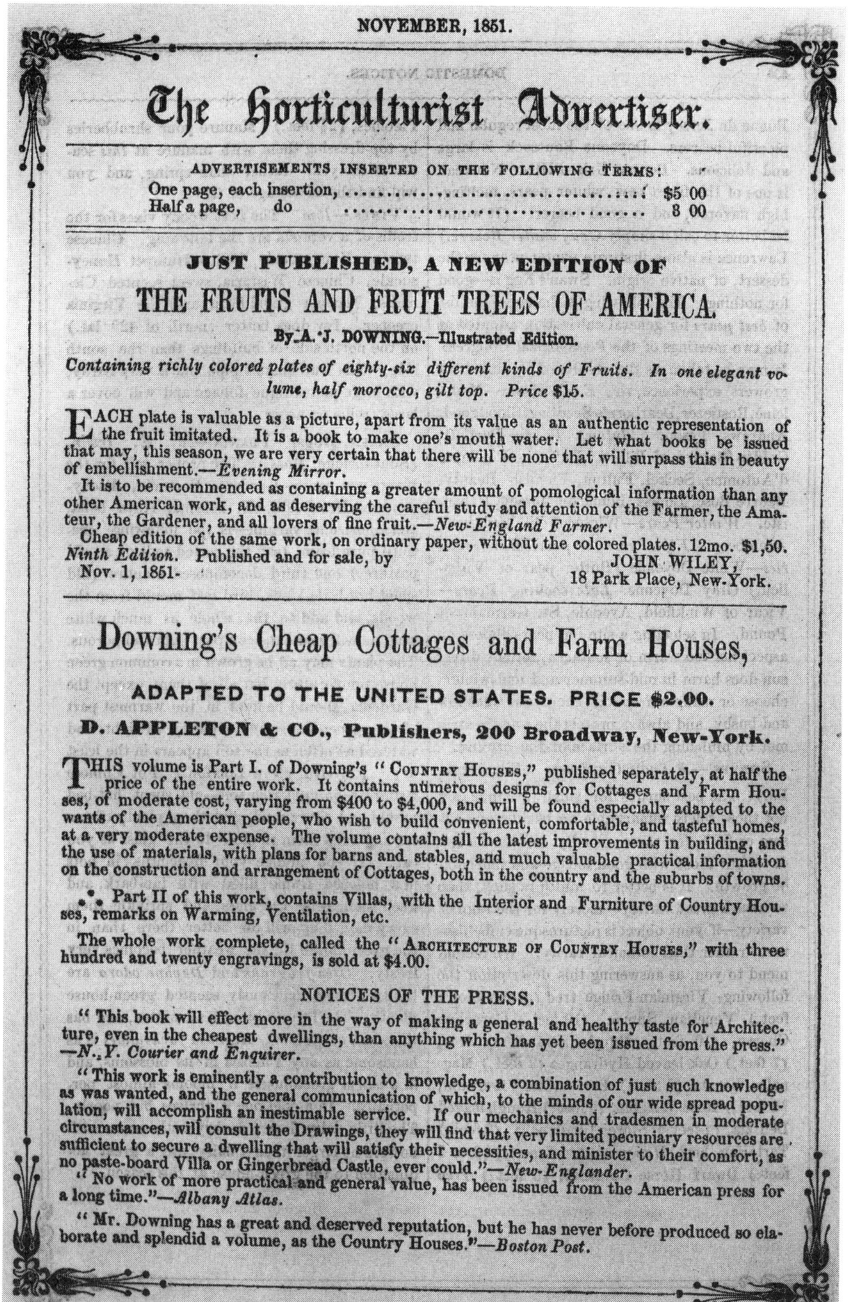

NOVEMBER, 1851.

The Horticulturist Advertiser.

ADVERTISEMENTS INSERTED ON THE FOLLOWING TERMS:

One page, each insertion,	$5 00
Half a page, do	3 00

JUST PUBLISHED, A NEW EDITION OF

THE FRUITS AND FRUIT TREES OF AMERICA.

By A. J. DOWNING.—Illustrated Edition.

Containing richly colored plates of eighty-six different kinds of Fruits. In one elegant volume, half morocco, gilt top. Price $15.

EACH plate is valuable as a picture, apart from its value as an authentic representation of the fruit imitated. It is a book to make one's mouth water. Let what books be issued that may, this season, we are very certain that there will be none that will surpass this in beauty of embellishment.—*Evening Mirror.*

It is to be recommended as containing a greater amount of pomological information than any other American work, and as deserving the careful study and attention of the Farmer, the Amateur, the Gardener, and all lovers of fine fruit.—*New-England Farmer.*

Cheap edition of the same work, on ordinary paper, without the colored plates. 12mo. $1,50. *Ninth Edition.* Published and for sale, by JOHN WILEY,
Nov. 1, 1851. 18 Park Place, New-York.

Downing's Cheap Cottages and Farm Houses,

ADAPTED TO THE UNITED STATES. PRICE $2.00.

D. APPLETON & CO., Publishers, 200 Broadway, New-York.

THIS volume is Part I. of Downing's "COUNTRY HOUSES," published separately, at half the price of the entire work. It contains numerous designs for Cottages and Farm Houses, of moderate cost, varying from $400 to $4,000, and will be found especially adapted to the wants of the American people, who wish to build convenient, comfortable, and tasteful homes, at a very moderate expense. The volume contains all the latest improvements in building, and the use of materials, with plans for barns and stables, and much valuable practical information on the construction and arrangement of Cottages, both in the country and the suburbs of towns.

⁂ Part II of this work, contains Villas, with the Interior and Furniture of Country Houses, remarks on Warming, Ventilation, etc.

The whole work complete, called the "ARCHITECTURE OF COUNTRY HOUSES," with three hundred and twenty engravings, is sold at $4.00.

NOTICES OF THE PRESS.

"This book will effect more in the way of making a general and healthy taste for Architecture, even in the cheapest dwellings, than anything which has yet been issued from the press." —*N. Y. Courier and Enquirer.*

"This work is eminently a contribution to knowledge, a combination of just such knowledge as was wanted, and the general communication of which, to the minds of our wide spread population, will accomplish an inestimable service. If our mechanics and tradesmen in moderate circumstances, will consult the Drawings, they will find that very limited pecuniary resources are sufficient to secure a dwelling that will satisfy their necessities, and minister to their comfort, as no paste-board Villa or Gingerbread Castle, ever could."—*New-Englander.*

"No work of more practical and general value, has been issued from the American press for a long time."—*Albany Atlas.*

"Mr. Downing has a great and deserved reputation, but he has never before produced so elaborate and splendid a volume, as the Country Houses."—*Boston Post.*

Figure 66. Advertisement for *Downing's Cheap Cottages and Farm Houses,* "The Horticulturist Advertiser," *Horticulturist* 6 (Nov. 1851). Courtesy of Special Collections, Morris Library, University of Delaware.

ৄ Downing's writings on architecture between 1846 and 1850, and his crusade for an American architectural expression, reached thousands of readers, at least some of whom followed his advice and erected dwellings according to the plans he published. But Downing was not a practicing architect, and when he was requested to design a residential or institutional building he usually passed the commission to A. J. Davis. There were at least three instances, however, when Downing and Davis collaborated on architectural projects: the design of the Angier cottage in Medford, Massachusetts, the preparation of plans for the New York State Agricultural College, and the design of the entrance gate and chapel of the Cemetery of the Evergreens in Brooklyn, New York.[76]

Given Downing's increasing stature as a tastemaker, it seems likely that he perceived for himself a lucrative business in architectural design. In January 1848, when he invited Davis's collaboration in preparing *The Architecture of Country Houses,* Downing, optimistically anticipating that the book would generate additional architectural commissions, suggested to Davis that their previous working relationship might evolve into a partnership able to take advantage of those opportunities: "I think together we can build up a large business & if so perhaps I may eventually . . . go to town & enter into *closer alliance* with you."[77] How much this allusive offer was a reflection of Downing's financial problems, and perhaps his fear that he would lose his home to creditors, is impossible to determine. But whether or not Downing was serious in suggesting that he and Davis form a partnership, the older architect must have demurred. As Jane B. Davies has pointed out, "Davis had experienced the problems of partnership and surely realized that such an arrangement for them would not work, as neither man would have accepted a subordinate role."[78] Downing did not, however, abandon his idea of establishing an architectural practice. He looked elsewhere for a talented professional willing to collaborate in translating his thoughts into buildings and eager to promote his crusade for an American style of architecture.

Downing & Vaux, Architects

∽

He had both the will and the power to exercise a marked influence for good over the taste of his countrymen.

—Calvert Vaux

∽ On July 6, 1850, Downing boarded the steamship *Pacific* bound for England. His purpose, he explained to A. J. Davis, was to conduct "a little business,"[1] which included studying English landscapes and buildings and obtaining woodcuts and engravings for Luther Tucker, presumably for use in the *Horticulturist*.[2] Although he did not admit it to Davis, his longtime collaborator, Downing apparently also hoped to find an architect whose professional training would complement his own abilities and who was willing to return with him to the United States. Calvert Vaux recalled that Downing traveled to England "partly with a view to form an architectural connection so as to be enabled to put in practice on his return to America his aspirations with regard to that art."[3]

Downing arrived in Liverpool and journeyed through the midland counties to the capital. Over a period of roughly six weeks, he toured countryside and city alike, visiting notable estates and botanical gardens as well as the parks of London. The Duke of Northumberland invited him to Sion House to study its ancient trees, and the Duke of Devonshire made him a guest at Chatsworth, where Downing stood in awe of its numerous fountains, which he described as the "crowning glory" of that estate's famous garden. There Downing also saw a superb *Victoria Regia,* an enormous water lily that had recently been discovered in Brazil and that was one of the botanical sensations of the time. Chatsworth, he concluded, showed "more *refined taste,* joined to magnificence, both externally and internally, than any place I have ever seen." The Duke of Bedford invited him to Woburn Abbey, notable both for its scientific farming and for its arboricultural and botanical riches. In addition to studying its garden, set amid a three-thousand-acre park, Downing visited a "whole settlement of farm cottages," which he found to be models, "combining the utmost convenience and comfort for dwellings of this class, with so much of architectural taste as is befitting to dwellings of this size." And he was a guest at Wimpole, the seat of the Earl of Hardwicke, where he admired the "picturesque" pleasure grounds, the rhododendrons and laurel, and the formal flower garden.[4]

During his travels through central England Downing visited Haddon Hall, Dropmore, Matlock, and Stratford-on-Avon, where he toured Shakespeare's birthplace and marveled at the "power of genius" evident in the cottage, which far outstripped the "pomp and external circumstance of high birth or heroic achievements." He also examined the Derby Arboretum, which had been established only ten years earlier as a public benefaction by a leading citizen, Joseph Strutt. The arboretum would become "one of the most useful and instructive public gardens in the world," Downing predicted, because of its skillful combining of "the greatest possible amount of instruction, with a great deal of pleasure for all classes, and especially the working classes." During a four-day visit to the Isle of Wight, he was enchanted by the landscape and scenery and discovered a scale and style of architecture he thought appropriate to the United States. Everywhere he turned on the island he found precisely the "kind of rural beauty, the tasteful embellishment of small places," that he had been promoting in his writings.[5]

Upon his arrival in London Downing met Sir William Hooker, who spent a day guiding him through the Royal Botanical Gardens at Kew. There Downing admired the rare specimens of plants and noble trees as well as the palm house, built in 1848, which he described as "fairy-like and elegant in its proportions, though of great strength." Sir Charles Barry spent a morning leading Downing through the new Houses of Parliament, where the visiting American was charmed by "the elegance, resulting from the union of fine proportions and select forms of modern cultivated tastes, with the peculiarly grand and venerable character of Gothic architecture." Downing was equally enthralled by the botanical garden in Regent's Park, a private subscription garden he described as an arboreal oasis "in the midst of a vast city."[6]

Judging from the published descriptions of his English travels, Downing was clearly infatuated with the taste and cultivation of his hosts, the sheer elegance of their homes and gardens. But although he experienced the "thorough *full-dress* air of the great English country places," Downing kept returning to the contrasts between English and American society. There were perhaps "20,000 private houses in Great Britain, larger than our President's House," he observed, but none could sway him from the republicanism of his native land.[7] At Warwick Castle, which had been built centuries before the first European settlement of the Americas and had remained in the same family since that time, Downing stood at the highest tower and gazed westward, musing about the differences between the land of his ancestors and that of his birth. Whereas to England "had been given to show the growth of man in his highest development of class," he wrote, "to America has been reserved the greater blessing of solving for the world the true problem of humanity—that of the abolition of all castes, and the recognition of the divine rights of every human soul."[8]

Downing shaped his prose carefully, and in noting that to America had been "reserved" the destiny of a classless society, he was admitting that it had not yet come to pass. A necessary step in achieving that goal, he believed, was the creation of public parks. Two years before sailing to England Downing had urged the establishment of public parks and gardens in a lead essay in the *Horticulturist*. Written in the form of a dialogue between the editor and an American traveler who had just returned from Europe, the essay celebrated the public pleasure grounds of the Continent. What most struck the traveler in Germany was the availability of "[p]ublic enjoyments, open to all classes of people, provided at public cost, maintained at public expense, and enjoyed daily and hourly, by all classes of persons." The conversation contrasted German provisions for public recreation with those in the New World and found the latter wanting. Although European societies were more stratified than that of the United States, parks on the Continent promoted a "*social freedom,* and an easy and agreeable intercourse of all classes, that strikes an American with surprise and delight." In Munich's Englisher Garten as well as in the new park constructed on what formerly had been the ramparts of Frankfurt, king and commoners alike enjoyed public recreational facilities. In the parks, they gained "health, good spirits, social enjoyment, and a frank and cordial bearing towards their neighbors, that is totally unknown either in England or America."[9]

During his visit to England Downing became more positive in his assessment of that country's parks, especially those in the West End of London. He dismissed John Nash's architecture with the faint praise that it was similar to buildings found in the most fashionable neighborhoods of other European capitals. The distinguishing "luxury" of the West End, he discovered, was "its holding the country in its lap." Comparing the open landscape of London's parks with a Pennsylvania countryside, Downing revised his earlier assessment of German recreational grounds. London's West End parks, he wrote, were "laid out and treated, in the main, with a broad and noble feeling of natural beauty, quite the reverse of what you see in the public parks of the continental cities. This makes these parks doubly refreshing to citizens tired of straight lines and formal streets, while the contrast heightens the natural charm." The landscape at St. James Park, he wrote, "seems to you more like a glimpse into one of the loveliest pleasure-grounds on the Hudson, than the belongings of the great Metropolis"; the vast size of Hyde Park and Kensington Gardens left Downing in a state of "bewildered astonishment," as he marveled at the "wealth of a city which can afford such an illimitable space for the pleasure of air and exercise for its inhabitants."[10] The kind of park most appropriate to American cities, he concluded, was one that grafted the republicanism he associated with German recreational grounds to the naturalistic landscape he admired in Britain.

In London Downing also visited an exhibition sponsored by the Architectural Association, where he was impressed with several sketches of European buildings and landscapes. When he asked about the author of some of the drawings, the secretary of the association, Anthony Seddon, sent for Calvert Vaux (fig. 67), who promptly appeared, perhaps expecting to meet a potential client.[11] Downing evoked in the young architect an instant rapport. "I was in a settled position and surrounded by friends," Vaux wrote shortly after Downing's death, "but I liked him so much, his foresight and observa-

Figure 67. Calvert Vaux, undated photograph. Courtesy of National Park Service, Frederick Law Olmsted National Historic Site, Brookline, Mass.

tion were so apparent in the conversations we had and above all his style was so calculated to win confidence that without a fear I relinquished all and accompanied him." The two men exchanged references, and the following evening made arrangements to meet in a week and depart for the United States. Downing then left for a brief visit to Paris. Upon his return the two men journeyed by train to Liverpool and sailed aboard the *Canada* for New York.[12]

That Downing sought an English-trained architect to help him translate his ideas into buildings may seem surprising, particularly given his articulate plea for the development of a distinctive American architecture. A cursory look at the architectural plans he presented in the *Horticulturist* between July 1850 and August 1852 suggests that Downing's fondness for English taste may have been overwhelming his preference for an architecture that sprang from American social and political conditions. Twenty-one of the twenty-six issues included a frontispiece devoted to architecture, and of these, thirteen were English designs or subjects, while another, Messina, a Livingston estate in the Hudson Valley, had been designed by British engineer I. K. Brunel.[13] Moreover, throughout 1851 Downing published lengthy excerpts from such English journals as the *London Builder* and the *Gardeners' Magazine of Botany*.[14]

While there is little doubt that Downing increasingly relied on English sources for articles and illustrations he published in the *Horticulturist*, the use of that material did not necessarily mark a turning away from his ideal of an American architectural expression. Several other explanations seem more persuasive. First, he acquired the illustrations at the request of Luther Tucker, which suggests that the publisher wanted a supply of images that could be prepared well in advance of publication, and, in the absence of an international copyright law, at little or no cost. Second, Downing may have turned to articles drawn from the English press as a way of lessening his own literary tasks at a time when his other professional responsibilities were increasing. Certainly the clustering of English architectural designs in late 1851 and early 1852 coincided with his frequent absences from Newburgh while superintending construction of his design for the public grounds at Washington. Third, and perhaps most important, when he published English designs he was presenting either styles for which there was not yet a good example in the United States, such as Romanesque and Lombard churches, or building types, such as schoolhouses, that, he believed, needed significant improvement. The church and the school, he asserted, contributed "more essentially to the architectural education of the country at large, than any private buildings," and in illustrating good models he hoped to banish "the present deformities" that marred such structures.[15]

In presenting English designs for his American audience, Downing carefully analyzed the "beauties and defects" of each plan and explained how it might best be adapted to American conditions.[16] His comments about the birthplace of Sir Walter Raleigh praised the simplicity of the dwelling and suggested two modifications that would make it a tasteful dwelling appropriate to the United States: "Diminish the size of this house to suit our wants, and add a veranda."[17] Similarly, Horace Walpole's Strawberry Hill was both "amusing"—a "kind of bastard imitation, or rather jumble of various eras of gothic architecture, without unity, harmony, or correctness of detail or proportion"—as well as "instructive" to American readers as an example of how an otherwise talented man could utterly fail when he attempted to serve as his own architect.[18] Downing employed English designs as "starting-points," in Calvert Vaux's words, for the improvement of American architecture.[19] Just as he had done prior to his tour of England, Downing continued to educate readers in matters of taste in a way that would contribute to the development of an American expression in architecture.

Whatever the reason for Downing's increasing reliance on English materials for the *Horticulturist,* there is little question that in fulfilling his hope of establishing an architectural practice he had few alternatives other than to hire an English-trained architect. There was not yet a professional school of architecture in the United States, and only a few Americans, most notably Davis, had followed a rigorous apprenticeship program and possessed the requisite skill to meet Downing's expectations. The majority of practicing architects had simply progressed from builder to self-proclaimed professional architect, designing in one or more of the classical revival styles. Most architects working in the Gothic or Italianate styles that Downing favored were immigrants who had come to the United States in search of better opportunities. John Notman was Scottish and Gervase Wheeler was English, as was Richard Upjohn, who had trained as a cabinetmaker.[20] An important exception was James Renwick, Jr., the son of a Columbia College professor and a socially prominent mother, who learned structural engineering from his father and architectural style through the study of books.[21] Whatever his training, Renwick would have been an unlikely choice as partner because of Downing's disdain for his most important commission, the Smithsonian Institution in Washington, D.C.[22] In forming a practice with any of these men, or another well-known professional architect, Downing would have confronted at least two potential problems. Since the resolution of his financial difficulties, he had shown no inclination of a willingness to leave Newburgh, so anyone who joined him in practice would have had to relocate. And the same issue that may have affected Davis's decision not to pursue a "closer alliance" with Downing—who would be the dominant personality in the partnership—might well have complicated an affiliation with an already estab-lished architect.[23]

In employing a young English architect as his associate, Downing ac-quired the requisite professional expertise and avoided potential problems of authority within the partnership. He may well have expected that he could mold that man's talents to conform to his ideas of what American architec-ture should become. As Vaux explained, architects who trained abroad needed "to learn and unlearn much before the spirit instilled in their designs can be truly and genuinely American."[24] Vaux, who was nine years younger than Downing, had been educated at the Merchant Tailors' School in Lon-don and had completed an apprenticeship in the office of Lewis Nockalls Cottingham, a leader in the Gothic Revival movement. He combined pre-cisely the skills in draughtsmanship and construction technology that Down-ing needed with strongly republican sympathies that the American must have found appealing.[25] Together, Downing must have anticipated, he and Vaux would establish a successful practice and design the kinds of buildings that would spread his gospel of taste.

᷼ The first architectural project Downing and Vaux undertook following their return to the United States was probably the construction of an office addition to Downing's residence (the office wing is visible in fig. 100, below). The new wing consisted of two rooms, an office for the architectural firm and Downing's private study. The office, which measured approximately fif-teen by twenty-five feet, was a "delightful" work space, in Clarence Cook's words. "On one side the southern windows let in the warm and cheerful sun-light," he wrote, "on another the rows of books gave a grace and charm to the apartment, and opposite them the bright wood fire warms body and soul with its crackling flames." Functional though the room was, Downing had designed it to be "agreeable in color and proportion." The walls were stained wood, divided into panels, and "fine architectural prints" hung on the west wall. Between the office and the library of the residence was Downing's study, a much smaller room. According to Cook, "the whole air of the place is that of taste and refinement."[26]

Only a small vignette of the exterior of the office addition has survived, and certainly in roof line and material it appears to have replicated the style of the dwelling Downing had designed twelve years earlier. Two features of the entrance porch (fig. 68), however, are novel: the almost Moorish line of the decorative wood trim and the use of different-colored shingles to give tex-ture to the roof. Vaux later described the "very agreeable effect" that could

Figure 68. A. J. Downing and Calvert Vaux, office porch addition to Downing residence, Newburgh, N.Y., 1850–51, from "A Visit to the House and Garden of the Late A. J. Downing," *Horticulturist*, n.s. 3 (Jan. 1853), p. 21. Courtesy of Shadek-Fackenthal Library, Franklin & Marshall College.

be produced by the use of "stripes or patterns" in a slate roof.[27] From the porch a curving path led to the entrance drive, thus making it possible to conduct business with little if any intrusion upon domestic life.

Having established an architectural office, Downing began seeking clients. The first major commission he received came from Matthew Vassar, the Poughkeepsie, New York, brewer who had acquired Springside, a forty-four-acre farm a mile south of the village, initially on behalf of a group of residents interested in establishing a rural cemetery. In the autumn of 1850 he began making improvements to the grounds. According to his biographer, Benson J. Lossing, Vassar engaged Downing to "suggest a plan of avenues for walks and drives" and to design several buildings.[28] Vassar appeared to vacillate between using the farm for a cemetery and developing it as a site for a house and gardens befitting his status in the community. Although discussion of the property's being used as a cemetery continued throughout much of 1851, in late 1850 Downing was clearly working under a different impression, and in February 1851 he published a plan for a carriage house and stable in the "Rustic Pointed style" (fig. 69). Downing described it as intended "for the villa residence of a gentleman on the Hudson, whose whole establishment will be remarkable for the completeness, convenience, and good effect of the various buildings, joined to much natural beauty of features of the locality in which they are placed." The carriage house was a board-and-batten structure that, he wrote, combined "picturesque effect" with "all the convenience demanded in a building of this class." Two features are noteworthy, sliding stable doors, with the rollers affixed to the top, and a cupolalike ventilator, which Downing described as an invaluable convenience that added to the "picturesqueness of the building."[29] As Downing had not included ventilators in his farm building designs in *The Architecture of Country Houses* yet they would be a staple of Vaux's architectural vocabulary for decades, it seems likely that Vaux played a significant role in the development of Vassar's estate, even though only Downing's name appears on surviving plans.

Downing and Vaux also designed at least two other structures that were erected at Springside, an ice house and a cottage for the farmer or gardener, as well as an entrance lodge that was never constructed.[30] The ice house, located adjacent to the stable, was also a board-and-batten design with a ventilator, and although no plans have survived, its similarity to the carriage house, and the fact that it was standing in 1852, suggest that it was designed by Downing and Vaux. The cottage (fig. 70), which stood until 1976, when the entrance façade was removed, bears a striking similarity to the "symmetrical bracketed cottage" Downing published as Design III of *The Architecture of Country Houses* (see fig. 52, above). As was true of the building in Design III,

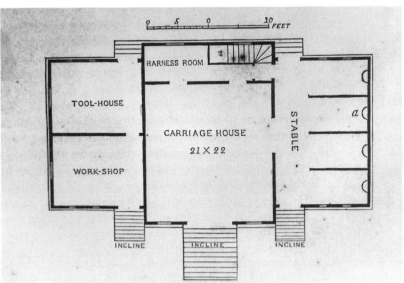

Figure 69. A. J. Downing and Calvert Vaux, plan for a carriage house and stable in the "Rustic Pointed style," commissioned by Matthew Vassar, Poughkeepsie, N.Y., from the *Horticulturist* 7 (Feb. 1851). This was reprinted in *Cottage Residences,* 4th ed. (New York, 1852), p. 186. Courtesy of Special Collections, Morris Library, University of Delaware.

Figure 70. A. J. Downing and Calvert Vaux, gardener's cottage for Matthew Vassar's Springside, built 1851. Undated photograph. Courtesy of Special Collections, Vassar College Libraries.

Vassar's cottage was a board-and-batten structure with a projecting entrance porch sheltered by an overhanging second-story room. Another feature common to both plans was the use of simple wooden window hoods. The Vassar design differs from Design III in numerous ways: the gable contains a decorative verge board, the details of the porch railing and brackets supporting the overhang are more elaborate, the roof is hipped and apparently intended to be covered with different-colored slate shingles in a striped pattern, and the kitchen wing was eliminated and its functions transferred to a full-story basement. These differences are attributable to topography and the role of the cottage as part of an ensemble of ornamental buildings for the estate of a wealthy individual rather than the home of a family of limited means, a situation in which Downing would have insisted on greater simplicity.[31] The cottage faced east, and the façade looked over the kitchen garden and farm fields in the distance, a telling indication of its proposed use, while the west front, labeled "back of elevation" in Downing's plan, had a veranda that extended almost the length of the building facing the ornamental garden. Taking advantage of the hilly topography, Downing supported the veranda on an arched foundation that provided light and access to the basement.

The various farm structures, Vaux wrote in 1857, "interfere less than is often the case with the general result, each having been studied with some reference to its position and artistic importance in the landscape."[32] The principal building he and Downing designed, Vassar's proposed brick and stone mansion, was an enormous structure, with a projecting hall and drawing room, surrounded on three sides by a veranda that would function as "a lengthened covered promenade." Other rooms on the main floor included a library, a dining room, and service areas, while the bedroom accommodations on the second story were "liberal." This was an extravagant home, with an exterior punctuated by large Flemish gables and clustered chimneys (fig. 71). Even with a "simple interior finish" Vaux estimated the cost at $16,000, a higher figure than the most expensive villa included in *The Architecture of Country Houses*. The mansion was never erected, however, as Vassar chose instead to use the cottage as a summer residence for the remainder of his life.[33]

In 1857 Vaux described the property at Springside as "somewhat secluded and park-like in its character, fine healthy trees being scattered in groups and masses over its whole extent." When Downing began to project improvements to the landscape, the ultimate use of the property may not have been determined: certainly the drives (fig. 72) were far more extensive than would have been necessary for domestic use, which suggests that he was designing a rural cemetery, for which the numerous roads would have provided convenient access to grave plots. The gently curving drives followed topography and, as Vaux noted, existing trees were "sparingly and judiciously thinned." The ornamental grounds, an area of approximately twenty acres, were "thoroughly drained," and the soil "enriched wherever it was thought necessary," while several ornamental fountains took advantage of one of the natural features of the site, its numerous springs. Many of the elements of Downing's plan for the grounds, the new structures he and Vaux designed for Vassar, and what appear to be several older farm buildings, are evident in a series of views painted in 1852 by Henry Gritten, an English landscape artist whom Vassar had hired to record the improvements to his property (fig. 73).[34] Those paintings capture visually what a contemporary described in words: the grounds combined "every variety of park-like and pictorial landscape that is to be found in any part of our country."[35] According to Vaux, what best characterized the "peculiar charm" of Springside was its "bold horizontal lines, and the broad, free stretches of richly-wooded intermediate distance contrasting, and yet in harmony, with the home landscape."[36]

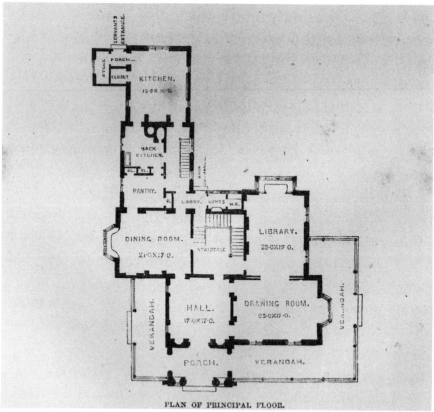

Figure 71. A. J. Downing and Calvert Vaux, villa of brick and stone, designed for Matthew Vassar but not built, from Vaux, *Villas and Cottages* (New York, 1857), facing p. 276.

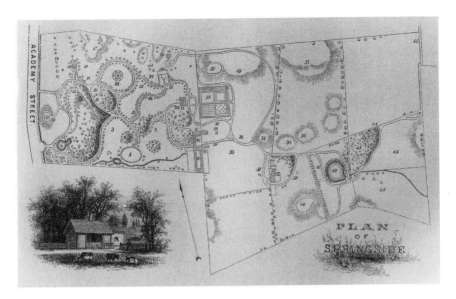

Figure 72. Plan of Springside, with ornamental grounds located adjacent to Academy Street and farm to the east, from Benson J. Lossing, *Vassar College and Its Founder* (New York, 1867), p. 62. Courtesy of Special Collections, Vassar College Libraries.

Figure 73. Henry Gritten, one of four paintings of Springside executed ca. 1852, this illustrates the view south from the lawn terrace. Private collection. Courtesy of Special Collections, Vassar College Libraries.

Springside was not the only architectural commission Downing received in the year following his return from England. When Fredrika Bremer visited the Downings in September 1851, she found her friend's "outward sphere of activity . . . very wide and effective." Together with Vaux and perhaps an apprentice, Downing was "preparing plans for houses which he is commissioned to erect for private persons, who in their villas and cottages desire to combine the beautiful with the useful. Downing's engagements and correspondence is at this time incredibly great," Bremer observed, "and extends over the whole Union."[37] A month later Downing wrote his friend John J. Smith, "I am deeply immersed in practical works—architectural and rural— turning my theories into practice all over the country."[38] The demand for Downing's architectural services was so great that he engaged another young English architect as his assistant. Frederick Clarke Withers, who had been employed in the London office of Henry Wyatt, joined Downing's staff in February 1852. The following month Downing informed Smith, "I am really a man of no leisure—except *after dinner,* at home. I wish I could show you my 'Bureau of Architecture,' in the new wing of my residence—full of commissions, and young architects, and planning for all parts of the country."[39]

Because no records from the architectural office appear to have survived, the best indication of the numerous commissions Downing and his associates received is Calvert Vaux's 1857 pattern book, *Villas and Cottages.* In addition to the plan of Vassar's mansion, Vaux's book illustrates eight other houses identified as having been designed by "D & V," six of which were built, as well as a study for a "villa on a large scale." For William L. Findlay the architects designed a "symmetrical country house" in Balmville, just north of Newburgh, and a stable with coachman's quarters. For Findlay, Downing and Vaux had to meet the needs of a client who wanted a spacious, airy house in summer, and a warm, intimate dwelling in winter, when there would be fewer residents. They accomplished this by creating a cross plan. The rooms were comparatively small for a house of its size and could be "readily warmed" during the colder months of the year, while during the summer, sliding doors could be opened to provide ample ventilation throughout the principal rooms of the first floor. In the published illustration (fig. 74) Vaux kept the ventilating turret he had designed but the client had not built. The architect considered it a "prominent feature," important to the overall effect of the dwelling, and estimated it could be added for $70 or $80.[40]

When Downing's neighbor David Moore acquired a property on which a house foundation had already been completed, he too turned to the architects. The foundation was square, which limited the range of possibilities for design, and was located very close to the street rather than nearer the middle

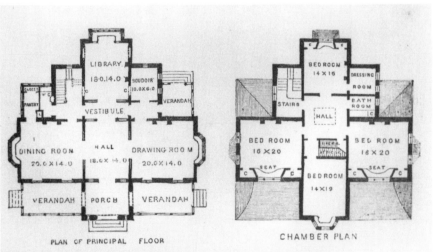

Figure 74. A. J. Downing and Calvert Vaux, "Symmetrical Country House of W. L. Findlay, Balmville, N. Y.," from Vaux, *Villas and Cottages* (New York, 1857), facing p. 187. Courtesy of Special Collections, Morris Library, University of Delaware. The hollow areas in some walls on the principal floor indicate sliding portions of doors designed to provide better ventilation in warm weather.

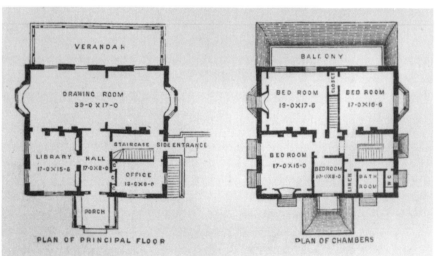

Figure 75. A. J. Downing and Calvert Vaux, "Picturesque Square House of David Moore, Newburgh, N. Y.," from Vaux, *Villas and Cottages*, (New York, 1857), facing p. 213. Courtesy of Special Collections, Morris Library, University of Delaware.

of the lot. The house Downing and Vaux planned (fig. 75) became, in Vaux's description, an example of a "generally picturesque effect" attainable in a dwelling without the inconvenience or cost of "irregularities in the internal arrangement, or uneconomical projections in carrying up the brick-work." Several features of this plan are distinctive: the drawing room, which extended the length of the house and opened on a veranda overlooking the Hudson River; the use of encaustic tile paving in the entrance hall, in red, black, and buff colors, a decorative motif that would become popular in the post–Civil War years; and the location of the outhouse on the basement level, connected to the house by a vine-covered passage so that this most necessary of buildings did not intrude upon the landscape. The plan for the grounds (fig. 76) took advantage of the house's siting to create "stretches of open lawn," which, Vaux noted, "have a much better effect than small plots intersected by gravel walks," and also included a "pretty fountain" near the principal entrance to the house.[41]

For Robert P. and Francis Dodge, Downing and Vaux designed Italianate villas for their property in the Georgetown section of the District of Columbia. The brothers "wished for a general similarity in the two designs," but not identical houses (fig. 77). The architects created designs that were almost mir-

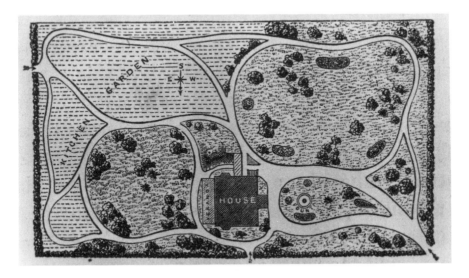

Figure 76. A. J. Downing, plan of the grounds of the Moore house, Newburgh, N.Y., from Vaux, *Villas and Cottages* (New York, 1857), p. 218. Courtesy of Special Collections, Morris Library, University of Delaware.

ror images; they altered the position of the library, to provide some variation on the interior and, on the exterior, changed the window treatment, giving one house rectangular fenestration shaded by window hoods, the other "circular heads and stone label mouldings."[42]

For Dr. William A. M. Culbert, Downing and Vaux designed a mansard-roofed structure (fig. 78) that combined residence and office. A second entrance led to a lobby and office, which was spatially separate from the private rooms of the house. The design was clearly their interpretation of the latest Parisian fashion and included brick walls with recessed panels, brownstone pilasters, and horizontal accents. The overall effect was "so richly and artistically" striking that Vaux was "very sorry indeed" when the exterior was painted.[43]

The sixth and most ambitious of the houses Downing and Vaux designed that was constructed was a "marine villa" for Daniel Parish (fig. 79). Located on fashionable Bellevue Avenue in Newport, Rhode Island, with "an uninterrupted view of the sea," this was a large Italianate structure with a broadly projecting roof supported by brackets. Classical details—quoins, an arcaded carriage porch, and a double arcade on the ocean façade—lent distinction to the exterior, while bay windows and a veranda so extensive it was called a pavilion provided light and attempted to unite this very formal house with its gardens. An unusual feature of the interior was an oval room, designated a "cabinet," located between the dining and drawing rooms.[44]

Two other designs by Downing and Vaux included in *Villas and Cottages* were not built. One was a "villa residence with curved roof" for Downing's friend Frederick J. Betts (fig. 80), who found the house more expensive than he expected and "concluded to postpone building till a more favorable opportunity." The other was an "irregular stone villa with tower" for S. D. Dakin (fig. 81), an enormous stone house with Flemish gables and an octagonal tower, located on a commanding site overlooking the Hudson. Construction of the foundation had commenced when "the sudden death of the proprietor put a stop to the works." Also left unbuilt was a "villa on a large scale" (fig. 82), which, according to Vaux, had been "prepared in detail some time before Mr. Downing's death, in accordance with instructions we received." Unfortunately, Vaux provided no information on the identity of the client who commissioned what would have been their most ambitious project, an enormous Gothic mansion to be built of stone, topped by a tall tower. Other unusual features of this plan were the fountain included in the entrance hall, and the terrace, a formal element made necessary by the slope of the ground, which served to link the house to its gardens. Vaux published this plan "to show how a large amount of accommodation may be arranged and combined."[45]

Figure 77. A. J. Downing and Calvert Vaux, suburban villa designs for Robert P. Dodge and Francis Dodge, Washington, D.C., from Vaux, *Villas and Cottages* (New York, 1857), facing p. 221. Courtesy of Special Collections, Morris Library, University of Delaware.

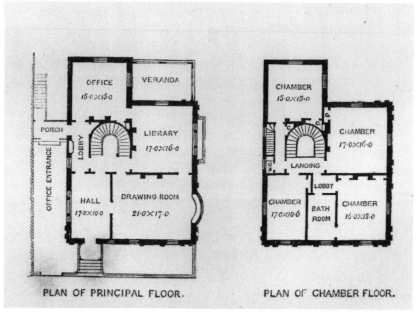

PLAN OF PRINCIPAL FLOOR.   PLAN OF CHAMBER FLOOR.

Figure 78. A. J. Downing and Calvert Vaux, "Suburban House with Curved Roof," designed for Dr. William A. M. Culbert, Newburgh, N.Y., from Vaux, *Villas and Cottages* (New York, 1857), facing p. 241. Courtesy of Special Collections, Morris Library, University of Delaware.

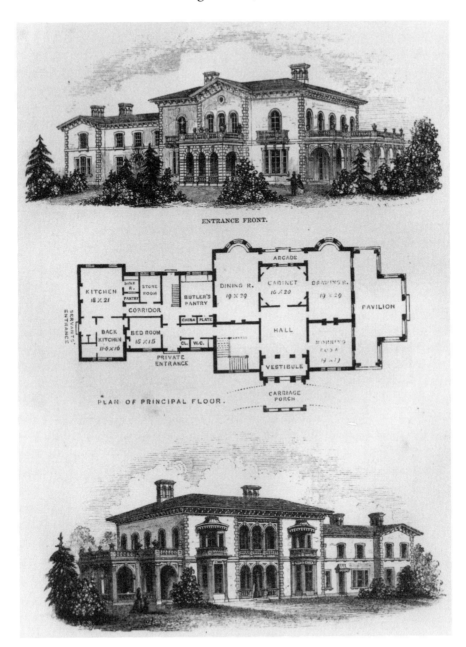

ENTRANCE FRONT.

PLAN OF PRINCIPAL FLOOR.

Figure 79. A. J. Downing and Calvert Vaux, "Marine Villa," designed for Daniel Parish, Newport, R.I., from Vaux, *Villas and Cottages* (New York, 1857), facing p. 307. Courtesy of Special Collections, Morris Library, University of Delaware.

Figure 80. A. J. Downing and Calvert Vaux, "Villa Residence with Curved Roof," designed for Frederick J. Betts, Newburgh, N.Y., but not built, from Vaux, *Villas and Cottages* (New York, 1857), facing p. 227. Courtesy of Special Collections, Morris Library, University of Delaware.

Figure 81. A. J. Downing and Calvert Vaux, "Irregular Stone Villa with Tower," designed for S. D. Dakin, but not built, from Vaux, *Villas and Cottages* (New York, 1857), facing p. 311. Courtesy of Special Collections, Morris Library, University of Delaware.

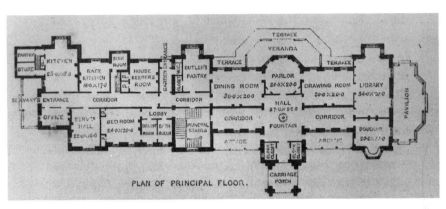

Figure 82. A. J. Downing and Calvert Vaux, design for "Villa on a Large Scale," not built, from Vaux, *Villas and Cottages* (New York, 1857), facing p. 317. Courtesy of Special Collections, Morris Library, University of Delaware.

In addition to its plans and descriptions for nine buildings designed by Downing and Vaux, *Villas and Cottages* also provides information on their charges for professional services. Vaux's business card (fig. 83), published at the end of his book, listed his fees as 2½ percent for plans and specifications, 1 percent for detailed drawings, and 1½ percent for superintendence. The text indicates that Downing and Vaux employed the same fee structure for the houses they designed between 1850 and 1852. For example, they superintended construction of the Findlay house, which cost $9326.51, and added a 5 percent architects' commission, which Vaux described as the usual fee. Thus, Downing and Vaux charged Findlay $466.33 for the house and $85 for the stable. They also superintended construction of their designs for the Moore house, at the same rate, and charged an additional $60.00 for "laying out the grounds." By contrast, the architects did not superintend construction of the Dodge houses in Washington, D.C. Because the owners made considerable changes in plans as the work progressed and "spared no expense, either in labor or materials," the cost far exceeded Downing's estimate. Presumably Downing and Vaux charged the Dodges the 2½ percent for plans, and perhaps the additional 1 percent for detailed drawings, but it is not clear whether the fee was a percentage of the estimated or the final cost.[46]

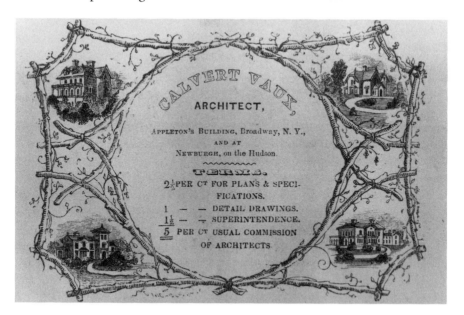

Figure 83. Calvert Vaux, business card listing charges for professional services, from Vaux, *Villas and Cottages* (New York, 1857), facing p. 318. Courtesy of Special Collections, Morris Library, University of Delaware.

Together, Downing and Vaux enjoyed a flourishing architectural practice. Vaux's comment that the nine plans labeled "D & V" in *Villas and Cottages* were "the latest over which the genial influence of the lamented Downing was exercised"[47] is confusing if not misleading, because these were not the last designs Downing prepared or the only ones the two men completed as partners. The office addition to Downing's residence was not included in Vaux's list, and there were other omissions as well, most notably the additions that transformed a two-story brick dwelling purchased by Warren Delano into an Italianate villa he renamed Algonac.[48] Vaux informed Marshall P. Wilder that, at the time of Downing's death, the firm had "commissions in Newburgh, along the Banks of the Hudson, Boston, Newport, Georgetown, Albany, etc."[49] He and Downing had "made many designs, particularly of villas, cottages, etc. with their accessories,"[50] Vaux wrote, which appears to suggest that not all of their plans were reproduced in *Villas and Cottages*. The need to hire a second architect, Withers, to help with the firm's business, is yet another indication that the commissions were more numerous than *Villas and Cottages* would suggest. Given the absence of the firm's records, with the exception of Algonac only the residential designs Vaux published can be identified with certainty; but it seems likely that his intent was to represent different types and styles of houses, not to present an exhaustive catalogue of works undertaken.

Indeed, Downing continued to prepare plans for simple rural dwellings after Vaux joined the firm. In the July 1851 *Horticulturist,* for example, he sketched a simple rural cottage suitable for a clergyman. Downing had received a letter from the minister, who was a subscriber to his journal. The plans the minister studied in *Cottage Residences* did not meet his needs because the smaller dwellings lacked a study. Anxious to avoid "sinning against architectural propriety and law" and unwilling to build a "house that shall be an eye-sore to those who may rightly judge it," the minister sought Downing's help. What he wanted was not simply a "snug cottage" but a dwelling that would be "a *standing lesson* to those who belong to my parish, of the manner in which a pleasant, unpretending home may be constructed—with the hope that it may not be without a certain tendency in its influence upon their minds, to an increased refinement and moral elevation." Here was a minister of the Gospel who wanted to become an apostle of taste, and Downing eagerly provided the requisite design (fig. 84). Following his correspondent's sketch and description of his needs, Downing published a plan for a simple yet picturesque board-and-batten cottage, with a rustic arbor-veranda and trellises that would add "an air of rural refinement and poetry to the house without expense."[51]

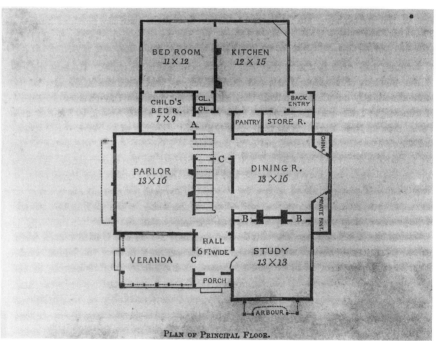

Figure 84. A. J. Downing, "Design for a Cottage for a Country Clergyman," *Horticulturist* 6 (July 1851); reprinted in *Cottage Residences*, 4th ed. (New York, 1852), facing p. 173. Courtesy of Special Collections, Morris Library, University of Delaware.

Prior to establishing an architectural practice, Downing had received a number of such letters, and when they promised a commission he usually sent them to A. J. Davis.[52] Surely he received similar requests for assistance after he established the architectural firm. Downing may well have responded to such inquiries by offering to provide plans at what he considered an appropriate fee. In much the way that he prepared designs for gardens based on a survey provided by a client, such as Joel R. Poinsett, at lower cost when he had not visited the property, so might Downing have developed designs for buildings based on descriptions of the client's needs and a sketch of the type of dwelling he or she wanted.[53] Vaux's schedule of fees, which clearly were in place during the time of Downing & Vaux, Architects, charged a percentage for the preparation of plans and additional fees for construction drawings and superintendence. For original designs of substantial buildings the partners might have charged a percentage of the estimated cost, while for smaller dwellings they might have offered the plans at a modest fee.[54]

If, as seems likely, Downing provided these or similar services to other individuals who wrote him, then the question remains how accurately the designs published in *Villas and Cottages* represent the work of Downing & Vaux, Architects. Vaux dedicated the book to Caroline E. Downing and the memory of her husband; this, together with the "D & V" designs he published, was an attempt to claim his place as successor to Downing and to assume his mantle as tastemaker to the nation. What is most striking about *Villas and Cottages,* which Vaux published almost five years after Downing's death, is the major shift in audience it represented. Whereas each of Downing's architectural books had included some plans for exceedingly modest dwellings, the cottages Vaux designed were much larger and more expensive. The cheapest was estimated at $1500 to $1600, four times the cost of the first design in *The Architecture of Country Houses*; of the cottages Downing illustrated in that book, only two exceeded the price of the least expensive Vaux design, G. J. Penchard's elaborate Swiss cottage and a brick and stucco suburban dwelling. The buildings depicted in *Villas and Cottages* identified by "D & V" were also larger and more expensive than were the smaller dwellings in *The Architecture of Country Houses,* but this does not necessarily imply that Downing had abandoned his longstanding effort to improve the dwellings of all Americans, starting with the simplest cottage. After all, his *Cheap Cottages and Farm Houses* and his plan for a country clergyman's house were published in 1851, at the very time he and Vaux were designing several of the homes represented in *Villas and Cottages.* Thus, the designs Vaux published undoubtedly reflected the author's choice of what buildings to represent, for surely he prepared *Villas and Cottages* at least in part with the hope of attracting prospective clients for his professional services: it included the types of residential buildings Vaux wanted to design, which did not necessarily extend to the same concern for the improvement of taste among all classes of citizens that Downing considered essential to the refinement of American society and to the process of adaptation that would contribute to the development of a national expression in architecture. Vaux embraced only part of Downing's mission as an apostle of taste.

An equally important reason that *Villas and Cottages* cannot be relied on as wholly representative of the firm's work is that residential designs were not the only commissions Downing received. The Boston commission Vaux mentioned in his 1852 letter to Marshall P. Wilder was probably the business block he and Downing designed for Milton J. Stone on Commercial Wharf.[55] Also, at the time of his death, Downing had completed "a postscript to a set of working plans to illustrate a design for an observatory proposed to be erected in one of our principal cities," which was the Dudley Observatory in Albany, New York.[56] Downing submitted a plan to the competition for the design of the New York Crystal Palace, a large structure that was erected on Reservoir Square in New York City to house the first American international exhibition in 1853. Whereas most of the designs in the competition were iron and glass variations on Joseph Paxton's London Crystal Palace, Downing planned a circular building (fig. 85), topped by a "colossal dome," that the published record of the exhibition's organizers applauded for its "great novelty and bold

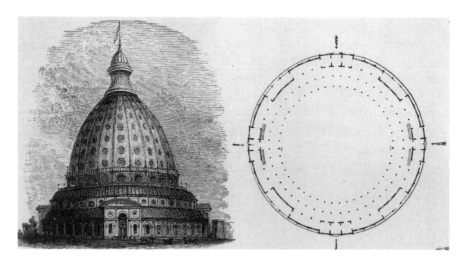

Figure 85. A. J. Downing, plan for building to house the international exhibition to be held in New York City, 1853, from Benjamin Silliman and C. R. Goodrich, eds., *The World of Science, Art, and Industry Illustrated* (New York, 1854), p. 2. Courtesy of Special Collections, Morris Library, University of Delaware.

conception." The palace Downing envisioned would not have been crystal but wood and canvas, supported by cast iron columns and iron ties and covered on the exterior with "tin and glass tiles." The building would have been economical to construct and have incorporated the spacious interior needed for an international exhibition. The committee selecting the plan, however, decided on a design submitted by Carstensen and Gildemeister, a cast-iron and glass structure that supposedly was fireproof, instead of Downing's, which, it conceded, would have been a highly visible landmark, "conspicuous at a distance and adapted to its position."[57]

In the course of implementing Downing's plan for the public grounds in Washington he and Vaux also took on several important architectural projects. For a fence surrounding Lafayette Park they echoed Benjamin H. Latrobe's American architectural motif—the corn and tobacco capitals he used on columns in the U.S. Capitol—by topping the fence palings with "an adaptation of the American Corn" (fig. 86). They also prepared a plan for modifying Robert Mills's Washington Monument, then a partially complete shaft, with a more "appropriate finish" than that provided by the architect, and sketched the general lines of a grand triumphal arch they hoped would become a fitting monument to the capital and the principal entrance to the public grounds.[58] Whatever other buildings Downing and his associates designed in these years, it is clear that Vaux's *Villas and Cottages* was not wholly representative of the firm's output.

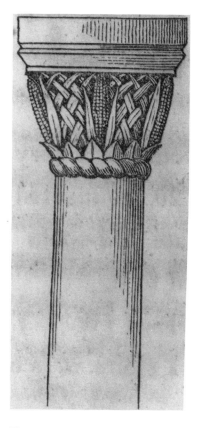

Figure 86. A. J. Downing, sketch for a new capital using the foliage and ear of Indian corn, which Downing believed would "give a distinctly American or local expression to all the architectural decoration." This image undoubtedly reflects the theme of the new capital he and Vaux sketched for the fence surrounding Lafayette Park in Washington, D.C. From *The Architecture of Country Houses* (New York, 1850), p. 362. Courtesy of Special Collections, Morris Library, University of Delaware.

୬୬ In the twenty-two months between his return from England and his death, when Downing presided over a growing architectural practice, he was also deeply involved in other projects. He continued to edit the *Horticulturist,* brought out a significantly enlarged edition of *Cottage Residences,* and worked as a professional landscape gardener. He actively supported the cause of agricultural education in New York State and projected writing a book on shade trees as well as preparing a completely revised and expanded edition of *Fruits and Fruit Trees of America.*[59]

Downing's wide-ranging activities and his frequent absences from the office to meet with clients and superintend the construction of works in progress[60] raise the question of how much he was involved in the day-to-day operations of the architectural firm. This, together with the paucity of documented designs by "D & V," makes any assessment of the ultimate influence of the firm little more than speculation. To be sure, Vaux introduced a number of new elements into Downing's design repertoire, from functional devices such as ventilating turrets to encaustic tile flooring and other decorative touches. The board-and-batten construction that Downing considered a beginning in the evolution of a distinctively American style gave way in Vaux's later work to horizontal clapboarding, the houses became larger in scale and style as simplicity gave way to ornamentation, and new Parisian fashions invaded the American hinterland. In an 1853 essay entitled "American Architecture" Vaux echoed many of Downing's concerns:

> [A] simple, well planned structure, costs less to execute for the accommodation obtained, than an ill planned one, and the fact of its being agreeable and effective or otherwise, does not depend on any ornament that may be superadded to the useful and necessary forms of which it is composed, but on the arrangement of the forms themselves, so that they may balance each other and suggest the pleasant idea of harmonious proportion, fitness, and agreeble variety to the eye, and from the eye to the mind.[61]

Downing surely encouraged Vaux to incorporate these sentiments in his designs, to "unlearn" those aspects of his English training that were inappropriate in a republican society, and to promote a "genuinely American" spirit in the buildings he created.

8

The Metropolitan Landscape

He intended to have made the Public Grounds at Washington as nearly perfect as his taste and experience would allow him and trusted that they might act favorably towards the accomplishment of his great desire—Public Pleasure grounds *every where*. —Calvert Vaux

Downing thought of himself as a champion of rural life. He devoted most of his energies to the improvement of the American countryside, and, like many of his contemporaries, considered agriculture the most virtuous pursuit in a republican society. Yet Downing was living during the period of the fastest rate of urban growth in American history. Together, the growth of cities and the beginnings of industrialization created new social, cultural, and economic conditions. Downing witnessed these changes on his frequent trips to major metropolitan centers. He visited Boston to tour nurseries, to attend the annual exhibition of the Massachusetts Horticultural Society, and to study new examples of architectural and landscape design, while professional consulting took him to numerous other cities. He often traveled to New York City and Albany, where his books and the *Horticulturist* were published, and while in New York he attended the annual exhibitions of the American Art-Union and other events important to the emerging artistic community. Downing nevertheless believed that the only reason to live in a city was to make enough money to retire to the country, and he recoiled from the human tragedies that accompanied urbanization and industrialization (he refused, for example, to take Fredrika Bremer to the Five Points, New York's most notorious slum). Still, he conceded that cities were the centers of culture as well as economic life, and in the last five years of his life he became increasingly concerned with reforming the landscape of metropolitan America as well.

When Downing met Fredrika Bremer in New York in October 1849, the first place he took her was Green-Wood Cemetery, in Brooklyn. Established in 1838, Green-Wood was located on a hilly, 175-acre site overlooking Gowanus

Bay and New York Harbor. Designed by engineer David B. Douglass in the natural style of landscape gardening, the cemetery was just the place for Bremer to escape the crush of visitors who wanted to greet the Swedish author. She was enchanted by Green-Wood, which she compared to Père-Lachaise, a famous cemetery on the outskirts of Paris. The Brooklyn cemetery was far larger than its Parisian counterpart, however, and its design was more naturalistic. As Downing drove the carriage along Green-Wood's gently curving drives, Bremer was struck by how much the place resembled "an extensive English park." The contrast between the bustling streets of the city, where she was appalled by the "restless, deeply-sunk eyes, the excited, wearied features" of many New Yorkers, and the serenity of the landscape at Green-Wood, was as striking to Bremer as it was to Downing. "Better [to] lie and sleep on Ocean Hill" (fig. 87), the highest point in the cemetery, she concluded, "than live thus on Broadway!"[1]

The "rural" cemetery was created in response to a number of problems: the skyrocketing value of urban real estate, which made land once set aside for burial more valuable for other uses; the sheer increase in the number of residents and burials, which led to the closing of many older urban cemeteries and necessitated additional grounds for interment; and the wave of epidemics that swept through America's cities in the nineteenth century, which, before the widespread acceptance of germs as causes of disease, raised the specter that miasmas, or gases escaping from graves, were a threat to public health. The first "rural" cemetery, Mount Auburn, in Cambridge, Massachusetts, was consecrated in 1831. Located some distance from the densely built city, Mount Auburn guaranteed permanence in burial and incorporated a new symbolism, the curvilinearity of the naturalistic landscape, as an important part of metropolitan life. Almost immediately after their opening Mount Auburn and Green-Wood became favorite places of resort: some sixty thousand New Yorkers visited Green-Wood between April and December 1848.[2]

Perhaps the most surprising reason so many New Yorkers thronged the paths and drives of Green-Wood was its scenery. Until the establishment of the "rural" cemetery there was very little open space in the built areas of the metropolis. The Commissioners Plan of 1811 had set aside a number of squares in Manhattan, but by 1842 most of this land had been sold or occupied with buildings. In Brooklyn, Hezekiah Pierrepont had hoped to establish a promenade on the Heights, but that land was instead developed privately and few other members of his generation considered the creation of open recreational areas a public responsibility.[3] But as the two cities on opposite banks of the East River expanded in physical size and soared in population, Green-Wood's spacious landscape came to represent a naturalistic counterpoint to the walls of brick, brownstone, and marble that otherwise

Figure 87. Egyptian Obelisk, Ocean Hill, Green-Wood Cemetery, engraving by James Smillie, from Nehemiah Cleaveland, *Green-Wood Illustrated. In Highly Finished Line Engraving, from drawings taken on the spot, by James Smillie. With Descriptive Notices by Nehemiah Cleaveland* (New York, 1847), facing p. 72.

characterized the city. The cemetery's directors succeeded in the effort to create a landscape characterized by *"verdure, shade, ruralness, natural beauty;* every thing, in short, in contrast with the *glare, set form, fixed rule* and *fashion* of the city."* Green-Wood, they explained, would stand forever as a place of repose, an escape from the "whirl and fever of artificial life" in the city, which the popular author Nehemiah Cleaveland described as a "discordant Babel."[4] As Downing noted, the "great attraction" of rural cemeteries was not their sculpture or solemnity, which might be found in a well-maintained churchyard, but the "natural beauty of the sites" and their "tasteful and harmonious embellishment."[5]

Drawing upon the success of cemeteries, most of which were organized as private joint stock corporations, Downing suggested a similar cooperative strategy for the creation of public gardens. A group of interested citizens could incorporate, acquire a tract of fifty to one hundred acres, and establish a garden. As part of his crusade to educate the public taste, Downing suggested that such a garden might include "an example of the principal modes of laying out grounds,—thus teaching practical landscape-gardening." Another feature might be a botanical garden, embracing "a collection of all the hardy trees and shrubs that will grow in this climate, each distinctly labelled." A "magnificent drive" could extend through the wooded portions of the garden, while other parts could be landscaped to serve as the "great promenade" of the community. Here, in a private setting, were most of the features Downing associated with the public park. He believed that many citizens would subscribe to the cost of creating the garden, just as they purchased lots in a rural cemetery, and that others would willingly pay a "small admission fee" to be able to enjoy the music, the scenery, and the festivities that would take place there. "If the road to Mount Auburn is now lined with coaches, continually carrying the inhabitants of Boston by thousands and tens of thousands," he pointed out, "is it not likely that such a garden, full of the most varied instruction, amusement, and recreation, would be ten times more visited." Indeed, he predicted, for an annual expenditure of less than the rent of P. T. Barnum's American Museum, such a garden would prove far more attractive than the showman's "stuffed boa-constrictors and *un*-human Belgian giants."[6]

Downing designed at least one rural cemetery, the Cemetery of the Evergreens in Brooklyn and Queens, New York. He was identified as the "Landscape Gardener and Rural Architect" in one of the cemetery's publications, though he worked in collaboration with A. J. Davis, who prepared plans for a gateway and chapel (probably from Downing's preliminary sketches).[7] The engraving that illustrated Downing and Davis's Lombard chapel depicts the building standing in a parklike setting, with curvilinear paths and other elements of the beautiful or the graceful that Downing incorporated in the landscape (fig. 88). Unfortunately, excepting a single letter to Davis, no surviving correspondence suggests Downing's intent in designing the cemetery, nor do the published records of the company that was developing the grounds, but the engraving conveys an openness and tranquility that contemporaries associated with rural cemeteries.

Although the extent of Downing's involvement with the Cemetery of the Evergreens remains uncertain, his writings on rural cemeteries surely contributed to the transformation of the metropolitan landscape. In 1833, only two years after the consecration of Mount Auburn, a Baltimore clergyman, Stephen Duncan Walker, pointed to the rural cemetery as the most expeditious way of creating a "public walk."[8] As numerous other writers celebrated the scenic beauties of Mount Auburn, Green-Wood, or Philadelphia's Laurel Hill Cemetery, Downing lent his authority to the cultural significance of these burial grounds. Rural cemeteries, he wrote in 1841, were "the first really elegant public gardens or promenades formed in this country."[9] Downing be-

Figure 88. Chapel of the Cemetery of the Evergreens, Brooklyn, N.Y., designed by A. J. Downing and A. J. Davis, grounds by A. J. Downing, from *Rules and Regulations of the Cemetery of the Evergreens* (New York, 1852). Courtesy of General Research Division, the New York Public Library, Astor, Lenox and Tilden Foundations.

lieved that the success of rural cemeteries stimulated the public's recognition of the importance of large parks as essential components of a new urban landscape. Eight years before the commencement of construction of New York's Central Park, Downing wrote, "[I]n the absence of great public gardens, such as we must surely one day have in America, our rural cemeteries are doing a great deal to enlarge and educate the popular taste in rural embellishment." The crowds that visited these cemeteries were proof, he added, of "how much our citizens, of all classes, would enjoy public parks on a similar scale."[10]

The example of rural cemeteries, and the vast expanse of parks in London's West End that he visited in 1850, convinced Downing that public parks were essential to the health and well-being of residents in America's cities, and he concluded that public rather than private financing was the best way of extending the benefits of parks to all citizens. Parks would not only prove attractive to residents of cities, he pointed out, but would become reformist

Figure 89. View of Washington, D.C., showing the
condition of the public grounds between the Capitol
and the Washington Monument prior to commencement of implementation of Downing's plan. Undated
lithograph by E. Sachse. Courtesy of Prints and
Photographs Division, Library of Congress.

institutions. They would be "better preachers of temperance than temperance societies, better refiners of national manners than dancing schools, and
better promoters of general good feeling than any lectures on the philosophy of happiness ever delivered in the lecture room."[11]

Shortly after returning from England Downing eagerly accepted the opportunity to put his ideas into practice and create what he hoped would become the first "*real* park in the United States." In the fall of 1850 Joseph
Henry, first secretary of the Smithsonian Institution, and Washington fi-
nancier W. W. Corcoran, convinced President Millard Fillmore to improve
the public grounds of the nation's capital. Henry, Corcoran, Mayor Walter
Lenox, and Commissioner of Public Buildings Ignatius Mudd "concluded to
send for some competent landscape gardener, to give a general plan of the
improvements" to be made, and they persuaded Fillmore to invite Downing
to undertake the project.[12]

The area the government commissioned Downing to landscape was an
L-shaped tract of approximately 150 acres that extended west from the foot of
the hill on which the Capitol sat to the site of the Washington Monument
and from that point north to the President's House. In his plan of the capital,
Pierre Charles L'Enfant anticipated that this area would develop into a "grand
avenue," the aesthetic centerpiece of the federal city. To his dismay, and that

of visitors from the United States and Europe alike, the federal government did little to improve the site. In 1841 Robert Mills had prepared a plan for landscaping the grounds of the Washington Monument, and later in the same decade Joseph Henry had attempted to improve the area adjacent to the Smithsonian, but these efforts were unsuccessful. Contemporary images corroborate one journalist's description of the site of the proposed park as a "bleak, unhospitable common," traversed by muddy roads, scarred by "deep gullies," and devoid of trees "except one or two scraggy and dying syca-mores"[13] (fig. 89). When Downing arrived in Washington on November 25, 1850, he and Henry called on the president, who "entered with much interest into the plans." Then, according to Henry, Downing "examined all the ground between the Capitol and the [Potomac] river," which he found "ad-mirably adapted to make a landscape garden and drive." Downing spent much of the next two months drafting and completing a plan of improvement, which he presented to the Regents of the Smithsonian on February 27, 1851.[14]

Downing's plan (fig. 90) attempted to transform the public grounds into an "extended landscape garden, to be traversed in different directions by gravelled walks and carriage drives, and planted with specimens, properly la-belled, of all the varieties of trees and shrubs which will flourish in this cli-mate."[15] The text accompanying the plan outlined three purposes: to "form a

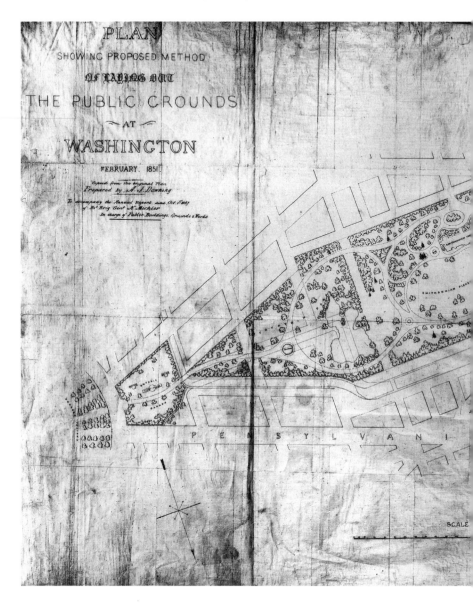

Figure 90. A. J. Downing, plan of the public grounds at Washington, February 1851. Courtesy of Geography and Maps Division, Library of Congress.

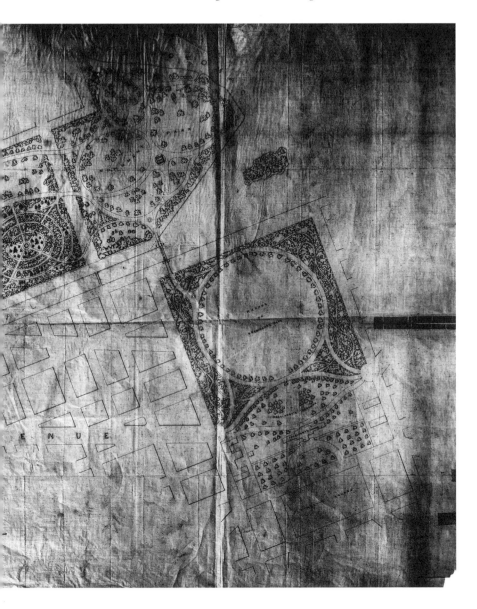

national Park, which should be an ornament to the Capital of the United States"; to "give an example of the natural style of Landscape Gardening which may have an influence on the general taste of the Country"; and to "form a public museum of living trees and shrubs." The commission, as Downing perceived it, was not simply to improve the public grounds but to create a great public park that would contribute to the improvement of individual taste and demonstrate to other cities the importance of open spaces within the urban environment. The Washington project, Downing predicted, "would exercise as much influence on the public taste as Mount Auburn Cemetery," which had inspired the creation of similar handsomely landscaped burial grounds in numerous other communities. If his plan was adopted, Downing wrote, the public grounds at Washington would become a "Public School of Instruction in every thing that relates to the tasteful arrangement of parks and grounds."[16]

Downing's plan divided the public grounds into six areas, with the type of landscape treatment for each determined by function yet united by an overall conception. The first, the President's Park or Parade, was located directly behind the executive mansion. Downing proposed "to keep the large area of this ground open, as a place for parade or military reviews, as well as public festivities or celebrations." The greensward was encircled by a row of elms

Figure 91. A. J. Downing, drawing showing the intended effect of the President's Arch, Washington, D.C., February 1851. Courtesy of National Archives and Records Administration, Washington, D.C.

shading a carriage drive, outside of which Downing placed serpentine paths amid dense plantings, thereby demarcating separate spaces for public ritual and for the quiet contemplation of nature. He also suggested the construction of a "large and handsome Archway of marble" (fig. 91) at Fifteenth Street and Pennsylvania Avenue, which would serve as the ceremonial entrance to the grounds. The arch would create a new terminus to the vista L'Enfant had designed for the avenue, a symbolic expression of the relationship between the executive and legislative branches that had been blocked by the construction of Robert Mills's Treasury building, and would, Downing hoped, become "one of the principal Architectural ornaments of the city."

The second element of Downing's plan, Monument Park, was a meadowlike garden of American trees surrounding Mills's still incomplete obelisk. Between the President's House and Monument Park flowed the Tiber Canal, and Downing proposed a wire suspension bridge (fig. 92) to carry paths and drives across the water. The third element of the plan was the Evergreen Garden, which Downing suggested be a museum of every evergreen that would thrive in the capital, including broad-leaved species such as laurels, rhododendrons, and magnolias. He considered this garden especially valuable because the city was most crowded in the winter and early spring months, when Congress was in session. The fourth area, Smithsonian Park or Pleasure Grounds, he designed as an "arrangement of choice trees in the natural style," along with carefully placed evergreens that would enhance the irregular outlines of James Renwick's castlelike building. East of the Smithsonian Downing located the fifth feature of his plan, Fountain Park, with its fountain, curvi-

Figure 92. A. J. Downing, drawing showing the intended effect of the suspension bridge proposed to span the Tiber Canal, Washington, D.C., February 1851. Courtesy of National Archives and Records Administration, Washington, D.C.

linear drives, and artificial lake. He then offered advice on landscaping the sixth area, the grounds surrounding the three greenhouses of the national botanical garden at the foot of Capitol Hill. Downing ran the carriage drives to the eastern end of the public grounds, where a large gateway opposite the entrance to the Capitol grounds marked the termination of the plan. Almost five miles of curvilinear drives and pedestrian paths led the visitor through the open spaces of the President's Park or Parade, Monument Park, the Smithsonian grounds, and Fountain Park. If his plan was implemented, Downing asserted, it would provide relief from and contrast to the "straight lines and broad Avenues of the Streets of Washington" and make it possible for residents to enjoy "all pleasant and healthful intercourse with gardens and green fields"[17] (fig. 93).

The Regents of the Smithsonian Institution adopted Downing's plan and

forwarded it to Fillmore, who, on April 12, 1851, approved construction of the part of the plan west of Seventh Street, "subject to such modifications as may be deemed advisable in the progress of the work." Presumably because of the cost of excavating the lake and altering the course of the Tiber Canal, the president did not authorize work on the eastern part of the plan until February 8, 1853. Downing was given an annual salary of $2500 for superintending the implementation of his design.[18]

Downing undoubtedly commenced the work in Washington optimistically. After all, the commission was an opportunity both to translate theory into practice and to demonstrate the value of public parks in American society. But he very quickly experienced frustration at the obstacles that impeded construction. The delays were predictable: Alexis de Tocqueville, whom Downing read favorably and quoted, had been shocked by the Washington

Figure 93. "Washington, D. C., The Projected Improvements." Lithograph by B. F. Smith, Jr., 1852. Courtesy of Prints and Photographs Division, Library of Congress.

he had visited two decades earlier. Like numerous other commentators, Tocqueville observed that Washington, D.C., was a capital in name only, not the metropolitan center of the nation; he was appalled that the federal government lacked the will and the resources to complete L'Enfant's grand design. "Unless one is Alexander or Peter the Great," he concluded, "one must not meddle with creating the capital of an empire."[19] Lacking the near-absolute power possessed by Baron Haussmann, who at the same time was beginning the transformation of Paris, Downing had to work with the executive and legislative branches as well as an entrenched bureaucracy to translate his plans into physical form.

In the spring of 1851 Downing oversaw the commencement of grading and draining of the grounds surrounding the Smithsonian. Because of numerous other commitments, and because the early stages of construction involved "the roughest operations of ground labor," Downing spent only a part of each month (usually a week) in the capital. To compensate for his absences from Washington, Downing devised a "rigid system of daily *overseeing*," which he entrusted to William D. Breckenridge, who directed the activities of the forty to seventy laborers who were engaged in the construction. Downing had apparently made this arrangement before accepting the commission and intended to spend greater periods of time in the capital as the more refined work—planting and the grading of paths and drives—necessitated his direct supervision.[20]

Nevertheless, Downing's absences provoked the ire of William Easby, the new commissioner of public buildings, who evidently told Fillmore that on his most recent visit Downing had remained "only long enough to draw his pay." Downing thought Easby was "ambitious to *manage* everything relating to Washington—and among other matters *myself*." He insisted that his role in the improvement of the public grounds was an artistic one and informed Joseph Henry, "If I am interfered with or trammelled by any petty commissioner I will throw up the matter at once—as I am wholly independent of both it & the President." At the urging of Henry and Corcoran, however, Downing journeyed to Washington, where he met with Fillmore "to settle the matter as to who has the jurisdiction of the grounds." As a result of this conference the president extended Downing's authority to include all public spaces within the city.[21]

The bureaucracy was only one source of Downing's frustration. In February 1852 he spent most of his week-long visit to the capital attempting to justify the cost of improvements to congressional committees responsible for Washington's public grounds. Learning of congressional resistance to the expenditures, which he estimated would be $50,000 that year, Downing sought the support of friends such as Joseph Henry. "I have a great interest in the work in Washington," he wrote, "& if you gentlemen who have influence in Washington will stand by me I will make the capital 'blossom like a rose.'" But to achieve this result he demanded absolute control of the work and freedom from "all mean acts of patronage."[22]

On March 24, 1852, the House of Representatives debated a resolution appropriating additional funds to continue the improvements to the grounds adjacent to the President's House. During the debate several congressmen again raised the issue of Downing's compensation and absentee supervision and otherwise objected to the cost of the project. Equally telling was the appearance of partisanship in the debate, with some Democrats demanding to know why it was so necessary to embellish the grounds of the executive mansion while a Whig was president. And although Downing's plan was one of a series of public works undertaken at least in part to make the capital a symbol of national union, sectional differences were apparent in this and subsequent congressional discussions of the improvements. Supporters of the appropriation described Downing as a man of "rare skill as a 'rural architect' and landscape gardener, as well as a man of great scientific intelligence." Congressman Richard Henry Stanton of Kentucky, for example, pointed out that the project attempted "to render the neighborhood of the Executive Mansion healthy enough to enable the President and his family to reside there without endangering their lives." He described Downing's plan as "admirable" and predicted that when completed it would be "a credit to the city and the nation." Stanton and other supporters of the improvements carried the day: passage of the spending resolution allowed construction to continue.[23] While supervising construction of the western half of the plan, Downing assumed responsibility for two other projects. Together with Calvert Vaux he planned and oversaw improvements to Lafayette Square, directly across Pennsylvania Avenue from the President's House, and he commenced preparation of a design for completing the Washington Monument with a more "appropriate finish" than that provided in Mills's plan.[24]

Downing's death in the fire that destroyed the Hudson River steamboat *Henry Clay* on July 28, 1852 ended the momentum behind the improvements to the public grounds. Indeed, the following month, one congressman testified that it was "universally understood" the project would not have been undertaken "if it had not been known that Mr. Downing would be employed."[25] Although Fillmore adopted the design for the improvements east of Seventh Street six months after Downing's death, thereafter the plan was in large part altered or ignored. In 1856 the editor of the *Horticulturist* described the grounds of the Smithsonian as being "in a neglected state"; on the eve of the Civil War the President's Park was still "an unsavory marsh which had formerly been an outlet for sewage" and the grounds south of the Tiber Canal were only "half-developed."[26] After the war Downing's plan fared no better. In 1868, for example, Supervising Architect of the Treasury A. B. Mullett recommended that Downing's design "be carried out at the earliest moment," but nothing came of his plea. Then, in the early 1870s, when Washington's Haussmann, Alexander Shepherd, was directing a series of public works projects, he allowed the tracks of the Baltimore and Potomac Railroad to cross the public grounds at grade and the construction of a large depot near Sixth Street. According to historian Constance McLaughlin Green, under Shepherd, "romantic landscaping" gave way to "commercial utility," and for the rest of the nineteenth century what Downing intended to be the first example of a public park in the United States remained only partly developed.[27]

The commission to improve the grounds of the capital in Washington was Downing's only major public landscape design. According to Vaux, Downing had hoped that the successful completion of the improvements would encourage every city in the United States to establish a public park.[28] However, left unfinished at the time of his death, and never completed as he intended, the Washington plan did not have the powerful influence Downing intended. His writings would have a greater impact in transforming the metropolitan landscape than did his incomplete design for the public grounds in the capital.

In the summer of 1851, Downing had taken up pen to urge the creation of a large public park in New York City. Mayor Ambrose C. Kingsland had proposed the establishment of a park at the Jones Wood, a 160-acre site overlooking the East River that extended from 64th to 75th streets. While Downing was pleased that New York was considering construction of a park, he had specific ideas about the qualities of landscape that would be necessary to relieve the tedium of a city he described as an "arid desert of business and dissipation." A park had to be more than city squares, which Downing characterized as children's playgrounds, and needed to embrace "broad reaches of park and pleasure-grounds, with a real feeling of the breadth and beauty of green fields, the perfume and freshness of nature." He then advocated the establishment of a park of at least 500 acres in the central area of Manhattan Island north of 39th Street.[29]

"The New-York Park," the leader Downing published in the August 1851 *Horticulturist,* outlined both a rationale for park development and a comprehensive reformist agenda he termed "popular refinement." During his visit to England he had praised the "elevating influences of a wide popular enjoyment of galleries of art, public libraries, parks and gardens, which have raised the people in *social* civilization and social culture to a far higher degree than we have yet attained in republican America." Downing conceded that the common school was merely a beginning, that in order to fulfill its republican destiny the United States needed to promote the kinds of institutions that would provide "the refining influence of intellectual and moral culture" to the working class. His prescription, breathtaking in scope, simultaneously condemned the limitations of a supposedly classless society and held out the possibility of a more enlightened future: "Open wide, therefore, the doors of your libraries and picture galleries, all ye true republicans! Build halls where knowledge shall be freely diffused among men, and not shut up within the narrow walls of narrower institutions. Plant spacious parks in your cities, and unloose their gates as wide as the gates of morning to the whole people." The program of popular refinement Downing advocated included "common enjoyments for all classes, in the higher realms of art, letters, science, social recreations and enjoyments." If successfully implemented, he predicted, it would "banish the plague-spots of democracy" and raise the level of civilization in the United States.[30]

"The New-York Park" was much broader in scope than the report accompanying Downing's plan for the public grounds in Washington, which he had written only six months earlier. Whether the difference was attributable to the intended audience or reflected a maturation of Downing's understanding of the importance of parks to American society is impossible to determine. Fredrika Bremer believed the latter was the case. When she first met Downing in 1849, she found him somewhat "exclusive and aristocratic." Two years later, however, she could "rejoice to see the development of life and activity which has taken place in Downing." She was pleased that he had accepted the commission to design the public grounds in Washington and applauded the reformist sentiments he had expressed in *The Architecture of Country Houses*. But Bremer was most taken by the commitment to republicanism she found expressed in "The New-York Park." In that essay, Bremer believed, Downing "declared from his sphere the mission of the New World."[31]

Downing conceived of the park as part of the evolving metropolitan landscape. It was, as well, an omnibus recreational and educational institution, a naturalistic setting for the promotion of "popular refinement." As an apostle of taste Downing expected that a public park would have space for "noble works of art, the statues, monuments, and buildings commemorative at once of the great men of the nation, of the history of the age and country, and the genius of our highest artists." It would be an appropriate setting for institutions of public education, which, he anticipated, might include the New York Crystal Palace as well as botanical gardens, grounds for zoological and horticultural societies, and "spacious buildings" to house galleries of art. His vision of the park combined the recreational uses of a pleasure garden, the setting for institutions of popular education, and the quiet contemplation of natural scenery.[32]

✌ Downing also became an effective proponent of the suburb as part of the metropolitan landscape. In 1848 he applauded the "rapid multiplication of pretty cottages and villas in many parts of North America," and while he used the terms *country house* and *suburban cottage* interchangeably, he was actually describing the beginnings of suburbanization. The key, he recognized, was the network of railroads that was extending outward from major cities. Although the railroads were originally built for commerce, Downing insisted that they could not "wholly escape doing some duty for the Beautiful as well as the useful" by making land on the periphery of cities suitable for metropolitan homes. "Hundreds and thousands," he wrote, "formerly obliged to live in the crowded streets of cities, now find themselves able to enjoy a country cottage, several miles distant,—the old notions of time and space being half annihilated." The development of suburbs was a positive good that enabled families "to breathe freely" and to enjoy natural surroundings while maintaining proximity to urban jobs, friends, and cultural attractions.[33] Indeed, Downing recommended a suburban home for individuals who enjoyed society and would feel a certain deprivation should they "let go the cord that binds them to their fellows."[34]

Downing quickly discovered that the emergence of the commuter suburb[35] brought problems as well as promises of a more spacious metropolitan landscape, particularly when real estate promoters and transportation companies laid out rectangular streets and advertised lots for sale in what they described as ideal communities. The plat of the village of Dearman (now Irvington, N.Y.) exemplified what Downing considered the worst kind of suburban development. Located on a large, hilly tract overlooking the Hudson River twenty miles north of New York City, the site was connected to the metropolis by the Hudson River Railroad, the Albany Post Road, and frequent steamboat excursions. Dearman (fig. 94) possessed all the requisites for advantageous development in what Downing termed the modern or natural style of landscape gardening. Given the topography of the site, curvilinear streets and irregularly shaped lots following the contours of the land would not only have enhanced Dearman's attractiveness as a location for suburban homes but would have reduced the cost of grading and filling the property. The real estate promoters, Cole and Chilton, instead imposed a rectangular gridiron on the site, with a central avenue, seventy feet wide, running east from the river, directly up a steep hill, intersected by eight narrower streets running north and south. They then subdivided the tract into uniform lots of fifty by one hundred feet.[36]

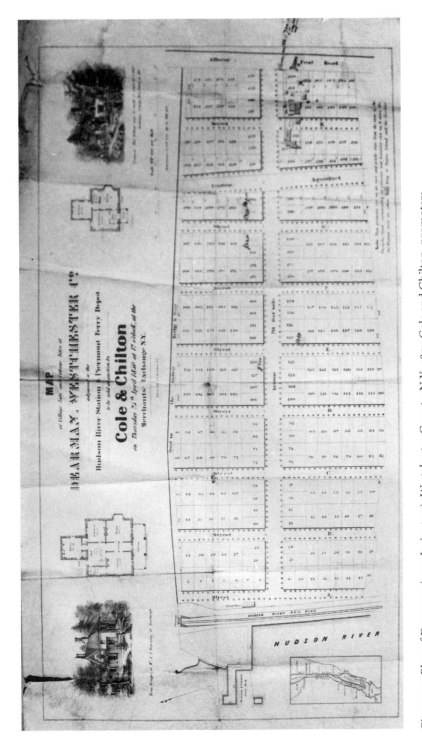

Figure 94. Plan of Dearman (now Irvington), Westchester County, N.Y., 1851, Cole and Chilton, promoters. Courtesy of The Hudson River Museum of Westchester (INV. 1992), Yonkers, N.Y.

Downing had special cause for concern with the Dearman plan. Although the developmental scheme violated every precept of landscape theory he had promulgated in the preceding decade, Cole and Chilton attempted to capitalize on Downing's cultural authority by placing engravings from *Cottage Residences* in the upper left and right corners of the subdivision map published prior to the auction of their lots. Downing must have been enraged. With this misrepresentation as incentive, he offered a devastating critique of the speculative suburban community. His response, "Our Country Villages," also established the general outlines of the suburban ideal in mid-nineteenth-century America.[37]

Because of the rapid development of communities throughout the United States, Downing argued, "the plan and arrangement of new towns ought to be a matter of national importance." He cited the example of recently platted suburbs along the Hudson River, which claimed to combine "the advantages of the country with easy railroad access" to the city. In a veiled reference to Dearman, Downing wrote that fifty-foot lots and rows of houses along shaded streets amounted to "the sum total of the rural beauty, convenience and comfort of the latest plan for a rural village in the Union." Alas, in forsaking the city the purchaser acquired only "his little patch of back and front yard, [and] a little peep down the street, looking one way at the river, and the other way at the sky." A resident sacrificed urban amenities, yet found himself in a village "with houses on all sides, almost as closely placed as in the city, which he has endeavored to fly from."[38]

Other arbiters of taste echoed Downing's criticism of the gridiron suburb. From the Editor's Easy Chair at *Harper's*, his friend George William Curtis chastised the "taste which would carve up such a town site as Dearman or Abbottsford, upon the steep slope of a river bank, into rectangular squares." Curtis, who had only recently completed the memoir of Downing that served as the introduction to *Rural Essays*, asserted that "roads in country villages *ought to wind*," both because such streets were cheaper to construct and because they increased the number of scenic views.[39] H. W. S. Cleveland, a landscape gardener who was a contributor to Downing's *Horticulturist*, similarly lamented the "experiments of speculators, who lay out rectangular villages with the aid of a surveyor, and offer rural felicity for sale in lots of thirty by fifty feet," while the authors of *Village and Farm Cottages* denounced the subdivider who laid out a suburban community with the "checker-board exactness which is supposed to be necessary in a city."[40] These commentators, like Downing, thought of the gridiron as urban form and found it completely inappropriate for use in a suburban community. A properly designed suburb, Downing argued, "should aim at something higher" than small lots aligned along rectangular streets.[41]

If the suburb was to be a handsomely landscaped community where families escaped the congestion of cities, Downing believed, it had to offer more than "mere rows of houses upon streets crossing each other at right angles, and bordered with shade trees." He conceded that either by choice or by necessity "people must live in towns and villages," but he could not accept that they should live in a place such as Dearman, which was devoid of the attractions he considered essential to residential life. Downing therefore outlined what he considered the requirements of an ideal suburban community. Most important was the provision of a "large open space, common, or park, situated in the middle of the village." This area, jointly owned by all lot holders, should be at least twenty acres in extent, though preferably much larger, and "should be well planted with groups of trees, and kept as a lawn." Such a park, Downing explained, would be the "nucleus or *heart of the village,* and give it an essentially rural character." He then recommended that wide, tree lined avenues and the "best cottages and residences" front the park, much as the largest dwellings in New England towns faced the common, and that through the "imperative arrangement" of surrounding streets the village proprietors secure "sufficient space, view, circulation of air, and broad, well-planted avenues of shade-trees."[42]

Important as they were, platting curving streets, building houses, and reserving a park were but the first steps in developing a true community. After a few years, Downing predicted, residents "would not be contented with the mere meadow and trees" and would decide to make the park into "pleasure-grounds." Using funds obtained from a small assessment paid by each family, the park could be planted with "rare, hardy shrubs, trees and plants" as well as beds of flowers and orchards. One advantage of such an arrangement, Downing explained, was that families that possessed "neither the means, time, nor inclination to devote to the culture of private pleasure-grounds, could thus enjoy those which belonged to all." Still later, residents would decide that they wanted additional amenities, and so would construct rustic seats and arbors, organize summer concerts on the lawns, and provide refreshments to all those in attendance.[43]

Here was Downing's ideal of a "*republican*" village, a private space that enshrined the "power and virtue of the *individual home*" and at the same time promoted communal activities. Private dwellings provided the optimal surroundings for nurture, while the park and its various entertainments offered positive "mental and moral influences" for all members of the community. A home in such a suburb enabled a family to reside free from the congestion, disease, and "immoral influences" of the city, to enjoy the beneficent surroundings of nature while remaining a part of the metropolitan landscape. The suburb itself was one of the many institutions Downing hoped would promote "popular refinement in the arts, manners, social life, and innocent enjoyments," and would, he believed, contribute to the realization of his ideal of "a virtuous and educated republic."[44]

✍ Downing's conceptualization of the metropolitan landscape remained incomplete at the time of his death. Although he castigated the practice of building cities "as though there was a fearful scarcity of space,"[45] he never had the opportunity to design a major subdivision or suburban community. In 1853, however, Downing's former client, Llewellyn S. Haskell, began assembling a large tract of land in West Orange, New Jersey, for what became Llewellyn Park (fig. 95). This was to be a community planned "with special reference to the wants of citizens doing business in the city of New York, and yet wishing accessible, retired, and healthful homes in the country." For the design of the suburb, Haskell turned to Downing's longtime collaborator, Alexander Jackson Davis, who was assisted by landscape gardeners Eugene A. Baumann and Howard Daniels. In overall conception Llewellyn Park closely resembled the ideal suburban community Downing had articulated

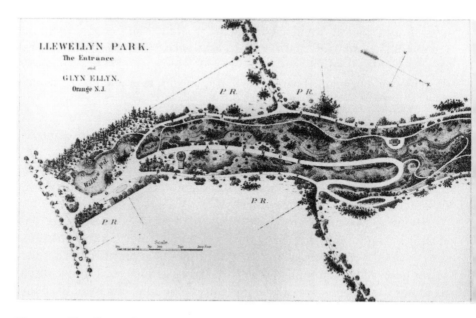

Figure 95. Llewellyn Park, entrance and the glen, from A. J. Downing, *Treatise on the Theory and Practice of Landscape Gardening,* 7th ed. (New York, 1875). Courtesy of the Winterthur Library: Printed Book and Periodical Collection, Winterthur, Del.

in "Our Country Villages." Its principal feature was a centrally located park of fifty acres, known as the Ramble (fig. 96), which was surrounded by sites for private residences. Throughout the Ramble Haskell placed a series of ornamental structures, including kiosks, summerhouses, rustic seats, and bridges. An annual assessment of all residents paid for the maintenance of the park, just as Downing had suggested. No fences separated individual properties, which contributed to the "appearance of a very large landscaped estate," while the communally owned park enabled a "family occupying a small place in the country, costing only a few thousands of dollars, to enjoy all the advantages of an extensive country seat, without the expense or trouble attending the latter."[46]

In physical form, at least, Llewellyn Park embodied Downing's suburban ideal. Yet even the smallest one-acre lots were beyond the financial reach of the urban workingman intent on erecting a humble suburban cottage. Downing "thought the millionaire sufficiently cared for," according to N. P. Willis, and devoted increasing energies in the last years of his life to dignifying "the homes of The Many."[47] Given his belief in the opportunities available to citizens in a republic, Downing was certain that sober, industrious individuals

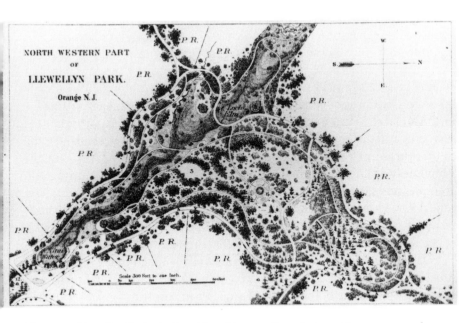

Figure 96. Llewellyn Park, the Ramble, with space for private residences arranged around it, from A. J. Downing, *Treatise on the Theory and Practice of Landscape Gardening*, 7th ed. (New York, 1875). Courtesy of the Winterthur Library: Printed Book and Library Collection, Winterthur, Del.

could attain a suburban home and a refined domestic environment for their families. However, the cost of transportation and the instability of job tenure precluded a home in the suburbs for most working-class Americans.[48]

Downing's death cut short his crusade for public parks as essential components of the metropolitan landscape. Although he hoped that his plan for the public grounds in Washington would inspire the creation of parks in other cities, because of the nature of the commission it was far more limited than the ideal of public recreational grounds he articulated in "The New-York Park." Nevertheless, Downing's ideas, and his personal commitment to parks, contributed significantly to the establishment of public parks in many of the nation's cities. Calvert Vaux persuaded the Board of Commissioners of the Central Park to reject a preliminary plan for development prepared by engineer Egbert L. Viele and to hold a competition to determine the park's design.[49] Together with Frederick Law Olmsted, Vaux entered a plan in the competition, "Greensward," that captured first premium. Olmsted, a Connecticut farmer who was a correspondent to Downing's *Horticulturist* in the 1840s and whose writings on parks Downing first published in his monthly, found in Downing the example for his own career in refining and civilizing American society.[50] After winning the competition, Olmsted and Vaux were entrusted with the responsibility for developing Central Park, and based on that success Olmsted became the dominant park builder and landscape architect of his generation.

Olmsted's conception of the park differed from Downing's in one important respect. Because of the value Olmsted placed on the psychological benefits residents of cities would derive from open space, especially seemingly boundless expanses of natural landscape, he rejected the park as a setting for institutional structures, arguing that other places were more appropriate for such uses and that the park was too important a part of the urban landscape to be compromised by unnecessary buildings. Thus, he and Vaux fought strenuously against most attempts to locate structures within Central Park, even projects such as Richard Morris Hunt's design for the New-York Historical Society and his plans for monumental entrances, both of which conformed to Downing's belief that the park should provide facilities for popular education and settings for important works of public art.[51]

Despite this difference, Olmsted and Vaux attributed much of their personal and collective success, as well as the popular embrace of public parks, to Downing's influence. In the spring of 1860, when construction had advanced to the point that the lower portion of Central Park was open to visitors, they attempted to place there "some appropriate acknowledgment of the public indebtedness to the labors of the late A. J. Downing, of which we feel the Park itself is one of the direct results." The printed circular accompanying their letters soliciting donations for the memorial included the passage from "The New-York Park" in which Downing outlined the social and cultural benefits of public parks.[52] Although nothing came of this effort, in 1882 Olmsted again attempted to honor Downing's memory by urging "special and reverent attention" to the surviving parts of Downing's plan for the public grounds in Washington, D.C. This was "the last and only important public work of Downing," Olmsted wrote, "who was not only a master of the art, but distinctly a man of genius, of whom his country should always be proud."[53] Once again, in 1887, Olmsted and Vaux paid homage to Downing when, at the urging of Caroline Downing Monell, they offered to donate their professional services to Newburgh, New York, for the design of a public park, "if the city should name the reservation 'Downing Park.'" The two men and their sons prepared a plan for the park in 1889, and Downing Vaux, the son Calvert Vaux had named after his former partner, superintended construction. Appropriately, the highest points in the park overlooked the community of Downing's birth, the towers and chimneys of the home he created, and the scenery of the Hudson River Valley he cherished.[54]

Shortly after Downing's death, James H. Watts, a member of the Genesee Valley Horticultural Society, called upon friends to honor Downing's memory by establishing a garden on the banks of the Hudson. Watts suggested that the grounds be planted with the "native trees of our country, and the ornamental ones of others—such as numerous nurserymen, and all his admirers, would be glad to appropriate for the purpose."[55] Downing Park was a more fitting if belated memorial to the individual whom his contemporaries considered the most articulate proponent of public parks as part of the metropolitan landscape. It was not simply an ornamental garden but a public park, which, together with suburban communities designed according to Downing's prescriptions, would provide for the poor and the middle class the handsomely landscaped grounds otherwise affordable only to the wealthiest Americans.

9

Tastemaker to the Nation

We mourn for one . . . who came and was welcomed just when the inhabitants of this western world had laid down the woodman's axe, and were anxiously waiting for lessons which should enable them to advance from the stern and rigid principles of mere *utility*, to the higher and more graceful pursuits of science and of art—from the rude cabin of the settler, to the vine-sheltered cottage or more lofty dwelling of the artist and the scholar.

—Henry Flagg French

On the morning of July 28, 1852, Downing was preparing to depart for New York City on the first leg of an extended trip to Newport, Rhode Island, where he would superintend construction of Daniel Parish's villa. He may well have paused on the steps of the house to survey his property. The Hudson River and the mountains on the eastern shore dominated the landscape (fig. 97) and stood as constant reminders of childhood and important events in his life, as did the wisteria vine and balsam fir planted by his father (fig. 98). Surely Downing looked with pride on the house he had designed and built, and on the handsome lawn that extended from the entrance drive east to a gently curving path (fig. 99). Beds of flowers and perhaps some tropical plants, moved from the greenhouse to bathe in the bright summer sunlight, were interspersed amid the "exquisitely tinted" grass that Clarence Cook compared to velvet. Perhaps Downing thought of how he would remove part of the vineyard that stood east of the path in order to enlarge the lawn and ornamental grounds, an intent he had expressed to Cook. The marks of Downing's taste were evident in several objects that embellished the lawn—a copy of the Warwick Vase, a sundial, and a rustic seat.[1] The scene, with the two towers and the veranda flanking the entrance to the house as viewed across the lawn, was instantly recognizable to Downing's readers, an icon of the taste and refinement he preached in his various writings.

Downing must have taken pleasure in the familiar, but the house and grounds had changed significantly in recent years. One major alteration was

Figure 97 *(top)*. View from the lawn of Downing's property toward the Hudson River and the mountains. Figure 98 *(bottom)*. Wisteria vine on Downing's property. Both figures from "A Visit to the House and Garden of the Late A. J. Downing," *Horticulturist,* n.s. 3 (Jan. 1853). Courtesy of Shadek-Fackenthal Library, Franklin & Marshall College.

Figure 99. "Residence of the Late A. J. Downing, Newburgh on the Hudson," drawn by Frederick C. Withers and engraved by Alexander Anderson, from "A Visit to the House and Garden of the Late A. J. Downing," *Horticulturist,* n.s. 3 (Jan. 1853). Courtesy of Shadek-Fackenthal Library, Franklin & Marshall College.

the addition of the office wing to the house sometime after September 1850, when he returned from England with Calvert Vaux and began practicing architecture. On the interior the new wing connected to the library of the residence through doorways cut into existing bookcases. Outside, a curving footpath led from the separate entrance to the drive and the streets beyond. A handsome lawn occupied the space between the new addition and the path, which formerly had been occupied by nursery stock. The trees that had been adjacent to the entrance drive (visible on an 1841 plan of the grounds, fig. 5, above), which would have screened the view of the working landscape, were undoubtedly removed when the nursery was transformed into lawn.[2]

Other parts of the grounds had changed since 1846, when, in the midst of a financial crisis, he had sold the nursery business. Most of the stock had been removed by early 1847, at which time Downing's property had been reduced to four and a half acres. The transformation from working nursery to pleasure grounds (fig. 100) probably began in the spring of 1848, when Downing began construction of a rustic summer house he called the Hermitage, but

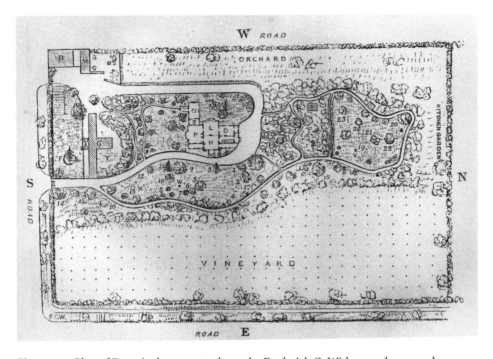

Figure 100. Plan of Downing's property, drawn by Frederick C. Withers and engraved by Alexander Anderson, from "A Visit to the House and Garden of the Late A. J. Downing," *Horticulturist*, n.s. 3 (Jan. 1853). Courtesy of Shadek-Fackenthal Library, Franklin & Marshall College. The letters on the plan indicate the following features: *L*, library; *H*, hall; *P*, parlor; *D*, dining room; *O*, office; *S*, study; *F*, fir tree; *W*, Warwick vase; *R*, Hermitage; *A*, arbor; *K*, rock work; *V*, Borghese vase; *G*, greenhouse; *Y*, yard to greenhouse; *M*, gardener's house; *B*, barn; *X*, sun dial. The numbers on the plan indicate the following trees or other features: *1*, Magnolia conspicua; *2*, Magnolia acuminata; *3*, deciduous cypress; *4*, Magnolia tripetala; *5*, European linden; *6*, Virgilia lutea; *7*, Salisburia adiantifolia; *8*, fern-leaved beech; *9*, English cork-barked elm; *10*, European larch; *11*, balsam fir; *12*, American white spruce; *13*, common weeping ash; *14*, white horse chestnut; *15*, yellow horse chestnut; *16*, cut-leaved birch; *17*, Dirca palustris (leather wood); *18*, Acer campester (common English maple); *19*, large bronze vase; *20*, weeping willow; *21*, weeping willow; *22*, Pinus excelsa; *23*, Abies Smithiana; *24*, Abies cephalonica.

undoubtedly accelerated a year later, following the resolution of his lawsuit with his father-in-law, John Peter DeWint. Although almost half of the property remained in cultivation, it was devoted to vineyards, an orchard, and the kitchen garden. These were located at the eastern, northern, and western areas of the property and were visually screened from the lawn and gardens. Where nursery stock once stood for sale, Downing grew fruits and vegetables for household consumption.[3]

Figure 101 *(top)* "The Hermitage" and Figure 102 *(bottom)* "View in the Grounds," with Borgese Vase in the foreground, the Hudson River in the middle distance, and the mountains in the distance. Both figures from "A Visit to the House and Garden of the Late A. J. Downing," *Horticulturist,* n.s. 3 (Jan. 1853). Courtesy of Shadek-Fackenthal Library, Franklin & Marshall College.

North of the house, another part of the nursery had been redesigned in a picturesque manner. Dense plantings separated this area from the more graceful landscape adjacent to the residence. Here were the "shadowy pathways" Fredrika Bremer found so enchanting. Just beyond the thick shrubbery was a rock garden Downing had added, which Cook termed "one of the pleasantest features" of the grounds. It was "a pretty sight in summer, with its fine beds of moss and thyme, and its stately ferns, under whose shadow the hare bells and columbines grew as in their native woods." From this enchanting scene the path led to the Hermitage (fig. 101), a rustic structure of logs and bark that was "a cool retreat from the burning heat of our midsummer noons." The north lawn, decorated with a bronze copy of the Borghese Vase (fig. 102), included weeping willows, spruces, and pines—the "arboretum planting" Downing mentioned to his friend J. J. Smith in February 1847—while a rustic arbor (fig. 103) provided seats with a pleasant view across the greensward toward the river.[4]

Figure 103. "Rustic Arbor," from "A Visit to the House and Garden of the Late A. J. Downing," *Horticulturist*, n.s. 3 (Jan. 1853). Courtesy of Shadek-Fackenthal Library, Franklin & Marshall College.

Hedges of English thorn and arbor vitae separated this private realm from the streets on three sides and the adjacent property to the north. Downing recommended such enclosures as more suitable than a wood, stone or iron fence, which, he wrote, appeared "hard and incongruous beside the pleasant verdure of a live hedge." A greenhouse, barn, and gardener's cottage stood near the southwest corner of the property, and all but the eastern part of the greenhouse, which abutted the entrance drive, was screened from view.[5]

Here was a landscape that, more than any other, bore the personal stamp of Downing's taste. It combined elements of the beautiful and the picturesque, the pillars of the "modern" style of landscape gardening he promoted, in a creative and harmonious way. Despite the relatively small extent of the garden, it demonstrated a point Downing had made in the *Treatise*, that the styles, though distinct, were "capable of intermingling and combining."[6] Although the garden was large compared to the house lots of working-class residents of Newburgh and required the labors of two gardeners, it was dwarfed by the estates of many of Downing's friends and clients. Nevertheless, Cook asserted, Downing's garden was indicative of "how much beauty and comfort lie at the doors of those whose means are not very extensive, but who are willing to bestow care, and able to bestow taste upon their places, however small."[7]

As Downing passed through the Gothic entrance gate of his property in 1852, he confronted a community that had similarly changed dramatically in the preceding decade. No pigs or poultry roamed the streets—an improvement he believed enhanced the appearance of the community and one he recommended to every village—so he might have left the gates ajar.[8] As Downing drove through town toward the steamboat landing, the return of prosperity was evident everywhere he looked. Newburgh had experienced a severe recession during the early 1840s, when completion of the Erie Railroad through the interior of western New York diverted trade from its docks. The number of new houses being built dropped dramatically, population declined as artisans moved elsewhere in search of jobs, and in 1843 a "general stagnation of business of all kinds" resulted in the need for a system to dispense public charity.[9] As historian Mark C. Carnes has demonstrated, Newburgh's economic redemption came through industrialization, the establishment of the Newburgh Steam Mills, which began operating in 1845. Organized by the merchant freighters to compensate for the loss of trade, which traditionally had powered the village's economy, the new five and a half story cotton mill, built of brick in a vaguely classical vernacular style, stood adjacent to the Hudson, just three blocks southeast of Downing's house. The mill employed approximately 300 workers, most of them unskilled women, and also attracted a number of iron foundries, which located nearby, whose employees were men.[10] The city's population soared as a result, reaching 11,415 in 1850, almost double the 6,000 residents enumerated in the census a decade earlier.[11]

Downing must have felt deeply ambivalent about the beginnings of industrialization in Newburgh. The factory system it introduced, predicated on cheap labor, portended a rigidly stratified society that was antithetical to the ideal of a cohesive republican community he had expressed in the late 1830s, when he helped found the Newburgh Library Association and the Newburgh Lyceum.[12] Moreover, the clustering of modest brick and frame houses throughout the village, on lots too small for anything but a postage stamp of a garden, marked a shift away from the independent rural existence he considered the optimal way of life for his countrymen. He nevertheless described the cotton mill as "one of the most useful of modern structures"[13] and surely realized that manufacturing was essential to the economic well-being of the town of his birth. Indeed, the wealth generated by industrialism, as well as the increases in property values that accompanied the return of prosperity, had swelled the ranks of prospective clients for his landscape gardening and architectural design services.

On his route to the steamboat landing Downing surely glanced at the "picturesque square house" of David Moore that stood less than a block from his entrance gate. Undoubtedly at some time he had thought of the ironies that dwelling represented. The lot on which the house stood had formerly been part of the family nursery, but Downing had been forced to sell it in 1847 to meet the demands of creditors. Though he may have been saddened by that turn of events, the handsome dwelling and grounds he and Vaux had designed were testament to a successful new stage in his career as tastemaker to the nation. Downing may also have passed Dr. William Culbert's elegant, mansard-roofed home, another building whose plans emanated from his new architectural office. The house was located on Grand Street, which Vaux described as the "handsomest thoroughfare" and the "principal promenade" of the village. The "beautiful elms and maples, with their wide-spreading and interarching branches," he wrote, "promise ere long to produce an effect that may equal the far-famed Hill-house Avenue in New Haven."[14]

Downing's architectural practice was flourishing: several handsome dwellings he and Vaux had designed had been erected in the suburbs of the village, while other commissions were taking him to various towns in the Hudson Valley, to eastern Massachusetts, Rhode Island, and Washington, D.C.[15] He must have anticipated that the successful completion of his design for the public grounds in the nation's capital would bring even greater opportunities in landscape gardening. And he envisioned launching a weekly entitled *Country Gentleman,* which would address "questions of manners, morals, social improvement, sanitary reform &c. &c." and have a "wider sphere of usefulness" than did the *Horticulturist*. Three years earlier Downing had been on the brink of financial ruin, but by the summer of 1852 his various professional endeavors were keeping him so busy that he could not find time for long-anticipated projects such as a new edition of *Fruits and Fruit Trees of America* and a book on shade trees.[16] The demand for his professional services amid a booming national economy portended a prosperous future.

Together with his wife, Caroline, several members of her family, and other friends, Downing boarded the steamboat *Henry Clay*, bound for New York, on the morning of July 28. One of the fastest of the Hudson River steamboats, the *Henry Clay* was "a fine specimen of our River craft," according to the *New York Times*, and "a favorite with the traveling public."[17] Fredrika Bremer, who with Downing had journeyed from New York City to Newburgh aboard the *Henry Clay* in October 1849, described it as "really a little floating palace, splendid and glittering with white and gold on the outside, splendid and elegant within: large saloons, magnificent furniture, where ladies and gentlemen reclined comfortably, talking or reading the newspapers."[18] On this day, however, the "utterly unprincipled" crew valued the boat's reputation for speed more that its renown for luxurious appointments: since departing Albany at 7:00 A.M the *Henry Clay* had been engaged in a furious race with a rival steamboat, the *Armenia*. In their effort to establish supremacy on the river the two boats had failed to stop at numerous towns north of Hudson, New York, leaving ticketed passengers standing on the wharves, and had collided in a narrow stretch of the river above Kingston, causing the *Armenia* "considerable damage" to its wheelhouse. The *Henry Clay* was the first to reach the dock at Newburgh, where the Downings boarded, and the race resumed. Gradually the *Henry Clay* outdistanced the *Armenia*, but at 2:45 P.M., within sight of Yonkers, fire broke out in its engine room. What followed was one of the worst steamboat disasters in the Hudson's long and storied history. At least seventy people died, including Stephen Allen, former mayor of New York City, Maria Hawthorne, sister of Nathaniel Hawthorne, and Downing.[19]

The *Henry Clay* was apparently without firefighting equipment, and the flames, abetted by a strong wind and perhaps by tar or resin added to the fuel, spread so quickly that there was no hope of extinguishing the blaze. Instead, the crew pointed the steamboat toward the east shore, where it ran aground about two and a half miles south of Yonkers.[20] For travelers at the stern of the boat, the fire blocked passage to the bow, leaving the deep water as their only escape from the flames. Several accounts, purportedly written by eyewitnesses, provided different explanations of Downing's actions as the disaster unfolded. A writer in the *Knickerbocker*, who lived near the scene of the tragedy and claimed to have seen the *Henry Clay* run aground, asserted that Downing, "after having rescued several from the deep, and returning again on his errand of mercy, was himself swallowed up by the waters, as if in revenge for the victims, of which he had deprived them."[21] Amelia A. Bailey, of Newburgh, who had been a passenger on the *Henry Clay*, attributed her surviving the fire to Downing's advice and informed the *Newburgh Gazette* that "the last she saw of Mr. Downing, he was struggling in the water with Mrs. [Matilda] Wadsworth clinging to his neck."[22] Still others believed that they floated to safety on chairs thrown from the deck by Downing.[23]

Downing's body was recovered from the Hudson at 11:00 A.M. the next day. At the coroner's inquest, Vaux identified the body, as well as the remains of Caroline Downing's mother, Caroline A. DeWint, and Mrs. Matilda Wadsworth, who were traveling with the Downings.[24] Vaux brought Downing's corpse to Newburgh, where Caroline Downing was being consoled by numerous mourners.[25] On the morning of the following day, July 30, the Reverend John Brown, minister of St. George's Episcopal Church, conducted the funeral service at the home Downing had built. His text was the Book of Job,

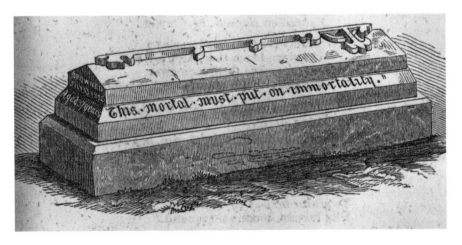

Figure 104. Gravestone of Andrew Jackson Downing, presumably designed by Calvert Vaux or Frederick C. Withers. Originally located in the Old Town Cemetery, Newburgh, N.Y., Downing's grave was moved to Cedar Hill Cemetery, Middle Hope, N.Y. (The date of Downing's death is incorrect on the woodcut but correct on the stone. He is described as "aged 37 years" because he was in his thirty-seventh year.) From "The Real Monument to Downing," *Horticulturist*, n.s. 7 (1857). Courtesy of Special Collections, Morris Library, University of Delaware.

chapter 24, verse 22: "He draweth also the mighty with his power: he riseth up, and no man is sure of life." Brown accompanied the funeral procession to the Old Town Cemetery, where Downing was interred.[26] The grave was marked by a tasteful stone, presumably designed by Vaux or Frederick C. Withers, in the Gothic style Downing favored, and bore the inscriptions "This mortal must put on immortality" and "Be not dismayed, I am thy God" (fig. 104).[27]

For Caroline Downing the ordeal was not finished: she then had to cross the river that had taken her husband, to Fishkill Landing, the home of her childhood, there to bury the mother after whom she was named. Nine weeks later her home, which carried $9,000 in mortgages, was sold at auction, as were dining room furnishings and other artifacts. Ironically, Downing had advised against building large houses because of the transience of wealth and the restless mobility of the American people, yet the property he had inherited from his parents, the house and gardens he had designed and loved, quickly passed to another family.[28]

Downing's death evoked outpourings of grief from across the nation. The *New York Tribune* expressed regret: "there is none whom the country could so little afford to lose, or whose services to the community could so little be replaced, as Mr. DOWNING," whom it described as a "man of genius and of high culture." Horticultural societies across the United States adopted resolutions lamenting the loss of one of their leaders, whom they invariably described as an "eminent and earnest advocate" of their interests. The Pittsburgh Horticultural Society termed Downing's death "a National loss to the cause of Horticulture," while members of the Pennsylvania Horticultural Society experienced "bereavement and affliction." Downing, the resolution of the latter society explained, was "endowed by nature with a vigorous intellect, which was elevated by liberal and practical cultivation, and directed by an expanded philanthropy and a glowing love of nature." The Genesee Valley Horticultural Society termed the loss of Downing "one of the greatest that could in this day befall the American people"; members of its kindred society in Columbus, Ohio, mourned the passing of "a brother, whose writings and teachings have been our pleasure and our guide, and whose memory we will cherish as one worthy our love and esteem." The *Ohio Cultivator* could identify "no man living whose loss would be a greater calamity at the present time, than is the death of Mr. Downing." Perhaps it was the resolution of the Massachusetts Horticultural Society that best captured Downing's singular role in American culture during his lifetime:

> Eminent alike as a Horticulturist, a Landscape Gardener, and an Architect, Mr. DOWNING has, in each character, made his mark upon the age.

Where the grateful gardener plucks the rich fruit from the laden bough, there is his name known. Where taste has turned the unsightly pasture into a lovely lawn, and adorned it with gems of the garden and the green wood, there are his labors felt.

The humble cot he has made a picture of beauty, and the elegant mansion, reared by his genius, fills and satisfies the most nicely critical eye.[29]

In September 1852, Marshall P. Wilder, Downing's longtime friend, delivered a eulogy at the meeting of the American Pomological Society, the organization Downing had helped to establish. Evidences of Downing's legacy, Wilder observed, "appear in the forests which he has preserved from the merciless axe" as well as in the improvements in horticultural, landscape, and architectural taste he championed. Few men had "left a mark so deep and broad on the generation in which they lived," Wilder concluded, for the fruits of Downing's labors, visible across the nation in tasteful homes and their gardens, were "his best eulogy—the most enduring monuments of his worth."[30]

Many of Downing's friends in the American Pomological Society were eager to honor his manifest contributions to their cause and to perpetuate his memory. Following Wilder's remarks, the society issued a circular soliciting donations toward the erection of a monument to honor Downing. Using contributions totaling $1676.50, the society in 1856 erected a marble monument, designed by Calvert Vaux and sculpted by Robert E. Launitz, on the grounds of the Smithsonian Institution in Washington, D.C. The monument (fig. 105), nine feet four inches tall, consisted of a classical vase, carved with acanthus leaves, "rich arabesque," and other appropriate allusions to the natural world Downing celebrated. Each of the four sides of the plinth supporting the vase bore inscriptions. The north front identified the vase as a monument to Downing and noted: "His life was devoted to the improvement of the national taste in rural art, an office for which his genius, and the natural beauty amidst which he lived, had fully endowed him. His success was as great as his genius, and for the death of few public men was public grief ever more sincere." On the south face was carved the quotation from "The New-York Park" in which Downing called for the creation of public parks and other institutions of popular refinement, while the east and west panels contained poems expressing the grief of his friends. The first four lines of the verse on the west front captured one anonymous poet's assessment of Downing's contributions to the transformation of the American landscape:

I climb the hills from end to end,
Of all the landscape underneath
I find no place that does not breathe
Some gracious memory of my friend.

Figure 105. Monument erected in Washington, D.C., to the memory of Andrew Jackson Downing by the American Pomological Society; designed by Calvert Vaux and sculpted by Robert Launitz, 1856. From "The Downing Monument," *Horticulturist*, n.s. 6 (Nov. 1856). Courtesy of Special Collections, Morris Library, University of Delaware.

The *Horticulturist,* eager to keep alive the reformist impulse of its founding editor, pointed to the didactic intent of the Downing memorial: "so long as his lessons are remembered, so long shall our country be far removed from that semi-barbarism which threatened the inland dweller when DOWNING'S spirit roused itself, and threw off the apathy to the love of the beautiful, which was fast overtaking us."[31]

∽ Downing was thirty-six when he died, and thus his work as an apostle of taste was left incomplete. To be sure, the progression from wilderness to civilization was rapidly transforming the American landscape: in 1835, the year in which Downing published the first of his reveries in the Hudson Highlands, Thomas Cole had lamented, "[The] ravages of the axe are daily increasing—the most noble scenes are made desolate, and oftentimes with a wantonness and barbarism scarcely credible in a civilized nation."[32] Downing's writings, which urged readers to set aside the axe and begin planting trees, stand with the concerns of Cole, the poet George P. Morris, and novelist James Fenimore Cooper among the earliest articulations of a conservationist ethos in nineteenth-century America.[33] But this was still largely an eastern and metropolitan phenomenon. As the Unitarian minister Henry W. Bellows pointed out in 1861, backwoods farmers hated trees, whereas residents of New York City were planting them by the thousands to recreate some semblance of the primeval landscape that urban development had destroyed.[34] Downing's vision of a reformed American landscape would not be realized during his life.

Downing's writings also constituted a path from utilitarianism toward a greater appreciation of the beautiful in the nation's homes and gardens. This was important both aesthetically and as an antidote to what Luther Tucker termed the "restless roving tendency of the times."[35] Downing was a prophet, who taught Americans the "eternal *principles* of taste" and "enabled our judgments to appreciate its true manifestations," asserted the New Hampshire attorney, farmer, and educator Henry F. French.[36] The *New York Evening Post* concurred, declaring that through his writings Downing had "worked a change in our style of building, and created a general improvement in taste."[37] The numerous designs he had published in his books and in the pages of the *Horticulturist* also pointed the way toward the development of a distinctive American architecture. But, as French noted with sorrow, Downing did not live long enough to stake the path to what he hoped would be its ultimate destination.

Downing's friends nevertheless confidently believed Marshall P. Wilder's words: "HIS MEMORY SHALL LIVE FOREVER."[38] Thus, it was both ironic and seemingly inevitable that in subsequent years his influence and his most important designs fell victim to changes in taste. In the aftermath of the Civil War the simplicity Downing had preached gave way to the bombastic eclecticism of High Victorian architecture and then, at the turn of the century, to Beaux-Arts classicism. Charles A. Platt, one of the most influential proponents of the Italian garden, helped popularize the very formal, geometric style Downing had attempted to banish in earlier years: the beautiful and picturesque elements of the naturalistic garden were replaced by axial formality, ornamental sculpture, and architectonic forms. Platt also argued, without apparent awareness of Downing's efforts, for the adaptation of European forms as the basis for an American architectural expression, though his chaste classical designs expressed a far different aesthetic than Downing's and testified, in a way, to the failure of the evolutionary process that, Downing expected, would result in a distinctive American architecture.[39]

Shortly after Downing's death several friends expressed hope that his house, his first architectural design, could be purchased and kept as a perpetual monument to him.[40] Only nine weeks after the burning of the *Henry Clay*, however, the property was sold and its new owner, C. C. Alger, immediately commissioned A. J. Davis to undertake significant alterations. Davis transformed the structure that Downing's readers considered an extension of the man, introducing asymmetrical castellated Gothic towers in place of simple Tudor details, extending the veranda around the south side of the building, adding an octagonal room for plants off the library and a bay window in the dining room, and remodeling Downing's office and study into a gallery of science and art. He also designed a stone coach house and stables. The property passed from Alger to his daughter in 1861, and in subsequent years to other owners, who sold several lots facing Grand Street for residential development. In 1918, following the death of the final owner, the remainder of Downing's domestic landscape devolved to the holder of the mortgage, the Columbus Trust Company. The bank in turn sold the property to the Miller-Hurley Realty Company, which demolished Downing's dwelling. The Historical Society of Newburgh Bay and the Highlands obtained one ornamental chimney, the only element of the house known to have survived, and the land on which the house had stood was carved into building lots. All other traces of Downing's house and its elegant grounds are gone.[41]

Similar fates befell most of the buildings Downing designed. Daniel Parish's marine villa in Newport, for example, burned in 1855. Although it was rebuilt the following year,[42] after Parish's death in 1880 the property was acquired by William B. Astor, who renamed the dwelling Beechwood and undertook significant alterations, particularly to the ocean façade.[43] The Moore house, in Newburgh, was greatly enlarged, as was Dr. Culbert's home. In each case the additions replicated important features of Downing's design but significantly altered the scale. More recently, the elegant, mansard-roofed house on Grand Street burned; it stands in ruin, a haunting reminder of Downing's optimistic hopes for American society. In nearby Poughkeepsie, Matthew Vassar's cottage and ancillary structures fell into disrepair: the carriage house and stables burned in 1969. Seven years later, the state removed most of the entrance façade of the cottage for preservation. Today none of the buildings erected during the period of Downing's involvement with Springside remains standing. Springside's landscape too suffered neglect over the years, and parcels were sold for development. But the threat of a 190-unit condominium development on the remainder of the site—Downing's best documented residential landscape design—inspired a group of dedicated preservationists to defend the historic importance of what was left of Vassar's ornamental grounds.[44]

Downing's plan for the public grounds in Washington, D.C., his only important public landscape design, was never completed as he intended and suffered intrusions such as railroad tracks and a train station during the last decades of the nineteenth century. As the centennial of the establishment of the capital city neared, Glenn Brown, secretary of the American Institute of Architects, called for major improvements to Washington, D.C. The Senate Park Commission, under the aegis of Senator James McMillan of Michigan and commission secretary Charles Moore, employed Daniel H. Burnham, Frederick Law Olmsted, Jr., and Charles Follen McKim, later joined by sculptor Augustus Saint-Gaudens, to prepare a design for the public grounds. These men proposed a European-inspired reinterpretation of L'Enfant's "grand avenue," a formal Beaux-Arts axis where, fifty years earlier, Downing had planted trees and laid out gently curving walks and drives. Over decades, new construction swept away the remnants of Downing's design as a new national imagery took shape on the public grounds.[45]

But even as the buildings and grounds Downing had designed were altered or neglected, many of the architectural forms he had championed became an indelible part of the American landscape. This seeming irony is testament to the importance of Downing's role as an apostle of taste, which was far greater than the sum of the buildings and grounds he designed. Because he so successfully encapsulated the aspirations of an emerging middle class, the appeal of Downing's ideas persisted and the sale of his books continued long after his death. Certainly the Surgeon's Quarters at Fort Dalles, Oregon (fig. 106), erected in 1856 and modeled closely after Design III of *The Archi-*

tecture of Country Houses, is remarkable only for its distant location. It was surrounded by several structures, built at the behest of Capt. Thomas Jordan, that similarly incorporated elements of designs from Downing's last book, though only the Surgeon's Quarters has survived from that outpost of Downing's taste in the Pacific Northwest. According to historian William H. Pierson, Jr., the Fort Dalles building "can be taken as typical of the scores of houses built in this country during the mid-nineteenth century which were directly inspired by specific illustrations in Downing's books."[46]

Figure 106. Surgeon's Quarters, Fort Dalles, Oregon, erected in 1856, following Design III of Downing's *Architecture of Country Houses* (fig. 52, above). Courtesy of Alan Gowans Collection, National Gallery of Art Slide Library, Washington, D.C.

Captain Jordan had relied upon a man named Louis Scholl to transform Downing's published designs into buildings. Similarly, Thomas H. Hyatt employed an architect to sketch his ideal home, which he named Elm-Wood Cottage (see fig. 44, above) and which clearly and admittedly owed much to Downing. Hyatt even claimed to have improved upon the plans he had studied, a demonstration of the validity of the "principle of progress" Downing considered one of the hallmarks of American domestic architecture.[47] But reliance on an architect was undoubtedly unusual. More representative of the way Downing's influence spread was the experience of the young couple Fredrika Bremer visited in Oxbridge, Massachusetts, who had pored over Downing's books, carefully studying the ideas he presented, and who then engaged a contractor to erect their dwelling. The young couple also turned to Downing's advice in the design of their garden.[48]

The reach of Downing's influence was not limited to the audience that read his books or the *Horticulturist*. The publication of his designs was followed by a process of imitation and modification, an American analogue to the adaptation of English forms he had practiced. Agricultural journals offered readers simplified versions of Downing's plans; authors of the next generation of pattern books, who aspired to the cultural authority Downing had acquired, incorporated many of his ideas in their publications; and individuals who built houses following those plans soon saw elements of their homes reflected in the appearance of more recently constructed dwellings, just as he had predicted. Ultimately, Downing's designs became part of the work of builders, who transformed them into a vernacular language of their own. Although later generations of builders and residents have long since forgotten Downing's name and his crusade to improve American domestic architecture, thousands of cottages and farmhouses, still standing amid handsome trees and gardens, display the central gable and veranda, ornamental brackets, board-and-batten construction, or other elements of residential design he popularized. Downing's greatest monument, H. F. French had predicted, would be found in "cultivated groves and gardens," in the improved architecture evident "in every valley, in every town and every village."[49] These anonymous homes, farm buildings, and landscapes testify to Downing's effort to democratize culture and are, fittingly, the most enduring legacy of this apostle of taste.

Appendix

Writings of Andrew Jackson Downing

Books (editions published during Downing's lifetime)

A Treatise on the Theory and Practice of Landscape Gardening, Adapted to North America; with a view to the improvement of country residences. Comprising historical notices and general principles of the art, directions for laying out grounds and arranging plantations, the description and cultivation of hardy trees, decorative accompaniments to the house and grounds, the formation of pieces of artificial water, flower gardens, etc. with remarks on rural architecture . . . (New York: Wiley and Putnam, 1841; 2d ed., enlarged, revised and newly illustrated, 1844; 4th ed., enlarged, revised, and newly illustrated, 1849, reissued 1850, 1852). No copies of a third edition are known to exist, so it is likely that none was issued.

Cottage Residences; or, A series of designs for rural cottages and cottage villas, and their gardens and grounds. Adapted to North America . . . (New York: Wiley and Putnam, 1842; 2d ed., 1844; 3d ed., 1847; 4th ed., revised and improved, 1852).

The Fruits and Fruit Trees of America; or, The culture, propagation, and management, in the garden and orchard, of fruit trees generally; with descriptions of all the finest varieties of fruit, native and foreign, cultivated in this country (New York: Wiley and Putnam, 1845, 1846, 1847, 1848, 1849, 1850, 1851, 1852; edition with color plates, 1847).

The Architecture of Country Houses; including designs for cottages, farm houses, and villas, with remarks on interiors, furniture, and the best modes of warming and ventilating. With three hundred and twenty illustrations (New York: D. Appleton, 1850, reissued 1850, 1852).

Collected Essays

Rural Essays. By A. J. Downing. Edited, With a Memoir of the Author, by George William Curtis; and a Letter to his Friends, by Frederika Bremer (New York: George P. Putnam, 1853).

Editions

John Lindley, *The Theory of Horticulture: Or, An attempt to explain the principal operations of gardening upon physiological principles. 1st American edition, with notes, etc., by A. J. Downing and A. Gray* (New York: Wiley and Putnam, 1841).

Jane Webb Loudon, *Gardening for Ladies; and Companion to the Flower Garden, by Mrs. Loudon. First American, from the third London edition. Edited by A. J. Downing* (New York: Wiley and Putnam, 1843, 1846).

George Wightwick, *Hints to Young Architects, Calculated to Facilitate their Practical Operations, by George Wightwick, . . With additional notes, and hints to persons about building in the country, by A. J. Downing* (New York: Wiley and Putnam, 1847).

Journal

Editor, *The Horticulturist, and Journal of Rural Art and Rural Taste*, Albany, N.Y., vols. 1–6 (July 1846–July 1852).

Articles
(excluding his writings published in the *Horticulturist*)

"Rural Embellishments," *New-York Farmer and Horticultural Repository* 5 (Sept. 1832): 329–30 (signed "X. Y. Z. *Newburgh*, Sept. 12, 1832").

"On the employment of Ornamental Trees and Shrubs in North America; more particularly the indigenous Species and Varieties, as regards their effect in the formation of Parks and Pleasure Grounds, and extensive Plantations for Landscape Beauty," *New England Farmer* 12 (1834): 225–26, reprinted in *Annales de l'Institut Horticole de Fromont* 6 (1834): 74–80, and in *American Gardener's Magazine* 1 (Dec. 1835): 445–52.

"Notes on Transplanting," *New-York Farmer and American Gardener's Magazine* 7 (Mar. 1834): 67.

"Vineyards in the United States," *New-York Farmer and American Gardener's Magazine* 7 (May 1834): 131–33.

"Horticultural Notes," *Horticultural Register and Gardener's Magazine* 1 (Feb. 1835): 65–69.

"American Highland Scenery. Beacon Hill," *New-York Mirror* 12 (Mar. 14, 1835): 293–94.

"On Hedges," *Horticultural Register* 1 (Apr. 1835): 142–44, reprinted in *New-York Farmer and American Gardener's Magazine* 7 (July 1835): 218–19.

"Horticultural and Scientific Notices," *Horticultural Register* 1 (June 1835): 225–27.

"An Account of some new Varieties of Fruit; communicated by Messrs. C. & A. J. Downing," *American Gardener's Magazine* 1 (Oct. 1835): 364–67.

"Introduction of the Filbert," "Fine specimen of the Caladium escluenium," "Coloring properties of the Venetian Sumach or Purple Fringe Tree," and "The splendid collection of Green and Hot-house plants," *American Gardener's Magazine* 1 (Nov. 1835): 433–34.

"The Dans Kamer. A Reverie in the Highlands," *New-York Mirror* 13 (Oct. 10, 1835): 117–18, reprinted in the *Newburgh Telegraph,* Nov. 5, 1835.

"The To Kalon Grape" and "The Papaw or Custard apple," *American Gardener's Magazine* 1 (Dec. 1835): 459.

"Useful qualities of the Chinese Ailanthus" (by Soulange Bodin, translated by A. J. Downing from *Annales des Fromont*) and "Note on the above,—the Ailanthus glandulosa, or Celestial Tree," *American Gardener's Magazine* 2 (Jan. 1836): 35.

"Singular anomaly in the Cherry Tree," *American Gardener's Magazine* 2 (Jan. 1836): 36–37 (co-authored with Charles Downing).

"Some Remarks on Temperature Considered in Relation to Vegetation and the Naturalization of Plants. Communicated to the Mass. Hort. Society by Mr. A. J. Downing, of Newburgh, N. Y.," *Horticultural Register* 2 (Feb. 1836): 68–72, and 2 (Mar. 1836): 99–105.

"Descriptive Notice of J. W. Knevels Esq.'s Collection of Exotic Plants at Newburgh, N. Y.," *American Gardener's Magazine* 2 (Mar. 1836): 96–102.

"The Bread-root of the western Indians," "Monograph of the North American Cyperaceae," "Transplanting Evergreen Trees," and "Flowering of Cycas revoluta," *American Gardener's Magazine* 2 (Apr. 1836): 155–56.

"Observations on the Culture of the Plum, with some Remarks upon the Insects infesting that Tree," *American Gardener's Magazine* 2 (May 1836): 161–65 (co-authored with Charles Downing).

"The New Zealand Flax, Phormium tenax," "Utility of the Prickly Pear (Cactus opuntia)" (extracted from Hooker's *Botanical Magazine*), and "Enkianthus quinqueflora," from *British Cyclopaedia, American Gardener's Magazine* 2 (May 1836): 192–94.

"Descriptive Notice of Mr. Hogg's new Method of Heating by Hot Water," *American Gardener's Magazine* 2 (July 1836): 248–50.

"Gama grass" and "The Crape Myrtle nearly hardy," *American Gardener's Magazine* 2 (July 1836): 273.

"Remarks on the Fitness of the different Styles of Architecture for the Construction of Country Residences, and on the Employment of Vases in Garden Scenery," *American Gardener's Magazine* 2 (Aug. 1836): 281–86.

"Rediscovery of the Scolopendrium" and "Poinsettia pulcherrima," *American Gardener's Magazine* 2 (Oct. 1836): 389–90.

"Programme of a Prize of one thousand Francs, offered by the Royal Horticultural Society of Paris, with the view of obtaining, by means of a repetition of the Experiments of Van Mons, and also by any other Method pursued with Seeds, the Improvement of the varieties of Apples and Pears. Translated by A. J. Downing," *American Gardener's Magazine* 2 (Dec. 1836): 446–49.

"Notices on the State and Progress of Horticulture in the United States," *Magazine of Horticulture* 3 (Jan. 1837): 1–10.

"Calls at Gardens and Nurseries," *Magazine of Horticulture* 3 (Jan. 1837): 26–32.

"New Method of sowing Grain, practised in the south of Europe," *Magazine of Horticulture* 3 (Jan. 1837): 33 (extracted from the *Reportons di Agricultura*, 1835).

"Floral Commerce of Paris," *Magazine of Horticulture* 3 (Jan. 1837): 34.

"The Mabille Pear," *Magazine of Horticulture* 3 (Feb. 1837): 53 (co-authored with Charles Downing).

"The Chinese Mulberry, morus multicaulis" and "Hardiness of young Fruit Trees in elevated situations," *Magazine of Horticulture* 3 (Feb. 1837): 74–75.

"Remarks on the Duration of the Improved varieties of New York Fruit Trees," *Magazine of Horticulture* 3 (Mar. 1837): 91–94.

"Remarks on the Natural Order Cycadaceae, with a description of the Ovula and Seeds of Cycas revoluta," *Silliman's Journal* (Apr. and May, 1837), reprinted in *Magazine of Horticulture* 3 (Aug. 1837): 308–11.

"Notes on the Cultivation of Vineyards in the United States," *Magazine of Horticulture* 3 (June 1837): 214–16.

"Origin of the Hermitage Vineyards," *Magazine of Horticulture* 3 (June 1837): 236–37.

"Improving strong Clay soils," *Magazine of Horticulture* 3 (July 1837): 273–74.

"Protection against Hail Storms. Notice and Description of the Paragrele, or Hail Rod," *Magazine of Horticulture* 3 (Aug. 1837): 281–83.

"Ringing Fruit Trees; with a notice of some Results following its application to the Pear Tree, discovered by M. Van Mons, of Brussels," *Magazine of Horticulture* 3 (Oct. 1837): 361–63.

"Hippophae rhamnoides fertilized by the Shepherdia" and "The yellow Locust," *Magazine of Horticulture* 3 (Oct. 1837): 389–90.

"Great collection of Dried Plants for sale" and "Death of Mr. Croom," *Magazine of Horticulture* 4 (Jan. 1838): 26–27.

"On the Cultivation of Hedges in the United States," *Magazine of Horticulture* 4 (Feb. 1838): 41–44.

"Pomological Notices; or Notices respecting new and superior varieties of Fruits, worthy of general cultivation. Notices of some new Plums, Pears, Strawberries, and other Fruits," *Magazine of Horticulture* 4 (Feb. 1838): 44–47 (co-authored with Charles Downing).

"Introduction of tropical plants," *Magazine of Horticulture* 4 (Feb. 1838): 75.

"Observations on the Culture of the Strawberry," *Magazine of Horticulture* 4 (May 1838): 161–64.

"Notice of the grafting of Evergreen Trees, as practised in Europe," *Magazine of Horticulture* 4 (June 1838): 201–3.

"Great Horticultural Society of the Valley of the Hudson," *Magazine of Horticulture* 4 (June 1838): 233–35.

"Horticultural Association of the Valley of the Hudson," *Magazine of Horticulture* 4 (Dec. 1838): 462–65.

"Remarks on preserving tender Shrubs and Plants during the winter, with some hints on Acclimation of Trees," *Magazine of Horticulture* 5 (Feb. 1839): 41–43.

"Notes on a novel method of preventing Mildew in the open air culture of Foreign Grapes," *Magazine of Horticulture* 5 (Apr. 1839): 121–23.

"The Horticultural Association of the Valley of the Hudson," *Magazine of Horticulture* 5 (June 1839): 231–32; also published as "Horticultural Exhibition," *Cultivator* 6 (June 1839): 80.

"Horticultural Association of the Valley of the Hudson," *Magazine of Horticulture* 5 (Aug. 1839): 310–13; also published as "Horticultural Report. Report of the second exhibition of the Horticultural Association of the Valley of the Hudson," *Cultivator* 6 (Aug. 1839): 97–98.

"Foreign Notices. North America," *Gardener's Magazine* (London) 15 (Jan. 1839): 38–39.

"Pomological Notices; or, Notices respecting new and superior varieties of Fruits, worthy of general cultivation. Some account of several new varieties of Pears, which have fruited in the Botanic Garden and Nurseries of A. J. Downing, Newburgh, N. Y.," *Magazine of Horticulture* 6 (June 1840): 206–9.

"Ribes sanguineum" and "Buist's 'American Flower Garden Directory,'" *Magazine of Horticulture* 6 (June 1840): 229.

"Notes on the Progress of Gardening in the United States," *Gardener's Magazine* (London) 16 (Dec. 1840): 642–45.

"Remarks on the cultivation of the Filbert," *Magazine of Horticulture* 7 (Feb. 1841): 57–59.

"Additional Notes on the Progress of Gardening in the United States," *Gardener's Magazine* (London) 17 (Mar. 1841): 146–47.

"Description of a new variety of Plum, called the Columbia; with Some Remarks on the Culture of the Plum, the destruction of the Curculio, &c.," *Magazine of Horticulture* 8 (Mar. 1842): 90–93.

"Notes on Belts of Trees in Ornamental Plantations," *Magazine of Horticulture* 8 (June 1842): 220–23.

"Figures and Descriptions of Five Varieties of Cherry, deserving a place in every Garden," *Cultivator* 10 (Sept. 1843): 150.

"Figures and Descriptions of Six varieties of Plum, worthy of general cultivation," *Cultivator* 10 (Oct. 1843): 167.

"Figure and description of Smith's Orleans Plum, with remarks on the confusion hitherto existing with regard to this variety," *Magazine of Horticulture* 9 (Nov. 1843): 410–13.

"Figures and Descriptions of Five choice varieties of Pears," *Cultivator,* n.s. 1 (Jan. 1844): 36–37.

"Figure and Description of the Jefferson Plum," *Magazine of Horticulture* 11 (Jan. 1845): 23–25.

"Remarks on re-establishing grafted Fruit Trees on their own Roots, especially applicable to Apples and Pears. Translated from the *Revue Horticole,* Tom. V., No. 30. By A. J. Downing," *Magazine of Horticulture* 11 (Apr. 1845): 138–40.

"Hints on the Construction of Farm-Houses," in New York State Agricultural Society, *Transactions* 5 (1846): 234–38, reprinted in *Cultivator,* n.s. 3 (June 1846): 184–85.

"Some Remarks on the Superiority of Native Varieties of Fruit" (1847), in Massachusetts Horticultural Society, *Transactions* 1 (1847-51): 29–32.

A. J. Downing et al., "Report of the Commissioners Appointed to Mature and Report a Plan for an Agricultural College and Experimental Farm," New York State Assembly, document number 30, Jan. 2, 1850.

"Address," Jan. 16, 1851, in New York State Agricultural Society, *Transactions* 10 (1850): 119–27.

Notes

In references to works of Andrew Jackson Downing, his name is abbreviated AJD.

Introduction

1. AJD, "On the Improvement of Country Villages," *Horticulturist* 3 (June 1849): 545–49.

2. AJD, quoted in "The Horticultural Festival at Faneuil Hall," *Horticulturist* 3 (Nov. 1848): 235.

3. AJD, *The Architecture of Country Houses* (New York, 1850), p. 394.

4. "Editor's Table," *Horticulturist*, n.s. 3 (Jan. 1853): 55.

5. L. Tucker, "The Publisher's Farewell," ibid. 7 (Dec. 1852): 538.

6. *Congressional Globe*, Aug. 26, 1852, p. 2375.

7. AJD, *Architecture of Country Houses*, pp. xixxx, 1.

8. N. H., "The Architecture of Country Houses," *Home Journal*, reprinted in *Horticulturist* 5 (Sept. 1850): 139–40.

9. H. F. French's remarks, published in *Home Journal*, reprinted in "Tributes to the Memory of Mr. Downing," *Horticulturist* 7 (Oct. 1852): 471.

10. AJD, "Introductory," *Horticulturist* 1 (July 1846): 10.

11. N. Harris, *Humbug: The Art of P. T. Barnum* (1973; Chicago, 1981), pp. 74, 4. See also idem, *The Artist in American Society: The Formative Years, 1790–1860* (Cambridge, Mass., 1966) and John Higham, *From Boundlessness to Consolidation: The Transformation of American Culture, 1848–1860* (Ann Arbor, 1969).

12. Geo. Jaques, "The Late A. J. Downing and his Writings," *Journal of Agriculture* 5 (Oct. 1852): 106–7. See also diary of George Jaques, Sept. 2, 1852, Oct. 16, 1852, Joseph Downs Manuscript and Microfilm Collection, Winterthur Museum, Gardens, and Library, Winterthur, Del.

13. Lillian B. Miller, *Patrons and Patriotism: The Encouragement of the Fine Arts in the United States, 1790–1860* (Chicago, 1966), pp. 160–72.

14. Russell Lynes, *The Tastemakers* (New York, 1955), p. 21.

15. L. Miller, *Patrons and Patriotism*, pp. 168–71.

16. N. P. Willis "Sale of Mr. Downing's Residence," *Home Journal*, reprinted in *Horticulturist* 7 (Nov. 1852): 527.

17. AJD, "The New-York Park," *Horticulturist* 6 (Aug. 1851): 348–49.

18. AJD, "Introductory," ibid., 1 (July 1846): 9.

19. AJD, quoted in "Horticultural Festival," p. 235; AJD, "A Reform Needed," *Horticulturist* 6 (Oct. 1851): 441–43.

20. Fredrika Bremer, *The Homes of the New World: Impressions of America*, trans. Mary Howitt, 2 vols. (New York, 1854), 2:632.

21. Jean Baker, "From Belief into Culture: Republicanism in the Antebellum North," *American Quarterly* 37 (fall 1985): 538. See also Daniel T. Rodgers, "Republicanism: The Career of a Concept," *Journal of American History* 79 (June 1992): 11–38.

22. AJD, "Reviews," *Horticulturist* 6 (Dec. 1851): 567–70.

23. AJD, *Architecture of Country Houses*, p. xix; AJD, "The New-York Park," pp. 348–49.

24. Kenneth T. Jackson, *Crabgrass Frontier: The Suburbanization of the United States* (New York, 1985), p. 63.

25. Higham, *From Boundlessness to Consolidation*, p. 26.

26. C. Vaux, *Villas and Cottages. A Series of Designs Prepared for Execution in the United States* (New York, 1857), p. 35.

27. D. W. Howe, "Victorian Culture in America," in Howe, ed., *Victorian America* (Philadelphia, 1976), p. 3.

Chapter 1 Downing's Newburgh and the Spirit of Place

Epigraph: Clarence C. Cook, "The Late A. J. Downing," *New York Quarterly* 1 (Oct. 1852): 378.

1. Because of an error by one of Downing's first biographers, the date of Downing's birth is often incorrectly cited as October 30, 1815. See *Rural Essays. By A. J. Downing. Edited, With a Memoir of the Author, by George William Curtis; and a Letter to His Friends, by Fredrika Bremer* (1853; reprint ed., with a new introduction by George B. Tatum, New York, 1974), p. IX.

2. Diedrich Knickerbocker, *A History of New York, From the Beginning of the World to the End of the Dutch Dynasty* . . . (1819; Philadelphia, 1871), p. 392.

3. The 1822 census tabulations are presented in Samuel W. Eager, *An Outline History of Orange County* . . . (Newburgh, N.Y., 1846–47), p. 228; Henry Bradshaw Fearon, *Sketches of America: A Narrative of a Journey of Five Thousand Miles Through the Eastern and Western States of America*, 2d ed. (London, 1818), p. 83.

4. N. H., "The Architecture of Country Houses," *Home Journal*, reprinted in *Horticulturist* 5 (Sept. 1850): 139–41; Cook, "The Late A. J. Downing," p. 371. Clarence Cook, who apparently had studied in Downing's office, was just beginning a long and distinguished career as a critic. In this essay he praised the "Western log hut, which even in its rudest shape has enough of beauty to redeem it from the charge of total vulgarity," as a "natural growth" and the "true type of our civilization" (ibid., p. 372). Perhaps because he was unaware of their grandeur, perhaps because he did not appreciate the style of architecture they embodied, Cook dismissed the buildings of the colonial and early national periods. He amplified his criticism of contemporary

buildings in New York City in a series of unsigned essays, "New-York Daguerreo-typed," which were published in *Putnam's Monthly* beginning in February 1853. He is best remembered as the author of *A Description of the Central Park* (1869) and *The House Beautiful* (1878).

5. AJD, "The Influence of Horticulture," *Horticulturist* 2 (July 1847): 9–10. Commentators who likewise decried the mobility of Americans in the antebellum years included James Fenimore Cooper and Alexis de Tocqueville. See Cooper's *Home As Found,* in *The Complete Works of J. Fenimore Cooper,* Leatherstocking Edition, 32 vols. (New York, 1893?), 14:326, 424, and Tocqueville, *Democracy in America,* ed. Phillips Bradley, 2 vols. (1835–40; New York, 1945), 2:144–45.

6. See, for example, Mark C. Carnes, "The Rise and Fall of a Mercantile Town: Family, Land, and Capital in Newburgh, New York, 1790–1844," *Hudson Valley Regional Review* 2 (Sept. 1985): 20–21; and, for local histories, Eager, *Outline History of Orange County,* pp. 175–77; E. M. Ruttenber, *History of the County of Orange: With a History of the Town and City of Newburgh* (Newburgh, N.Y., 1875); and John J. Nutt, *Newburgh: Her Institutions, Industries and Leading Citizens* (Newburgh, N.Y., 1891).

7. Will of Samuel Downing, May 10, 1822, Orange County Surrogate Court, Goshen, N.Y., liber G, pp. 74–76; Eunice Downing and Charles Downing, deed to James C. Clark, April 3, 1823, Recorder of Deeds Office, Orange County Government Center, Goshen, N.Y., liber BB, pp. 22–24.

8. The extent of these properties has been determined through the following deeds, all located in the Recorder of Deeds Office, Orange County Government Center, Goshen, N.Y.: Frederick J. Betts and George Cornwall, assignees for AJD, and Charles Downing, deed of sale to Nathan Reeve, May 5, 1847, liber 92, pp. 206–8; Charles Downing and AJD, deed of transfer to Charles Downing, Mar. 26, 1839, liber 66, pp. 135–38; Charles Downing and AJD, deed of transfer to AJD, Mar. 26, 1839, liber 66, pp. 138–41; George W. Downing, deed of sale to Samuel W. Eager, Oct. 7, 1841, liber 72, pp. 345–46. The advertisement of trees is cited in Eager, *Outline History of Orange County,* p. 175.

9. The other children of Samuel and Eunice Downing were Emily (1801–64), Charles (1802–85), George Washington (1804–46), and Fanny (b. 1808), who died in infancy. See George B. Tatum, "Introduction: The Downing Decade," in *Prophet With Honor: The Career of Andrew Jackson Downing, 1815–1852,* ed. George B. Tatum and Elisabeth Blair MacDougall (Washington, D.C., 1989), p. 3n.

10. See George William Curtis, "Memoir," in *Rural Essays,* pp. xi–xvi, and Charles Downing to Marshall P. Wilder, Aug. 24, 1852, in John Jay Smith Papers, Library Company of Philadelphia, placed on deposit at the Historical Society of Pennsylvania, Philadelphia, Pa. (hereafter cited as Smith Papers). In preparing his "Memoir," Curtis consulted several articles written shortly after Downing's death: Cook, "The Late A. J. Downing," pp. 367–82; Mrs. John J. Monell, "Tribute to the Late A. J. Downing," *Knickerbocker* 40 (Oct. 1852): 353–55; and Marshall P. Wilder, "Col. Wilder's Eulogy on Mr. Downing," *Horticulturist* 7 (Nov. 1852): 491–500.

For a useful critique of Curtis's "Memoir," see the review of *Rural Essays* published in *Horticulturist,* n.s. 3 (July 1853): 334–37.

11. Will of Samuel Downing, May 10, 1822, Orange County Surrogate Court,

Goshen, N.Y., liber G, pp. 74–76. The elder Downing is listed as a trustee of Newburgh in numerous documents, including a deed dated July 30, 1817, in liber T, p. 193, Recorder of Deeds Office, Orange County Government Center.

Clarence Cook's interpretation differed from Curtis's only slightly: he asserted that Samuel Downing was "not poor, but possessed of a moderate property, not sufficient, however, to give his sons many advantages for education." "The Late A. J. Downing," p. 370.

12. C. C., "A Visit to the House and Garden of the Late A. J. Downing," *Horticulturist*, n.s. 3 (Jan. 1853): 21–27, and editor's preface, pp. 20–21. The author of the essay, presumably Clarence C. Cook, is identified as "C. C." in ibid. (Feb. 1853): 104.

13. C. Downing to M. P. Wilder, Aug. 24, 1852, Smith Papers; Orange County Community of Museums and Galleries, *Museum Matters* 4 (1970): 1; *Catalogue of the Officers and Staff of Montgomery Academy for the Year Ending July 1837* (Montgomery, N.Y., 1837), p. 5.

Downing's copy of E. Chambers, *The Practice of Perspective, or an Easy Method of Representing Natural Objects According to the Rule of Art* (London, 1726), which may date from his years at Montgomery Academy, is in the collection of the Washington's Headquarters State Historic Site, Newburgh, N.Y.

14. C. Downing to M. P. Wilder, Aug. 24, 1852, Smith Papers; AJD, "A Chapter on Agricultural Schools," *Horticulturist* 4 (Dec. 1849): 251.

15. Carnes, "Rise and Fall of a Mercantile Town," pp. 20–21; idem, "From Merchant to Manufacturer: The Economics of Localism in Newburgh, New York, 1845–1900," *Hudson Valley Regional Review* 3 (Mar. 1986): 75.

A memorial to the state legislature of 1831 observed that, "in consequence of the construction of the Erie, and Hudson and Delaware canals, much of the business which had usually been transacted at Newburgh has been diverted to other places." "Memorial," *Newburgh Telegraph*, Dec. 29, 1831.

16. "Newburgh," *Newburgh Telegraph*, Oct. 8, 1835; "United States Hotel," ibid., June 19, 1834; "A Description of the Reformed Dutch Church," ibid., Nov. 12, 1835. Shortly before the dedication of the Dutch Reformed Church, the *Telegraph* described it as "a noble specimen of chaste architecture, the first structure in our village in which the rules of architecture have been at all consulted, and it now stands an ornament to the village and an honor to its projectors." Ibid., Nov. 23, 1837. See also Arthur Channing Downs, Jr., *The Architecture and Life of the Hon. Thornton MacNess Nevin (1806–1895)*, 2d ed. (Goshen, N.Y., 1972), pp. 19–20.

17. "Newburgh," *Newburgh Telegraph*, Oct. 8, 1835.

18. "Visit to Newburgh," *Newburgh Telegraph*, Dec. 6, 1832, which was extracted from the *New-York Farmer*; *Newburgh Telegraph*, May 9, 1833; A. Elwood Corning, "Little Known Facts and Well-Known Folks of Newburgh and Vicinity," 36 vols. of notebooks in the possession of the Historical Society of Newburgh Bay and the Highlands, Newburgh, N.Y., vol. 1, p. 38; [Freeman Hunt], *Letters About the Hudson River, And Its Vicinity. Written in 1835 & 1836*, 3d ed. (New York, 1837), p. 191. There is no history of the Newburgh Horticultural Society, but it is known to have been in existence as early as 1830 and to have remained active for several years. The Reverend John

Brown, who served as its president, frequently mentions the affairs of the horticultural society in his diary, which is located at St. George's Church, Newburgh, N.Y.

19. C. Downing to M. P. Wilder, Aug. 24, 1852, Smith Papers; Calvert Vaux to M. P. Wilder, Aug. 18, 1852, Smith Papers (Vaux was conveying information provided by Caroline DeWint Downing); Curtis, "Memoir," *Rural Essays,* p. xvii; George B. Tatum, "Andrew Jackson Downing: Arbiter of American Taste, 1815–1852," Ph.D. diss., Princeton University, 1950, p. 41. An obituary described von Lederer as "a gentleman possessed of a highly cultivated mind and amiable manners." *New York Daily Tribune,* Dec. 23, 1842.

20. C. Downing to M. P. Wilder, Aug. 24, 1852, and C. Vaux to M. P. Wilder, Aug. 18, 1852, both in Smith Papers; Corning, "Little Known Facts and Well-Known Folks," vol. 36, p. 61; Thomas S. Cummings, *Historic Annals of the National Academy of Design* (1865; reprint ed., New York, 1969), p. 143; *National Academy of Design Exhibition Record, 1826–1860,* 2 vols. (New York, 1943), 1:240–41; "The Fine Arts. National Academy of Design," *New-York Mirror* 13 (June 18, 1836): 406; Wilder, "Col. Wilder's Eulogy on Mr. Downing," p. 493.

21. "Died," *Newburgh Telegraph,* Aug. 16, 1838; will of Caroline Downing Monell, Box 20410, will 17–363, Dutchess County Surrogate Court, Poughkeepsie, N.Y.

22. C. Vaux to M. P. Wilder, Aug. 18, 1852, Smith Papers; Wilder, "Col. Wilder's Eulogy on Mr. Downing," p. 493.

23. Rev. John Brown diary, Sept. 11, 1833.

24. AJD, "American Highland Scenery. Beacon Hill," *New-York Mirror* 12 (Mar. 14, 1835): 293–94.

25. AJD, "The Dans Kamer: A Reverie in the Highlands," *New-York Mirror* 13 (Oct. 10, 1835): 117–18, which was reprinted in *Newburgh Telegraph,* Nov. 5, 1835. The editor of the *Telegraph* found the republication of Downing's essay a "just cause of pride" yet also expressed "mortification" that local papers did not print essays of such quality, and by the same author, more frequently.

Washington Irving's folklore described how members of Peter Stuyvesant's crew "were most horribly frightened, on going on shore above the [Hudson] highlands, by a gang of merry roistering devils, frisking and curveting on a flat rock, which projected into the river, and which is called the *Duyvel's Dans-Kamer* to this very day." Knickerbocker, *History of New York,* pp. 392–93.

26. C. Vaux to M. P. Wilder, Aug. 18, 1852, Smith Papers.

27. "Public Library," *Newburgh Telegraph,* Mar. 26, 1835; AJD, "Report of the Trustees of the Newburgh Library Association," ibid., Apr. 20, 1837. Other trustees of the Library Association included John W. Knevels, editor of the Whig newspaper *Newburgh Gazette,* and Downing's longtime friend John J. Monell.

28. "The Gala," *Newburgh Telegraph,* Sept. 15, 1836; "Library Notice," ibid., Dec. 1, 1836; "Trustees of the Newburgh Library Association," ibid., June 15, 1837; AJD, "Report of the Trustees of the Newburgh Library Association," ibid., Apr. 20, 1837.

29. AJD, "Report of the Trustees of the Newburgh Library Association," ibid., Apr. 20, 1837. See also AJD et al., letter to Charles U. Cushman, July 12, 1837, printed in ibid., July 20, 1837.

However much Downing intended that the library serve all citizens of the village, either the cost, the selection of materials, or simply a desire for their own institution led workingmen to establish the Mechanics' Library Association in 1839. The two libraries later merged and in time became the Newburgh Free Library. See *Newburgh Telegraph*, Dec. 12, 1839; "The Fete," ibid., Jan. 2, 1840; and "Mechanics," ibid., July 16, 1840.

30. "Newburgh Lyceum" and "Lyceums," ibid., Dec. 28, 1839. See also Carl Bode, *The American Lyceum: Town Meeting of the Mind* (New York, 1956).

31. "Constitution of the Newburgh Lyceum," *Newburgh Telegraph*, Jan. 18, 1838. Arthur Channing Downs, Jr., has asserted that Downing "helped draw up the constitution and by-laws" of the lyceum, but the subcommittee entrusted with that responsibility consisted of a Rev. Kennedy, Jonas Story, and J. W. Knevels. See Downs, *Thornton MacNess Nevin*, p. 19, and "Newburgh Lyceum," *Newburgh Telegraph*, Jan. 25, 1838.

32. The topics of the meetings, held every other week, were published in the *Newburgh Telegraph*. Downing remained president of the Newburgh Library Association until the spring of 1839. See "Library Notice," ibid., Mar. 7, 1839, and untitled editorial notice, ibid., Apr. 4, 1839.

33. "The Court of Common Pleas," ibid., Sept. 8, 1842; Downs, *Thornton MacNess Nevin*, p. 40.

34. AJD, "The New-York Park," *Horticulturist* 6 (Aug. 1851): 349.

35. "Married," *Newburgh Telegraph*, June 14, 1838.

36. On DeWint's horticultural interests see AJD's note on the yellow locust, *Magazine of Horticulture* 3 (Oct. 1837): 389–90; AJD, "Horticultural Association of the Valley of the Hudson," ibid., 4 (Dec. 1838): 463; and AJD, "Horticultural Association of the Valley of the Hudson," ibid., 5 (Aug. 1839): 312. DeWint's efforts in land development and speculation were noticed by Henry Bradshaw Fearon, who traveled to the United States as agent for thirty-nine English families considering immigration to the United States, and who examined a property owned by DeWint in Fishkill Landing. According to Fearon, the "property for sale consisted of one hundred acres of land, and fourteen small frame (not log) houses; the price for the whole is 25,000 dollars (£5625): there is on this lot a neat frame church, which may be purchased for 2500 dollars (£562. 10s.); it is not fitted up, except a few common seats, and a pulpit of rather primitive simplicity. A credit of four years will be given, charging the interest: the present cash price is not lower." Fearon, *Sketches of America*, pp. 79–80.

37. E. M. Ruttenber, *History of the Town of Newburgh* (Newburgh, N.Y., 1859), pp. 154, 170–71; "DeWint's Building" is identified on Stephen C. Parmenter's "Map of Part of the Village of Newburgh . . .," 1846, City Engineer's Office, City of Newburgh, N.Y., and is described in "Room for Public Meetings," *Newburgh Telegraph*, July 25, 1839; see also Carnes, "From Merchant to Manufacturer," p. 51. For DeWint's contribution toward the cost of acquiring and improving the court house lot see Downs, *Thornton MacNess Nevin*, p. 40.

38. Margaret Armstrong, *Five Generations: Life and Letters of an American Family, 1750–1900* (New York, 1930), p. 234; "Married," *Newburgh Telegraph*, June 14, 1838;

Fredrika Bremer, *The Homes of the New World: Impressions of America,* trans. Mary Howitt, 2 vols. (New York, 1854), 1: 22.

39. Bremer, *Homes of the New World,* 1: 39–41; idem., "To the Friends of A. J. Downing," *Rural Essays,* p. lxii: Frederick Law Olmsted to John J. Monell, n.d. [ca. 1868]; F. L. Olmsted, fragmentary draft of *Cottage Residences,* n.d.; and Caroline Downing Monell letters to Olmsted, July 14, 1887, June 7, 1889, and June 10, 1889, all in Frederick Law Olmsted Papers, Manuscript Division, Library of Congress, Washington, D.C. For Caroline Downing Monell's role in the creation of Downing Park, see David Schuyler, "Belated Honor to a Prophet: Newburgh's Downing Park," *Landscape* 31 (spring 1991): 10–17.

40. On the Greek Revival in Newburgh see Downs, *Thornton MacNess Nevin,* pp. 23–42.

41. See, for example, AJD, "On the Improvement of Country Villages," *Horticulturist* 3 (June 1849): 545–49.

42. C. C., "A Visit to the House and Garden," p. 23; AJD, *A Treatise on the Theory and Practice of Landscape Gardening, Adapted to North America . . . .* (New York, 1841), 1844 ed., pp. 386–87.

43. Arthur Channing Downs, "Downing's Newburgh Villa," *Bulletin of the Association for Preservation Technology* 4 (1972): 30–33.

44. Downing added the subtitle "Adapted to North America" to both the *Treatise* and *Cottage Residences* (1842). For the importance of expression of purpose, see AJD, *Treatise,* 1844 ed., pp. 344–48.

45. Dimensions of the building are derived from "Residence of A. J. Downing, Botanical Gardens and Nurseries, Newburgh, New York," *Magazine of Horticulture* 7 (Nov. 1841): 401–11, as well as the correction that appeared in ibid. 8 (Jan. 1842): 3n.

46. "The Architects and Architecture of New York," *Brother Jonathan* 5 (Aug. 12, 1843): 421; the Downing letter recommending Gill as plasterer is quoted in Mills Lane, *Architecture of the Old South: Mississippi and Alabama* (New York, 1989), p. 89.

47. Information on mortgages Downing carried on the house is contained in Charles Downing and Henry W. Sargent, executors for AJD, and Caroline E. Downing, deed of transfer to Charles C. Alger, Apr. 1, 1853, Recorder of Deeds Office, Orange County Government Center, Goshen, N.Y., liber 133, p. 139. On Downing's superintendence of construction see C. C., "A Visit to the House and Garden," p. 22, and Curtis, "Memoir," *Rural Essays,* p. xxiii.

48. Eunice Downing's death was noted in *Newburgh Telegraph,* Nov. 1, 1838. For information on the division of property see Charles Downing and AJD, deed of transfer to Charles Downing, Mar. 26, 1839, liber 66, pp. 135–38; Charles Downing and AJD, deed of transfer to AJD, Mar. 26, 1839, liber 66, pp. 138–41; Frederick J. Betts and George Cornwall, assignees for AJD, and Charles Downing, deed of sale to Nathan Reeve, May 5, 1847, liber 92, pp. 206–8, all in Recorder of Deeds Office, Orange County Government Center, Goshen, N.Y.

49. C. C., "A Visit to the House and Garden," p. 25. Because Downing's garden occupied much of the space formerly devoted to the nursery, and perhaps because of increasing business as well, much of the nursery was transferred to Charles Down-

ing's thirteen-acre property in Balmville, just north of Newburgh. After a visit to Charles's nursery, C. M. Hovey wrote: "Though residing separate from his brother, he is occupied exclusively in growing trees for him, through whom all orders are transmitted." C. M. Hovey, "Notes made during a Visit to New York, Philadelphia, Baltimore and Washington, and intermediate places, from Aug. 8th to the 23rd, 1841," *Magazine of Horticulture* 7 (Oct. 1841): 372.

50. "Residence of A. J. Downing," pp. 402–6; "Banks of the Hudson," *Cultivator* 11 (Oct. 1844): 299.

51. Freeman Hunt described the east lot as containing "an extensive walk just formed, exhibiting a complete botanical circuit of plants arranged in a scientific manner—a rockwork for alpine plants, and a pond for aquarium, in which the water-lilies and a number of other aquatic plants were thriving admirably." The pond is evident on S. Parmenter's 1846 map of Newburgh. See [Hunt], *Letters About the Hudson River,* p. 192.

52. Curtis, "Memoir," *Rural Essays,* p. xxxii.

53. C. C. "A Visit to the House and Garden," p. 23; AJD, *Treatise,* 1841 ed., fig. 35; 1844 ed., fig. 53. Downing was deeply concerned that the published view of his house be as attractive as possible. He criticized the proof of the engraving prepared by Alexander Anderson as "execrable" and added that it "affords me no pleasure whatever." In a letter to Alexander Jackson Davis he pointed out what he considered the "defects"—parts of the house "have a hard wooden look; the porch seems a ridiculous appendage being apparently flattened up against the house (vide the difference between this and Mrs. D's copy herewith); the base of the chimney is one-sided and monstrous—the shields jumbled and the distant arches of the piazza very bad. The outline of the vignette is awkward and too deep, not forming a graceful oval." Downing then asked Davis to redraw the house on block and transmit it to the engraver. See AJD to A. J. Davis, Oct. 18, 1840, A. J. Davis Collection, Department of Prints and Photographs, Metropolitan Museum of Art, New York.

54. "Landscape Gardening and Rural Architecture in America," *United States Magazine and Democratic Review* 16 (April 1845): 348.

55. Curtis, "Memoir," *Rural Essays,* pp. xxii, xxxiv; Cook, "The Late A. J. Downing," p. 368; see also C. C., "A Visit to the House and Garden," p. 23.

Chapter 2 The Making of the Treatise

Epigraph: Fredrika Bremer, "To the Friends of A. J. Downing," in *Rural Essays. By A. J. Downing. Edited, With a Memoir of the Author, by George William Curtis; and a Letter to His Friends, by Fredrika Bremer* (1853; reprint ed., with a new introduction by George B. Tatum, New York, 1974), p. lxiv.

1. See Charles B. Wood III, "The New 'Pattern Books' and the Role of the Agricultural Press," in *Prophet With Honor: The Career of Andrew Jackson Downing 1815–1852,* ed. George B. Tatum and Elisabeth Blair MacDougall (Washington, D.C., 1989), pp. 165–89.

2. "Rural Embellishment," *Cultivator* 5 (July 1838): 85; C. M. Hovey, "A Retrospective View of the Progress of Horticulture, in the United States, during the past year," *Magazine of Horticulture* 5 (Jan. 1839): 4.

3. C. M. Hovey, "Arboricultural Notices," *Magazine of Horticulture* 25 (Mar. 1859): 133–35; Luther Tucker, "Mr. Downing and the Horticulturist," *Horticulturist* 7 (Sept. 1852): 394.

4. Downing's letters were excerpted and printed, along with commentary by C. M. Hovey, in a review of Henry Winthrop Sargent's 1859 edition of the *Treatise* in "Arboricultural Notices," pp. 133–35. See also AJD to A. J. Davis, Mar. 29, 1839, Davis Collection, Department of Prints and Photographs, Metropolitan Museum of Art, New York (hereafter Davis Collection/MMA).

5. Hovey, "Arboricultural Notices," pp. 133–35.

6. AJD to Robert Donaldson, Dec. 26, 1840, collection of Richard Jenrette.

7. AJD, "Observations on the Culture of the Strawberry," *Magazine of Horticulture* 4 (May 1838): 162; AJD, "Ringing Fruit Trees," ibid., 3 (Oct. 1837): 363; AJD, "Remarks on the Duration of the Improved varieties of New York Fruit Trees," ibid., 3 (Mar. 1837): 91.

8. AJD, "Remarks on the Duration of Fruit Trees," pp. 90–91. Throughout his career Downing frequently reiterated his disagreement with Knight and Van Mons. Two years after publishing this essay, for example, he informed an English audience: "Some of the old fruits, which Mr. Knight and others of your best European physiologists considered nearly extinct and degenerate, bear and thrive in the Middle States yet, with all their primitive vigor." He also outlined his disagreements with them in the pages of the *Horticulturist* and in *Fruits and Fruit Trees of America*. AJD, "Foreign Notices. North America," *Gardener's Magazine* 15 (Jan. 1839): 38; AJD, "A Talk With Flora and Pomona," *Horticulturist* 2 (Sept. 1847): 105–8; AJD, "A Look About Us," *Horticulturist* 4 (Apr. 1850): 441–43; AJD, *The Fruits and Fruit Trees of America . . .* (New York, 1845), pp. 5–9.

9. J. Torrey and A. Gray, *A Flora of North America: Containing Abridged Descriptions of all the Known Indigenous and Naturalized Plants Growing North of Mexico; Arranged According to the Natural System* (New York, 1838–40), p. xi; Gordon P. De Wolf, Jr., "Andrew Jackson Downing and Pomology," in *Prophet With Honor*, p. 132n.

10. *Magazine of Horticulture* 3 (Aug. 1837): 308–11. On the Lyceum's role in the professionalization of science, see Thomas Bender, *New York Intellect: A History of Intellectual Life in New York City, from 1750 to the Beginnings of Our Own Time* (New York, 1987), pp. 71–72.

11. AJD, "Some Remarks on the Superiority of Native Varieties of Fruits" (1847), in Massachusetts Horticultural Society, *Transactions* 1 (1847–51): 29–32.

12. AJD, "Vineyards in the United States," *New-York Farmer and American Gardener's Magazine* 7 (May 1834): 131–33. In promoting the consumption of wine, Downing was responding to the tremendous magnitude of alcohol consumption in the United States during the early nineteenth century. See W. J. Rorabaugh, *The Alcoholic Republic: An American Tradition* (New York, 1979).

13. Asa Gray to M. P. Wilder, Aug. 23, 1852, John Jay Smith Papers, Library Com-

pany of Philadelphia, placed on deposit at the Historical Society of Pennsylvania, Philadelphia. Wilder used Gray's words, without acknowledgment, in "Col. Wilder's Eulogy on Mr. Downing," *Horticulturist* 7 (Nov. 1852): 495.

14. John Lindley, *The Theory of Horticulture: Or, An attempt to explain the principal operations of gardening upon physiological principles*, 1st American ed., with notes, etc., by A. J. Downing and A. Gray (New York, 1841). Downing's notes (pp. 33–34, 114–15, 116–18, 133, 134–35, 156, 191–92, 195, 204, 206–7, 229–30, 231, 233, 273–74, 318) generally provided information on practical aspects of gardening, especially grafting, pruning, and transplanting, while Gray's annotations usually involved matters of plant physiology. A contemporary review observed that the notes prepared by Downing and Gray had "greatly added to its value, and better adapted it to the American public." "Lindley's Theory of Horticulture," *Cultivator* 8 (Sept. 1841): 145. On the collaboration in preparing the edition of Lindley, see A. Hunter Dupree, "Asa Gray and Andrew Jackson Downing: A Bibliographical Note," *Rhodora* 58 (Sept. 1956): 243–45.

15. Compare Asa Gray, *Manual of the Botany of the Northeastern United States* (Boston, 1846), pp. 412–17, and AJD, *A Treatise on the Theory and Practice of Landscape Gardening, Adapted to North America . . .* (New York, 1841), 1859 ed., pp. 117–28; Bender, *New York Intellect*, p. 71.

16. AJD, "Preface to the American Edition," Lindley, *Theory of Horticulture*, p. ix.

17. AJD, "Some Remarks on Temperature Considered in Relation to Vegetation and the Naturalization of Plants," *Horticultural Register* 2 (Mar. 1836): 105.

18. See Tamara Plakins Thornton, *Cultivating Gentlemen: The Meaning of Country Life Among the Boston Elite, 1785–1860* (New Haven, 1989), pp. 147–72.

19. "Great Horticultural Society of the Valley of the Hudson," *Magazine of Horticulture* 4 (June 1838): 233–35; "Horticultural Association of the Valley of the River Hudson," ibid. 4 (Sept. 1838): 353–54. The circular was signed by Jesse Buel, John Torrey, and Downing. A copy is preserved in the Thompson Collection, DKI0367, Box 12, New York State Library, Albany. Downing was deeply involved in preparing the announcement of the association and in organizing its inaugural meeting. See AJD to Jesse Buel, May 8, 1838, ms. 5707, New York State Library, Albany. See also AJD, "Horticultural Association of the Valley of the Hudson," *Magazine of Horticulture* 4 (Dec. 1838): 462–65; AJD, "Horticultural Association of the Valley of the Hudson," ibid. 5 (Aug. 1839): 310–13; AJD, "Horticultural Exhibition," *Cultivator* 6 (June 1839): 80; AJD, "Horticultural Report," ibid., 6 (Aug. 1839): 97–98.

20. XYZ, "Rural Embellishments," *New-York Farmer and Horticultural Repository* 5 (Sept. 1832): 329–30. In addition to having obvious similarities in content and style with Downing's writings, the essay also criticized the placement of houses too close to the public road, a subject Downing addressed in numerous other writings.

21. AJD, "On the employment of Ornamental Trees and Shrubs in North America; more particularly the indigenous Species and Varieties, as regards their effect in the formation of Parks and Pleasure Grounds, and extensive Plantations for Landscape Beauty," *American Gardener's Magazine* 1 (Dec. 1835): 445–52. The essay originally appeared in the *New England Farmer* 12 (1834): 225–26, and was reprinted in *Annales de l'Institut Horticole de Fromont* 6 (1834): 74–80.

22. AJD, "Remarks on the Fitness of the different Styles of Architecture for the Construction of Country Residences, and on the Employment of Vases in Garden Scenery," *American Gardener's Magazine* 2 (Aug. 1836): 281–86.

23. Ibid.

24. AJD, "Notices on the State and Progress of Horticulture in the United States," *Magazine of Horticulture* 3 (Jan. 1837): 1–10; AJD, "Notes on the Progress of Gardening in the United States," *Gardener's Magazine* 16 (Dec. 1840): 642–45, and "Additional Notes on the Progress of Gardening in the United States," ibid. 17 (Mar. 1841): 146–47. Downing reiterated the call for a nationally supported experimental garden and "practical school for gardeners" in "A Look About Us," *Horticulturist* 4 (Apr. 1850): 441–43.

Downing's stricture on the total absence of an experimental garden needs qualification. The Massachusetts Horticultural Society did include precisely such a garden in Mount Auburn Cemetery (dedicated 1831), but by 1835 the cemetery had separated from its parent organization and annexed the ground originally set aside for experimental horticulture. See David Schuyler, *The New Urban Landscape: The Redefinition of City Form in Nineteenth-Century America* (Baltimore, 1986), pp. 43–44.

25. This is suggested in Brenda Bullion, "Hawthorns and Hemlocks: The Return of the Sacred Grove," *Landscape Journal* 2 (fall 1983): 114–24.

26. A. Halsey, "Report of the Visiting Committee of the New-York Horticultural Society for 1828," reprinted in *New-York Farmer and American Gardener's Magazine* 7 (Apr. 1834): 107–8.

27. AJD, *Treatise*, p. ii.

28. The first page of text of the *Treatise* bears the head, "Essay on Landscape Gardening, &c.," which may well have been an overall description of the first three chapters. In Oct. 1838 Downing had explained to C. M. Hovey that part of the book he was writing was "a short treatise on modern Landscape Gardening," while the remainder was a description of trees and their effect in the garden. It is possible that the "Essay" head referred to the opening sections of the *Treatise* and that Downing intended to add another head, of the same size and type, to introduce the three chapters devoted to trees, vines, and climbing plants. Perhaps the final arrangement of the chapters, with the placement of the sections on ground, water, rural architecture, and embellishments after the chapters devoted to trees, made Downing's original scheme unworkable. It is also possible that Downing considered "Essay on Landscape Gardening" an apt description of the entire book, though that seems less plausible given his choice of a different title. In any case, subsequent editions of the *Treatise* retained the head above the first section. For Downing's letter to Hovey, see Hovey, "Arboricultural Notices," pp. 133–34.

29. AJD, *Treatise*, p. 20; 1844 ed., pp. 10, 29–30. M'Mahon's essay referred to a "Pleasure-ground, according to modern gardening," which required "consulting rural disposition, in imitation of nature," and avoiding straight lines and other elements of the ancient or formal garden. *The American Gardener's Calender, Adapted to the Climates and Seasons of the United States* (Philadelphia, 1806), p. 55.

30. AJD, *Treatise*, pp. 20–21; 1844 ed., pp. 29–30. In a tenor strikingly similar to

that which Downing later employed, Parmentier roundly criticized the "exactness of geometric forms" in the ancient or formal garden, which he considered "totally ruinous to the beauty of the prospect" and destructive of the "charms of nature." The landscapes he designed avoided formal elements and emphasized natural scenery. Parmentier's essay "Landscapes and Picturesque Gardens" was published in Fessenden's *New American Gardener,* 6th ed. (Boston, 1832), pp. 184–87. See also J. E. Spingarn, "Henry Winthrop Sargent and the Early History of Landscape Gardening and Ornamental Horticulture in Dutchess County, New York," *Year Book of the Dutchess County Historical Society* 22 (1937): 36–70.

31. AJD, *Treatise,* 1844 ed., pp. 10, 20, 48–49; 1859 ed., pp. 46–47.

32. AJD, *Treatise,* pp. 53–54; 1844 ed., pp. 10, 73; 1859 ed., p. 288.

33. See Edmund Burke, *A Philosophical Enquiry into the Origin of our Ideas of the Sublime and Beautiful,* ed. J. T. Boulton (London, 1958), pp. 91, 39. The literature on the eighteenth-century and early-nineteenth-century English garden, as well as the debate over the beautiful and the picturesque, is summarized in George B. Tatum, "Nature's Gardener," in *Prophet With Honor,* pp. 43–80.

34. Tatum, "Nature's Gardener," *Prophet With Honor,* pp. 43–80. See also Melanie Louise Simo, *Loudon and the Landscape: From Country Seat to Metropolis, 1783–1843* (New Haven, 1988).

35. AJD, *Treatise,* p. iv; 1844 ed., pp. x, 26, 54–55, 312–13; Tatum, "Nature's Gardener," *Prophet With Honor,* pp. 43–80.

36. AJD, "English and American Landscape Gardening," *Horticulturist* 2 (Dec. 1847): 263.

37. AJD, *Treatise,* 1844 ed., pp. 312–13, passim; Roger B. Stein, *John Ruskin and Aesthetic Thought in America, 1840–1900* (Cambridge, Mass., 1967), pp. 46–56. Loudon's discussion of utility, fitness, and variety, which itself drew upon the writings of other writers, including Archibald Alison and Humphry Repton, appears in his *Encyclopedia of Cottage, Farm, and Villa Architecture . . . ,* new ed. (London, 1839), pp. 1106–24.

38. AJD to A. J. Davis, Mar. 8, 1839 (misdated 1838 in original), Davis Collection/MMA.

39. AJD, *Treatise,* pp. 29ff.; 1844 ed., pp. 49, 55–56; 1859 ed., pp. 53–54. Downing's description of the graceful is strikingly similar to Thomas Cole's characterization of the beautiful. In a letter to Daniel Wadsworth describing his *Garden of Eden* (1827–28), Cole wrote: "There are in it lofty distant Mountains, a calm expansive lake . . . undulating grounds, a meandering river, cascades, gentle lawns, . . . banks of beauteous flowers . . . harmless and graceful animals." Cole is quoted in Angela Miller, *The Empire of the Eye: Landscape Representation and American Cultural Politics, 1825–1875* (Ithaca, 1993), p. 50.

40. AJD, *Treatise,* 1844 ed., pp. 56–57; 1859 ed., pp. 53–54, 59–60. On the symbolic masculinity of mountains, see Yi-Fu Tuan, *Topophilia: A Study of Environmental Perception, Attitudes, and Values* (Englewood Cliffs, N.J., 1974), pp. 70–74, and A. Miller, *Empire of the Eye,* pp. 266–71.

41. In the 1844 edition of the *Treatise* (p. 59) Downing suggested that the picturesque was the style of choice for the "imaginative few," who appreciated Nature's

"more free and spirited charms." He was pleased that during the previous five years his countrymen had begun to express a preference for the picturesque. In the 1850 edition (p. 76) he again noted with approbation that "many minds" were choosing the picturesque over the beautiful.

42. AJD, *Treatise*, 1844 ed., pp. 58, 64ff. In his famous injunction, contained in his "Epistle to the Earl of Burlington," Pope wrote: "Consult the Genius of the Place in all;/That tells the Waters or to rise, or fall." The importance of *genius loci* extends back to antiquity: it is also mentioned in the fifth book of Virgil's *Aeneid*. See M. R. Brownell, *Alexander Pope and the Arts of Georgian England* (Oxford, 1978), pp. 108–9.

43. AJD, *Treatise*, 1844 ed., pp. 61–64.

44. Ibid., pp. 79–80.

45. Ibid., pp. 93–103 (quotation p. 103).

46. Ibid., pp. x, 340–41.

47. Ibid., pp. 343–47.

48. Ibid., pp. 348, 353–54. Downing also pointed out that the temple form was probably not used for domestic purposes in ancient Greece, a fact "which easily accounts for our comparative failure, in constructing well arranged, small residences in this style" (p. 354).

49. Ibid., pp. 356–59.

50. Ibid., pp. 362–63.

51. Ibid., pp. 363–64.

52. Ibid., pp. 364–72.

53. Ibid., pp. 372–74.

54. Ibid., p. 378.

55. AJD to A. J. Davis, Dec. 12, 1838, collection of the late Anthony N. B. Garvan; A. J. Davis, *Rural Residences, Etc.: Consisting of Designs, Original and Selected, for Cottages, Farm-Houses, Villas, and Village Churches: With Brief Explanations, Estimates, and a Specification of Materials, Construction, etc.* (1838; reprint ed., with an introduction by Jane B. Davies, New York, 1980), unpaginated advertisement; Jane B. Davies, "Davis and Downing: Collaborators in the Picturesque," in *Prophet With Honor*, pp. 81–84.

56. Davies, "Davis and Downing," *Prophet With Honor*, p. 85; AJD to A. J. Davis, Mar. 8, 1839, Davis Collection/MMA.

57. Davies, "Davis and Downing," *Prophet With Honor*, pp. 85–86; AJD to A. J. Davis, Apr. 8, 1839, Davis Collection/MMA.

58. "Downing's Landscape Gardening," *New York Review* 9 (July 1841): 256–60; "Landscape Gardening and Rural Architecture," *United States Magazine and Democratic Review*, n.s. 9 (Dec. 1841): 554.

59. See, for example, Wiley and Putnam's advertisement, at the back of the first American edition of Lindley's *Theory of Horticulture*, which quotes the review that appeared in *Silliman's Journal*; "Reviews.—Downing on Landscape Gardening," *Magazine of Horticulture* 7 (July 1841): 268; "Downing on Landscape Gardening," *North American Review* 53 (July 1841): 262; and "Downing's Landscape Gardening, &c.," *Cultivator* 8 (Sept. 1841): 145. Another early review, "Downing's Landscape-Garden-

ing," appeared in J. C. Loudon's *Gardener's Magazine* 17 (Aug. 1841): 421–27, but it was almost entirely devoted to excerpts from the *Treatise*.

60. George William Curtis quoted these reviews in his "Memoir" in *Rural Essays*, p. xxv.

61. AJD, *Treatise*, pp. ii–iii.

62. Alexis de Tocqueville, *Democracy in America*, ed. Phillips Bradley, 2 vols. (1835-40; New York, 1945), 2: 144–45.

63. "Downing on Landscape Gardening," *North American Review*, pp. 259–60.

64. "Landscape Gardening and Rural Architecture," *New Englander and Yale Review* 1 (Apr. 1843): 207.

65. "Landscape Gardening and Rural Architecture in America," *United States Magazine and Democratic Review* 16 (Apr. 1845): 356–57.

66. Daniel Walker Howe, *The Political Culture of the American Whigs* (Chicago, 1979).

67. See, for example, "Landscape Gardening and Rural Architecture in America," p. 348.

68. AJD to John Jay Smith, May 21, 1842, Smith Papers.

69. AJD to Robert Donaldson, Nov. 15, 1841, collection of Richard Jenrette.

70. AJD to Robert Donaldson, Jan. 21, 1842, collection of Richard Jenrette.

Chapter 3 Theory and Practice

Epigraph: AJD to Dr. William Darlington, Oct. 8, 1846, New-York Historical Society, New York.

1. AJD to A. J. Davis, Mar. 29, 1839, A. J. Davis Collection, Department of Prints and Photographs, Metropolitan Museum of Art, New York (hereafter Davis Collection/MMA).

2. Although the designs for a number of Hudson Valley properties developed or improved during the 1830s, including the grounds of Blithewood and Montgomery Place, have been attributed to Downing, there is no surviving documentation of his working as a landscape gardener prior to publication of the *Treatise*. When C. M. Hovey visited Newburgh and described the Downing brothers' nursery in the summer of 1841, he noted that the proprietors advised purchasers "in regard to the selection of such fruits as are best adapted to general cultivation, or for the particular purposes of standards, dwarfs, espaliers, or wall fruit." Given Hovey's comment that "landscape gardening and rural architecture have lingered far in the rear of horticultural improvements," it seems reasonable to infer that if Downing had been actively practicing landscape gardening the author would have mentioned those efforts. C. M. Hovey, "Notes made during a Visit to New York, Philadelphia, Baltimore and Washington, and intermediate places, from Aug. 8th to the 23d, 1841," *Magazine of Horticulture* 7 (Oct. 1841): 371; AJD to Robert Donaldson, Nov. 15, 1841, collection of Richard Jenrette. See also George B. Tatum, "Andrew Jackson Downing: Arbiter of American Taste, 1815–1852," Ph.D. diss., Princeton University, 1950, pp. 96–100, and

idem, "Nature's Gardener," in *Prophet With Honor: The Career of Andrew Jackson Downing, 1815–1852,* ed. George B. Tatum and Elisabeth Blair MacDougall (Washington, D.C., 1989), pp. 67–68.

3. See, for example, Richard Schermerhorn, Jr., "Andrew Jackson Downing, the First American Landscape Architect," *House and Garden* 16 (Aug. 1909): 3–4.

4. AJD to A. J. Davis, Dec. 29, 1841, Davis Collection/MMA.

5. AJD to Robert Donaldson, Jan. 21, 1842, collection of Richard Jenrette.

6. Downing's preface bears the date June 1842.

7. AJD, *Cottage Residences; Or, A Series of Designs for Rural Cottages and Cottage Villas, and their Gardens and Grounds. Adapted to North America . . .* (New York, 1842), p. iv.

8. A. J. Davis, *Rural Residences, Etc.: Consisting of Designs, Original and Selected, for Cottages, Farm-Houses, Villas, and Village Churches: With Brief Explanations, Estimates, and a Specification of Materials, Construction, etc.* (1838; reprint ed., with an introduction by Jane B. Davies, New York, 1980), unpaginated introduction and end paper.

9. Henry-Russell Hitchcock, *American Architectural Books: A List of Books, Portfolios, and Pamphlets on Architecture and Related Subjects Published in America before 1895* (Minneapolis, 1962), p, iii; Vincent J. Scully, Jr., *The Shingle Style and the Stick Style: Architectural Theory and Design from Downing to the Origins of Wright,* rev. ed. (1955; New Haven, 1971), p. xxvii; Charles B. Wood III, "The New 'Pattern Books' and the Role of the Agricultural Press," in *Prophet With Honor,* pp. 181–83. Dell Upton refers to these types of publications as architectural handbooks and stylebooks. See "Pattern Books and Professionalism: Aspects of the Transformation of Domestic Architecture in America, 1800–1860," *Winterthur Portfolio* 19 (summer/autumn 1984): 107–50.

10. Davis, *Rural Residences,* unpaginated introduction.

11. Wood, "New 'Pattern Books,'" pp. 183–86.

12. The text was critically important to the education of the prospective home builder or owner. Downing criticized J. J. Smith and Thomas U. Walter's *Two Hundred Designs for Cottages and Villas* (Philadelphia, 1846) for the absence of adequate explanations accompanying the plans. The result, he wrote, was "asking from the architecturally uneducated person, who turns over a variety of designs, a good deal of the highest inventive powers of the best architect." "Reviews," *Horticulturist* 1 (Nov. 1846): 231–32.

13. This interpretation—that for all the efforts of Downing and others to establish a distinction between architecture and building, the house pattern book enabled the traditional builder to adapt to changing styles—differs from Dell Upton's "Pattern Books and Professionalism."

14. AJD, *Cottage Residences,* pp. i, 9–24. Downing did publish an octavo edition of *Fruits and Fruit Trees of America* that included color plates.

Four years after the publication of *Cottage Residences* Downing reflected on how contemporaries had adopted his advice on colors. "Some time ago, we ventured to record our objections to *white,* as a universal color for country houses," he wrote.

"We have had great satisfaction, since that time, in seeing a gradual improvement taking place with respect to this matter. Neutral tints are, with the best taste, now every where preferred to strong glaring colors." AJD, "On Simple Rural Cottages," *Horticulturist* 1 (Sept. 1846): 109, printed in *Rural Essays. By A. J. Downing. Edited, With a Memoir of the Author, by George William Curtis; and a Letter to His Friends, by Fredrika Bremer* (1853; reprint ed., with a new introduction by George B. Tatum, New York, 1974), p. 251.

James Fenimore Cooper echoed Downing's remarks on color in "American and European Scenery Compared," in *A Landscape Book, By American Artists and Authors* (New York, 1868), p. 9. By contrast, Henry David Thoreau stridently criticized Downing's aesthetic: see Richard N. Masteller and Jean Carwile Masteller, "Rural Architeture in Andrew Jackson Downing and Henry David Thoreau: Pattern Book Parody in *Walden*," *New England Quarterly* 57 (Dec. 1984): 483–510.

15. AJD, *Cottage Residences*, pp. ii, 10, 25.

16. Ibid., pp. 26–29

17. Ibid., pp. 30–34.

18. Jane B. Davies, "Davis and Downing: Collaborators in the Picturesque," in *Prophet With Honor*, pp. 86–91. Downing paid $255 for the seventy drawings that Davis prepared for *Cottage Residences*. Davis, Day Book, Jan. 1, 1842, Manuscript and Archives Division, Rare Book and Manuscript Division, New York Public Library, Astor, Lenox and Tilden Foundations, New York.

19. AJD to A. J. Davis, Dec. 29, 1841, Davis Collection/MMA; AJD, *Cottage Residences*, p. 171.

20. AJD, *Cottage Residences*, pp. 124–25.

21. Ibid., pp. 124–36.

22. AJD, "Cockneyism in the Country," *Horticulturist* 4 (Sept. 1849): 108.

23. AJD, *Cottage Residences*, pp. 79–87; AJD to A. J. Davis, Jan. 25, 1842, Davis Collection/MMA.

24. Davies, "Davis and Downing," *Prophet With Honor*, pp. 89–90. Davies believes that Downing was inspired by Davis's Vanderburg Cottage.

25. Davis would later use Design II in slightly modified form in the design of the Delamater House (1844), in Rhinebeck, New York.

26. AJD, *Cottage Residences*, pp. 40–48.

27. Davies, "Davis and Downing," *Prophet With Honor*, p. 86.

28. "Notices of New Publications," *Cutivator* 9 (Sept. 1842): 140; "Reviews," *Magazine of Horticulture* 8 (Nov. 1842): 414–17; "Literary Notices," *American Review, and Metropolitan Magazine* 1 (Jan. 1843): 95; Solon Robinson, "A Cheap Farm House," *Ohio Cultivator* 2 (Mar. 15, 1846): 41–42, reprinted in *Solon Robinson: Pioneer and Agriculturist, Selected Writings*, ed. Herbert Anthony Kellar, 2 vols. (Indianapolis, 1936), 1:553.

29. "Landscape Gardening and Rural Architecture," *New Englander and Yale Review* 1 (Apr. 1843): 211; "Our New Houses," *United States Magazine and Democratic Review* 21 (Nov. 1847): 392; *Broadway Journal* 1 (1845): 213.

30. Wood, "New 'Pattern Books,'" p. 166; Hitchcock, *American Architectural Books*, pp. 31–32.

31. Fredrika Bremer, *The Homes of the New World: Impressions of America,* trans. Mary Howitt, 2 vols. (New York, 1854), 1:46.

32. S. G. Fisher, *A Philadelphia Perspective: The Diary of Sidney George Fisher Covering the Years 1834–1871,* ed. Nicholas B. Wainwright (Philadelphia, 1967), p. 201.

33. AJD to J. J. Smith, Oct. 21, 1842, John Jay Smith Papers, Library Company of Philadelphia, placed on deposit at the Historical Society of Pennsylvania, Philadelphia. Hereafter cited as Smith Papers.

34. AJD, *Cottage Residences,* 1852 ed., p. 48.

35. *Cultivator* 9 (Sept. 1842): 144–45; Bremer, *Homes of the New World,* 1:111; Fredrika Bremer, "To the Friends of A. J. Downing," in *Rural Essays,* p. lxiv. In a letter dated Dec. 2, 1849, Bremer added, "I was there [Oxbridge] at a little beautiful cottage, built (theoretically) by you, my brother, and practically by a young happy couple who studied your books every day for three months before they set to work." Adolph B. Benson, ed., "Fredrika Bremer's Unpublished Letters to the Downings," *Scandinavian Studies and Notes* 11 (May 1930): 51.

36. Susan Fenimore Cooper, *Rural Hours* (New York, 1850), pp. 383–85. The agricultural reformer Lewis F. Allen concurred with Cooper's observation: "We may, in truth, be said to have no architecture at all, as exhibited in our agricultural districts, so far as any correct system, or plan is concerned, as the better taste in building, which a few years past has introduced among us, has been chiefly confined to our cities and towns of rapid growth." Lewis F. Allen, *Rural Architecture: Being a Complete Description of Farm Houses, Cottages, and Out Buildings, Comprising Wood Houses, Workshops . . . &c.* (New York, 1852), p. 13.

37. A copy of the advertisement is bound at the back of the Library of Congress's copy of Hovey's *Magazine of Horticulture,* vol. 8 (1842).

38. AJD to J. J. Smith, Nov. 15, 1841, Smith Papers (date is almost illegible and may be imprecise). Downing had called for the creation of botanical and experimental gardens in several essays he published.

39. Cynthia Zaitzevsky, *Frederick Law Olmsted and the Boston Park System* (Cambridge, Mass., 1982), p. 15; Kenneth B. Hawkins, "The Therapeutic Landscape: Nature, Architecture, and Mind in Nineteenth-Century America," Ph.D. diss., University of Rochester, 1991, pp. 174–76.

40. AJD to J. J. Smith, Oct. 21, 1842, in "Downing's Landscape Gardening. A Letter From Mr. Downing," *Horticulturist,* n.s. 8 (Sept. 1858): 412; AJD to A. J. Davis, Oct. 21, 1842, Davis Collection/MMA.

41. AJD to A. J. Davis, Oct. 21, 1842, Davis Collection/MMA; Davies, "Davis and Downing," *Prophet With Honor,* pp. 92–93

42. Fisher, *A Philadelphia Perspective,* pp. 202, 224, 228.

43. Bremer, *Homes of the New World,* 1:286–88, 299.

44. AJD to A. J. Davis, Oct. 21, 1842, Davis Collection/MMA.

45. C. A. Mann to AJD, Sept. 10, 1842, Oneida County Historical Society, Oneida, N.Y.

46. AJD, "A Chapter on School Houses," *Horticulturist* 2 (Mar. 1848): 395, printed in *Rural Essays,* p. 269.

47. AJD to A. J. Davis, Oct. 21, 1842, Davis Collection/MMA; AJD to C. A. Mann,

Oct. 26, 1842, Oneida County Historical Society, Oneida, N.Y.; Hawkins, "The Therapeutic Landscape," pp. 178–80.

48. *Thirteenth Annual Report of the Managers of the State Lunatic Asylum at Utica* (Albany, N.Y., 1856), p. 39.

49. Hawkins, "The Therapeutic Landscape," pp. 178–81.

50. Horace A. Buttolph, *Historical and Descriptive Account of the New Jersey State Lunatic Asylum* (Trenton, 1849), pp. 4, 34.

51. Hawkins, "The Therapeutic Landscape," pp. 180–81. As Ohio established its asylum for the insane, a local horticultural journal echoed Downing in asserting that the "*moral influence of gardening* places it in the foremost rank of remedial means, valuable in the treatment of insanity." "Ohio Lunatic Asylum—Gardening and Insanity," *Ohio Cultivator* 7 (Feb. 15, 1851): 59.

52. AJD to J. J. Smith, Aug. 11 and Sept. 9, 1843, Smith Papers.

53. "New Books," *Cultivator* 11 (Dec. 1844): 367.

54. AJD to A. J. Davis, Nov. 7, 1843, Davis Collection/MMA. On Davis's role in preparing the illustrations for the new edition, see Davies, "Davis and Downing," *Prophet With Honor,* p. 91.

55. AJD to J. J. Smith, Feb. 26, 1844, Smith Papers.

56. "New Books," *Cultivator* 11 (Dec. 1844): 367; "Landscape Gardening," ibid. 12 (Jan. 1845): 80, 83.

57. Quoted in "English and American Landscape Gardening," *Horticulturist* 2 (Dec. 1847): 261.

58. AJD, *The Fruits and Fruit Trees of America* . . . (New York, 1845), pp. v–vii.

59. Ibid., pp. vii, 1–9, passim.

60. See Gordon P. De Wolf, Jr., Andrew Jackson Downing and Pomology," in *Prophet With Honor,* pp. 132–33, and C. M. Hovey, "Reviews," *Magazine of Horticulture* 11 (Aug. 1845): 297.

61. See, for example, Hovey, "Reviews," pp. 297–305.

62. Henry Ward Beecher, "Review of Downing's Fruits and Fruit Trees of America," *Cultivator,* n.s. 3 (Apr. 1846): 117–19.

63. AJD, *Fruits and Fruit Trees of America,* pp. 555–56.

64. Hovey, "Reviews," pp. 304–7; S. B. Parsons, "Miscellaneous Intelligence," *Magazine of Horticulture* 11 (Aug. 1845): 308–13.

65. J. J. King, "Downing's Fruits and Fruit-Trees of America," *Cultivator,* n.s. 3 (May 1846): 149. See also Henry Ward Beecher, "Do Varieties of Fruit run out?" *Horticulturist* 1 (Oct. 1846): 181–82.

66. King, "Downing's Fruits and Fruit-Trees," p. 149; "Notices of New Publications," *Cultivator* 12 (May 1845): 155.

67. For the assessments of the *American Agriculturist* and *Broadway Journal,* see the publisher's advertisement in the "Horticulturist Advertiser," bound in vol. 3 of the *Horticulturist,* copy in Special Collections, Morris Library, University of Delaware.

68. George B. Tatum, "Introduction: The Downing Decade," in *Prophet With Honor,* pp. 28–29.

69. AJD to J. J. Smith, Dec. 29, 1847, Smith Papers.

70. See, for example, George William Curtis, "Memoir," in *Rural Essays*, p. xlvi.

Chapter 4 A Gospel of Taste

Epigraph: [Mary E. Monell], "Tribute to the Late A. J. Downing," *Knickerbocker* 40 (Oct. 1852): 354.

1. Fredrika Bremer, *The Homes of the New World: Impressions of America,* trans. Mary Howitt, 2 vols. (New York, 1854), 1:17, 2:121.

2. Ibid., 1:19–22, 253–54; Fredrika Bremer, "To the Friends of A. J. Downing," in *Rural Essays. By A. J. Downing. Edited, With a Memoir of the Author, by George William Curtis; and a Letter to his Friends, from Fredrika Bremer* (1853; reprint ed., with a new introduction by George B. Tatum, New York, 1974), pp. lxii–lxv; F. Bremer, letters dated Nov. 7, 1849 and Nov. 1849, published in Adolph B. Benson, ed., "Fredrika Bremer's Unpublished Letters to the Downings," *Scandinavian Studies and Notes* 11 (May 1930): 39, 48.

3. Bremer, *Homes of the New World,* 1:17, 19–20, 27. On Sedgwick, see Edward K. Spann, *Ideas and Politics: New York Intellectuals and Liberal Democracy, 1820–1880* (Albany, N.Y., 1972), pp. 85–91, and Richard Bushman, *The Refinement of America: Persons, Houses, Cities* (New York, 1992), pp. 432–33. For a different interpretation of Sedgwick, see Eric Homberger, *Scenes from the Life of a City: Corruption and Conscience in Old New York* (New Haven, 1994), pp. 38–39.

4. Bremer, *Homes of the New World,* 1:26, 35–38, 46, 56–65. Bremer's letters to the Downings give some indication of their extensive network of friends, acquaintences, and clients. Bremer wrote on Dec. 29, 1849, "Friends of your works and art I find everywhere." Adolph B. Benson, "Fredrika Bremer's Unpublished Letters to the Downings," *Scandinavian Studies and Notes* 11 (Aug. 1930): 77.

5. George William Curtis, "Memoir," in *Rural Essays,* pp. xxvii–xxix, xxxvii–xxxix.

6. Ibid., p. xxxviii; *Horticulturist,* n.s. 3 (July 1853): 334–37.

7. Curtis, "Memoir," *Rural Essays,* pp. xxxvi, xxxiii, xxxv.

8. Lenora Cranch Scott, *The Life and Letters of Christoper Pearse Cranch* (Boston, 1917), p. 174.

9. Bremer, "To the Friends of A. J. Downing," *Rural Essays,* p. lxv; "Col. Wilder's Eulogy on Mr. Downing," *Horticulturist* 7 (Nov. 1852): 496 (Wilder based this assessment on information provided by Calvert Vaux in a letter of Aug. 18, 1852, John Jay Smith Papers, Library Company of Philadelphia, placed on deposit at the Historical Society of Pennsylvania, Philadelphia); Curtis, "Memoir," *Rural Essays,* p. xxxvii.

10. Bushman, *Refinement of America,* p. 411.

11. Curtis, "Memoir," *Rural Essays,* pp. xxxvi–xxxix.

12. Calvert Vaux to Marshall P. Wilder, Aug. 18, 1852, Smith Papers. Vaux included handwritten recollections provided by Caroline Downing.

13. Curtis, "Memoir," *Rural Essays,* p. xlii; AJD to Luther Tucker, Apr. 19, 1849, Tucker Papers, Firestone Library, Princeton University; AJD to Robert Donaldson, Apr. 24, 1847, collection of Richard Jenrette.

14. AJD, assignment of deed to Frederick J. Betts et al., Nov. 26, 1846, liber 90, pp. 214–15, Recorder of Deeds Office, Orange County Government Center, Goshen, N.Y.; legal notice, *Newburgh Telegraph,* Dec. 17, 1846.

15. F. J. Betts and George Cornwall, assignees of AJD, and Charles Downing, deed of transfer to Nathan Reeve, May 5, 1847, liber 92, pp. 206–8, Recorder of Deeds Office, Orange County Government Center, Goshen, N.Y.

16. AJD to L. Tucker, Apr. 19, 1849, Tucker Papers.

17. *Horticulturist,* n.s. 3 (July 1853): 337; AJD to J. J. Smith, Feb. 19, 1847, printed in ibid., n.s. 6 (Jan. 1856): 23; advertisement announcing sale of Downing's greenhouse plants, *Newburgh Telegraph,* Dec. 17, 1846. See also Curtis, "Memoir," *Rural Essays,* p. xlii, which asserts that Downing's "interest in the management of the nursery, however, decreased, and he devoted himself with more energy to rural architecture and landscape gardening."

18. Bremer, *Homes of the New World,* 1:176–77, 36.

19. AJD, "A Few Words on Our Progress in Building," *Horticulturist* 6 (June 1851): 253.

20. Curtis, "Memoir," *Rural Essays,* p. xlii.

21. AJD, "Introductory," *Horticulturist* 1 (July 1846): 10; N. H., "Architecture of Country Houses," *Home Journal,* reprinted in *Horticulturist* 5 (Sept. 1850): 139.

22. U. P. Hedrick, *A History of Agriculture in the State of New York* (Albany, 1933), p. 395.

23. AJD, "On the Improvement of Country Villages," *Horticulturist* 3 (June 1849): 545.

24. AJD, "On the Moral Influence of Good Houses," *Horticulturist* 2 (Feb. 1848): 347.

25. AJD, "Improvement of Country Villages," pp. 545–48; AJD, *A Treatise on the Theory and Practice of Landscape Gardening, Adapted to North America . . .* (New York, 1841), 1844 ed., p. 80; AJD, "Rural Architecture. Hints for Improving an Ordinary Country House," *Horticulturist* 1 (July 1846): 13–15. In the 1844 edition of the *Treatise,* Downing asserted that tasteful rural dwellings would "exert an influence for the improvement in taste of every class in our community," while his essay "On Simple Rural Cottages" added that "every rural dwelling, really well designed and executed, has a strong and positive effect upon the good taste of the whole country." *Treatise,* 1844 ed., p. 378; *Horticulturist* 1 (Sept. 1846): 105. For a perceptive assessment of Downing as an architectural reformer see Clifford E. Clark, Jr., *The American Family Home, 1800–1960* (Chapel Hill, 1986).

26. Timothy Dwight, *Travels in New England and New York,* 4 vols. (1822; Cambridge, Mass., 1969), 2:346–47. Downing quoted this passage in "The Moral Influence of Good Houses," *Horticulturist* 2 (Feb. 1848): 546.

27. Quoted in Stanley K. Schultz, *Constructing Urban Culture: American Cities and City Planning, 1800–1920* (Philadelphia, 1989), p. 10.

28. S. F. Cooper, *Rural Hours* (New York, 1850), p. 384.

29. Alexis de Tocqueville, *Democracy in America,* trans. Phillips Bradley, 2 vols. (1835–40; New York, 1945), 1:6–7; T. B. F[ox], "The Education of the Public Taste," *Christian Examiner* 53 (Nov. 1852): 358–72.

30. AJD, "Hints to Rural Improvers," *Horticulturist* 3 (July 1848): 9–14. See also John F. Kasson, *Rudeness and Civility: Manners in Nineteenth-Century Urban America* (New York, 1990).

31. For a suggestive discussion of this point, as well as of Downing's belief that taste could be learned, see Kenneth L. Ames, "Downing and the Rationalization of Interior Design," in *Prophet With Honor: The Career of Andrew Jackson Downing, 1815–1852,* ed. George B. Tatum and Elisabeth Blair MacDougall (Washington, D.C., 1989), pp. 192–95.

32. See, for example, AJD, "A Few Words on Rural Architecture," *Horticulturist* 5 (July 1850): 9–11, and idem., *The Architecture of Country Houses* (New York, 1850), pp. 407–8. A classic statement of the distinction is Horace Bushnell's "Taste and Fashion," *New Englander and Yale Review* 1 (Apr. 1843): 153–68.

33. AJD, "Reviews," *Horticulturist* 1 (Nov. 1846): 231–32.

34. AJD, ibid. 6 (Dec. 1851): 567–70; AJD, "A Few Words on Rural Architecture," p. 9. Downing had published Wheeler's plan for an English cottage in *Horticulturist* 4 (Aug. 1849): 77–79, and in *The Architecture of Country Houses* (New York, 1850), pp. 298–304.

35. John Higham, *From Boundlessness to Conslidation: The Transformation of American Culture, 1848–1860* (Ann Arbor, 1969), p. 8; Bremer, *Homes of the New World,* 1:48.

36. AJD, *Treatise,* 1844 ed., p. 80.

37. AJD, "On Simple Rural Cottages," pp. 106–7.

38. Ibid., pp. 107–8. In a Sept. 2, 1846 letter to A. J. Davis, Downing explained that the vignettes illustrating the simple cottages were "defective in the details as they were hurried out before I could have time to make the proper corrections" (collection of the late Anthony N. B. Garvin).

39. AJD, "On Country Houses," *Horticulturist* 1 (Oct. 1846): 153–55.

40. A Young Architect, of New-York, "Hints on Swiss Cottages," *Horticulturist* 1 (Feb. 1847): 381.

41. AJD, *Architecture of Country Houses,* pp. 39–44, 135–39, 257–58.

42. Stuart Blumin, *The Emergence of the Middle Class: Social Experience in the American City, 1760–1900* (Cambridge, 1989), pp. 2–3, 311 n. 5.

43. AJD, *Architecture of Country Houses,* pp. 40, 257.

44. AJD, "Economy in Gardening," *Horticulturist* 3 (May 1849): 497.

45. Edgar Allan Poe, *Collected Works of Edgar Allan Poe: Tales and Sketches, 1843–1849,* ed. Thomas Ollive Mabbott et al. (Cambridge, Mass., 1978), pp. 1267–83, 1328–40; on the engendering of environment in landscape painting, see Angela Miller, *The Empire of the Eye: Landscape Representation and American Cultural Politics, 1825–1875* (Ithaca, 1993), pp. 243–88 (quotation p. 248).

46. AJD, "Review," *Horticulturist* 5 (Nov. 1850): 231.

47. See Kathryn Kish Sklar, *Catharine Beecher: A Study in American Domesticity* (New Haven, 1973), pp. 151–67, 306 n. 2.

48. "Model Cottages," *Godey's Lady's Book* 34 (Jan. 1847): 54. See also George L. Hersey, "Godey's Choice," *Journal of the Society of Architectural Historians* 18 (Oct. 1959): 104–11.

49. "Editor's Table," *Godey's Lady's Book* 23 (Aug. 1841): 93–94; Catharine E. Beecher, *A Treatise on Domestic Economy* (1841; Boston, 1843), pp. 37–38.

50. AJD, "On the Drapery of Cottages and Gardens," *Horticulturist* 3 (Feb. 1849): 353, reprinted in *Rural Essays*, p. 88–89.

51. There is no precise way of determining who read Downing's books or the *Horticulturist*. However, the authors of articles published in the monthly were overwhelmingly male, as were the correspondents whose letters or queries Downing included in each issue. One woman whose letter Downing published observed, "I don't think you have many lady correspondents to your delightful Horticulturist." Her call for "ladies in town" to enjoy the beauties of nature evoked Downing's enthusiastic endorsement. "A Letter to Ladies in Town," *Horticulturist* 4 (June 1850): 546–47.

52. AJD, *Architecture of Country Houses*, pp. 373, 403–4, 425, 457.

53. Bremer, *Homes of the New World*, 2:633.

54. AJD, "Review," *Horticulturist* 5 (Nov. 1850): 230–32.

55. Mrs. Loudon, *Gardening for Ladies; and Companion to the Flower-Garden*, ed. A. J. Downing (New York, 1843), p. iv. In preparing a single volume from Mrs. Loudon's two books, Downing eliminated several chapters from *Gardening for Ladies* that addressed the kitchen garden and that otherwise duplicated the content of the *Companion*. He also added notes to the *Companion* that, he judged, were "rendered necessary by differences resulting from our climate, &c."

56. "Review," *Horticulturist* 1 (Feb. 1847): 384–85.

57. AJD, "Review," *Horticulturist* 5 (Nov. 1850): 231.

58. AJD, "On Feminine Taste in Rural Affairs," *Horticulturist* 3 (Apr. 1849): 449–55, reprinted in *Rural Essays*, pp. 44–54. Catharine Beecher and her sister, Harriet Beecher Stowe, echoed Downing's correlation of women's health and activities in the garden. They acknowledged that "much of the instruction conveyed in the following pages is chiefly applicable to the wants and habits of those living either in the country or in such suburban vicinities as give space of ground for healthful outdoor occupation in the family service" (*The American Woman's Home: Or, Principles of Domestic Science* [New York, 1869], p. 24).

59. "Domestic Notices," *Horticulturist* 3 (Oct. 1848): 190; "The Horticultural Festival at Faneuil Hall, Boston," ibid. 3 (Nov. 1848): 234. In his account of the decorations in the hall, Downing omitted only one of the names of prominent horticulturists, his own.

Chapter 5 Reforming Rural Life

Epigraph: Luther Tucker, "Mr. Downing and the Horticulturist," *Horticulturist* 7 (Sept. 1852): 395.

1. The Buffalo Horticultural Society's resolution, adopted Aug. 26, 1846, was transmitted to Downing by Lewis F. Allen and printed in *Horticulturist* 1 (Oct. 1846): 194.

2. AJD, "Introductory," ibid. 1 (July 1846): 9–10. The owner of the *Horticulturist*, Luther Tucker, also published the *Cultivator*, so it seems likely that Downing hoped to

attract a different audience rather than compete with Tucker's own agricultural journal. See Gilbert M. Tucker, *American Agricultural Periodicals: An Historical Sketch* (Albany, N.Y., 1909).

3. AJD, "On Country Houses," *Horticulturist* 1 (Oct. 1846): 153–55.

4. "List of Agricultural Papers," *Ohio Cultivator* 6 (Feb. 1, 1850): 43; W. Miller, "Downing, Andrew Jackson," in Liberty Hyde Bailey, comp., *Cyclopedia of American Horticulture*, 4 vols. (New York, 1900), 1:501. See also "The Horticulturist, and Journal of Rural Art and Rural Taste," *Ohio Cultivator* 7 (Feb. 15, 1851): 61, which called Downing "one of the ablest writers of the age, on all branches of horticulture, landscape gardening, rural architecture, &c."

5. "The Horticulturist, and Journal of Rural Art and Rural Taste," *Cultivator*, n.s. 3 (Oct. 1846): 311.

6. Advertisement placed in *Cultivator*, n.s. 6 (June 1849): 200.

7. AJD to John Torrey, Feb. 1851, Academy of Natural Sciences, Philadelphia.

8. Letter from Edson Harkness, printed in "Domestic Notices," *Horticulturist* 2 (Aug. 1847): 96.

9. Clarence C. Cook, "The Late A. J. Downing," *New York Quarterly* 1 (Oct. 1852): 375.

10. AJD, "Cultivators—The Great Industrial Class of America," *Horticulturist* 2 (June 1848): 538, reprinted in *Rural Essays. By A. J. Downing. Edited, With a Memoir of the Author, by George William Curtis; and a Letter to His Friends, by Fredrika Bremer* (1853; reprint ed., with a new introduction by George B. Tatum, New York, 1974), pp. 385–89. Downing's figures were drawn from Edmund Burke's *Annual Report of the Commissioner of Patents* (1847), whose office was responsible for compiling agricultural statistics until the establishment of a separate Department of Agriculture in 1862. See Paul W. Gates, *The Farmer's Age: Agriculture, 1815–1860* (New York, 1960), pp. 329–37.

11. AJD, "Address," Jan. 16, 1851, in New York State Agricultural Society, *Transactions* 10 (1850): 121.

12. AJD, "Cultivators—Great Industrial Class," p. 539. See also Sally McMurry, *Families and Farmhouses in Nineteenth-Century America: Vernacular Design and Social Change* (New York, 1988), and Tamara Plakins Thornton, *Cultivating Gentlemen: The Meaning of Country Life among the Boston Elite, 1785–1860* (New Haven, 1989), p. 147.

13. AJD, "The Influence of Horticulture," *Horticulturist* 2 (July 1847): 9.

14. AJD, "Pomological Reform," ibid. 3 (Sept. 1848): 105.

15. AJD, "Pomological Gossip," ibid. 1 (Dec. 1846): 277–79. See also Marshall P. Wilder, "Col. Wilder's Eulogy on Mr. Downing," ibid. 7 (Nov. 1852): 495.

16. "The Rules of American Pomology," ibid. 2 (Dec. 1847): 273; "Rules of American Pomology," ibid. 2 (Apr. 1848): 480–81; Domestic Notices," ibid. 2 (Apr. 1848): 480–81; AJD, "Pomological Reform," ibid. 2 (Oct. 1847): 175–78. On Downing's authorship of the rules, see Wilder, "Col. Wilder's Eulogy on Mr. Downing," p. 498. Downing's *Fruits and Fruit Trees* had already been adopted as the standard for classification and nomenclature by numerous horticultural societies. See, for example, "Domestic Notices," *Horticulturist* 1 (Apr. 1847): 485.

17. AJD, "Pomological Reform," ibid. 3 (Sept. 1848): 105–9; "Domestic Notices," ibid. 3 (Nov. 1848): 246–48; *Proceedings of the Second Session of the American Pomological Congress* (Philadelphia, 1852), pp. 4–5.

18. "Domestic Notices," *Horticulturist* 4 (July 1849): 46–47; An Old Digger, "Something About the Fruit Conventions," ibid. 4 (Sept. 1849): 126–28. See also Lewis F. Allen's defense of the Buffalo organization and his rejoinder to Downing's promotion of a single national group in "Domestic Notices," ibid. 4 (Apr. 1849): 485–87.

19. "Domestic Notices," ibid. 4 (July 1849): 46–47. See also J. J. Thomas, "The New-York and Buffalo Fruit Conventions," *Cultivator*, n.s. 6 (Aug. 1849): 245.

20. An Old Digger, "Something About Fruit Conventions," pp. 126–28. Luther Tucker identified Downing as author of the "Old Digger" pieces in "Mr. Downing and the Horticulturist," p. 394.

21. "The Congress of Fruit-Growers," ibid. 4 (Nov. 1849): 226–28. See also Marshall P. Wilder et al., "Great National Convention of Fruit Growers," *Proceedings of the National Convention of Fruit Growers* 1 (1848): 5–6.

22. "American Congress of Fruit Growers," *Cultivator*, n.s. 6 (Nov. 1849): 341.

23. Wilder, "Col. Wilder's Eulogy on Mr. Downing," p. 499.

24. AJD, "The Horticultural Shows," *Horticulturist* 5 (Sept. 1850): 107.

25. AJD, "A Look About Us," ibid. 4 (Apr. 1850): 442.

26. Wilder, "Col. Wilder's Eulogy on Mr. Downing," p. 499; *Proceedings of Pomological Congress*, pp. 4–9, 14–15.

27. AJD, "Cultivators—Great Industrial Class," pp. 537–38.

28. Solon Robinson, "A Flight Through Connecticut" (1849), in *Solon Robinson: Pioneer and Agriculturist, Selected Writings*, ed. Herbert Anthony Kellar, 2 vols. (Indianapolis, 1936), 2:247–53, 307–10.

29. Solon Robinson, "A Day in Westchester County" (1850), in Kellar, *Solon Robinson*, pp. 437–40. See also John R. Stilgoe, *Borderland: Origins of the American Suburb, 1820–1939* (New Haven, 1988), pp. 69–76.

30. "Farming Life in New England," *Atlantic Monthly* 2 (Aug. 1858): 334, 336–37. See also AJD, "The National Ignorance of the Agricultural Interest," *Horticulturist* 5 (Sept. 1851): 393–96.

31. Johnston is quoted in Sarah Burns, *Pastoral Inventions: Rural Life in Nineteenth-Century American Art and Culture* (Philadelphia, 1989), p. 51.

32. See, for example, AJD, "Hints on the Construction of Farm-Houses," New York State Agricultural Society, *Transactions* 5 (1846): 234–38. This essay was also published in *Cultivator*, n.s. 3 (June 1846): 184–85.

33. Solon Robinson, "A Cheap Farm House," in Kellar, *Solon Robinson*, 1:553; H of Oneida Co., "Rural Architecture," *Cultivator*, n.s. 4 (Mar. 1847): 73–74.

34. Lewis F. Allen, *Rural Architecture: Being a Complete Description of Farm Houses, Cottages, and Out Buildings, Comprising Wood Houses, Workshops, &c. . . .* (New York, 1852), pp. 15–16.

35. T. H. Hyatt, "Monroe Co. Ag. Society—Rural Architecture, &c.," *Cultivator*, n.s. 1 (Nov. 1844): 354, and Thos. H. Hyatt, "Rural Architecture," ibid., n.s. 3 (Jan. 1846): 24–25. Hyatt's illustration and text were reprinted in *Ohio Cultivator* 2 (Oct. 1, 1846): 145–46.

36. "Plan of a Farm Cottage," New York State Agricultural Society, *Transactions* 7 (1848): 227–28. The article and plan were reprinted as "Plan of a Farm House" in *Cultivator*, n.s. 5 (Aug. 1848): 248–49, and as "Rural Architecture—Plan of a Farm House," *Ohio Cultivator* 5 (Feb. 15. 1849): 57–58. Mrs. Howard's earlier venture into domestic design was for an exceedingly modest one-and-a-half-story farm house. The principal element she carried forward and grafted to the overall frame of Downing's design was the extension to accommodate additional work space. See Matilda W. Howard to Messrs. Editors, *Cultivator* 10 (Apr. 1843): 69. See also McMurry, *Families and Farmhouses*, pp. 67–72.

37. AJD, "Hints on the Construction of Farm-Houses," pp. 234–38.

38. AJD, "How to Popularize the Taste for Planting," *Horticulturist* 7 (July 1852): 297.

39. AJD, "Our Country Villages," ibid. 5 (June 1850): 537–39.

40. AJD, "Trees, in Towns and Villages," ibid. 1 (Mar. 1847): 393–94.

41. AJD, "On the Improvement of Country Villages," ibid., 3 (June 1849): 545–47.

42. AJD, "Our Country Villages," p. 538.

43. Ibid.; AJD, "Trees, in Towns and Villages," p. 395; AJD, "On the Improvement of Country Villages," pp. 548–49.

44. AJD, "Shade-Trees in Cities," *Horticulturist* 7 (Aug. 1852): 345–47; AJD, "Trees, in Towns and Villages," pp. 395–97. Downing also published an excerpt of Susan Fenimore Cooper's *Rural Hours* under the title "A Plea for American Trees." See *Horticulturist* 4 (Sept. 1850): 136–39.

45. AJD, "Our Country Villages," p. 538; AJD, "A Reform Needed," *Horticulturist* 6 (Oct. 1851): 441–43.

46. W. H. Manning, "The History of Village Improvement in the United States," *Craftsman* 5 (Feb. 1904): 423–32. See also Hal S. Barron, *Those Who Stayed Behind: Rural Society in Nineteenth-Century New England* (Cambridge, 1984).

47. "Domestic Notices," *Horticulturist* 3 (Feb. 1849): 390.

48. Ulysses Prentiss Hedrick, *A History of Agriculture in the State of New York* (Albany, 1933), pp. 417–18.

49. AJD, "Cultivators—Great Industrial Class," pp. 539–40.

50. "Review," *Horticulturist* 1 (Dec. 1846): 282–84.

51. D. Tomlinson, "Notes on Vegetable Physiology and Agricultural Schools," ibid. 2 (Dec. 1847): 268–69.

52. "Prof. Shepard on Agricultural Schools," ibid. 3 (Aug. 1848): 85–91.

53. "Domestic Notices," ibid. 3 (May 1849): 533.

54. AJD, "Address," p. 119.

55. AJD, "A Chapter on Agricultural Schools," *Horticulturist* 4 (Dec. 1849): 250.

56. "Report of the Commissioners Appointed to Mature and Report a Plan for an Agricultural College and Experimental Farm," New York State Assembly Document Number 30 (Jan. 2, 1850), p. 2; Robinson, "A Flight Through Connecticut," Kellar, *Solon Robinson*, 2:247–53.

57. AJD, "A Chapter on Agricultural Schools," p. 251.

58. "Report of a Plan for an Agricultural College," pp. 3–14. See also "Agricultural College," *Cultivator*, n.s. 7 (Mar. 1850): 114–15.

59. "Report of a Plan for an Agricultural College," pp. 15–16.

60. Ibid., p. 16.

61. AJD, "How to Choose a Site for a Country Seat," *Horticulturist* 2 (Dec. 1847): 252.

62. "Report of a Plan for an Agricultural College," p. 17.

63. Ibid., pp. 17, 15; AJD to A. J. Davis, Dec. 3, 1849, A. J. Davis Collection, Department of Prints and Photographs, Metropolitan Museum of Art, New York.

64. AJD, "A Chapter on Agricultural Schools," p. 252.

65. AJD to A. J. Davis, Dec. 3, 1849, Dec. 11, 1849, Jan. 4, 1850, and Jan. 13, 1850, all in Davis Collection/Metropolitan Museum of Art.

66. "Domestic Notices," *Horticulturist* 4 (June 1850): 571–72; E. W. Leavenworth, "The N. Y. Agricultural School—Reasons Why the Bill was not Passed," ibid. 5 (Nov. 1850): 211–13.

67. AJD, "The National Ignorance," ibid. 6 (Sept. 1851): 394–95; AJD, "Address," p. 121. See also "Agricultural Schools," *Cultivator,* n.s. 8 (Nov. 1851): 353–54.

68. Tucker, "Mr. Downing and the Horticulturist," p. 395.

Chapter 6 Toward an American Architecture

Epigraph: AJD, "A Few Words on Our Progress in Building," *Horticulturist* 6 (June 1851): 251.

1. AJD, "On Country Houses," *Horticulturist* 1 (Oct. 1846): 153.

2. "Landscape Gardening," *Cultivator* 12 (Jan. 1845): 84.

3. George L. Hersey, "Godey's Choice," *Journal of the Society of Architectural Historians* 18 (Oct. 1959): 105.

4. See, for example, "Model Cottages," *Godey's Lady's Book* 34 (Jan. 1847): 54, 60.

5. AJD, "Reviews," *Horticulturist* 6 (Dec. 1851): 567–70.

6. AJD, "A Few Words on Rural Architecture," ibid. 5 (July 1850): 9–11.

7. AJD, "A Few Words on Building," pp. 249–50.

8. Ibid., p. 250.

9. AJD, "On Feminine Taste in Rural Affairs," *Horticulturist* 3 (Apr. 1849): 449.

10. J. Hector St. John de Crevecoeur, *Letters from an American Farmer and Sketches of Eighteenth-Century America* (New York, 1963), pp. 60–99.

11. AJD, "On Feminine Taste in Rural Affairs," pp. 449–50.

12. AJD, "A Few Words on Building," pp. 250–51.

13. Ibid., pp. 251–53.

14. George Wightwick, *Hints to Young Architects . . . With Additional Notes, and Hints to Persons About Building in the Country, by A. J. Downing* (New York, 1847), unpaginated preface; AJD, "Reviews," *Horticulturist* 2 (July 1847): 37–40.

15. Wightwick, *Hints to Young Architects,* pp. i–ii.

16. Ibid., pp. iii–xii.

17. Ibid., pp. xiii–xxiv. In response to a query from a reader, Downing reprinted much of this section of his "Hints" in "Domestic Notices," *Horticulturist* 2 (Nov. 1847): 239.

18. Wightwick, *Hints to Young Architects*, pp. xxv–xxxi.

19. This enumeration of architectural designs does not include descriptive visits to estates, such as Montgomery Place, which focused on the landscape more than the architecture and which were different in intent from the designs Downing presented. "A Visit to Montgomery Place," *Horticulturist* 2 (Oct. 1847): 153–60.

20. See "Design for a Rural Church," ibid. 2 (Mar. 1848): 433–34; "A Word or Two About Rural Churches," ibid. 4 (Sept. 1849): 120–21; "Hints and Designs for Rustic Buildings," ibid. 2 (Feb. 1848): 363–65; "A Few Words on Rustic Arbours," ibid. 4 (Jan. 1850): 320–21; "How To Build Ice-Houses," ibid. 1 (Dec. 1846): 249–53; and the frontispiece that accompanied Downing's review of Barnard's *School Architecture*, in ibid. 3 (Oct. 1848): 182–84. The two designs for schoolhouses, one bracketed, one Romanesque, were prepared by a "Mr. Teft, an architect of Providence." Downing described them as "especially worthy of commendation, as uniting rural beauty, and expression of purpose, with convenient accommodation in a high degree."

21. The cottage designs appeared in the *Horticulturist* 1 (Sept. 1846): 105–8; 1 (Feb. 1847): 381–82; 2 (July 1847): 19–20; 2 (Aug. 1847): 66–67; 2 (Dec. 1847): 272–73; 2 (Apr. 1848): 471–72; 3 (July 1848): 47; 3 (Dec. 1848): 287; 3 (May 1849): 521–22; and 4 (Aug. 1849): 77–79. The cottage villas were published in ibid. 1 (Mar. 1847): 413–14; 4 (Nov. 1849): 225; and 4 (Feb. 1850): 373–75. The farmhouse appeared in ibid. 1 (Oct. 1846): 153–55. The country houses were published in ibid. 1 (July 1846): 13–15; 4 (Dec. 1849): 263–64; 4 (Mar. 1850): 426; and 4 (June 1850): 563. The villas were included in ibid. 2 (Jan. 1848): 328; 2 (June 1848): 554–56; 3 (Jan. 1849): 334; 3 (Mar. 1849): 435; 3 (Apr. 1849): 483–84; 3 (June 1849): 560–61; 4 (July 1849): 28–29; and 4 (May 1850): 516–18. The mansion was published in ibid. 4 (Apr. 1850): 479–81.

22. These were the design for a country house, ibid. 4 (Mar. 1850): 426, which was published as Design XV in *The Architecture of Country Houses* (New York, 1850), and the farmhouse, published as Design for a Simple Country House, *Horticulturist* 1 (Oct. 1846), which appeared as fig. 142 on p. 316 of *Architecture of Country Houses*. The assertion that a country house was less pretentious than a villa is based on Downing's description of such a dwelling as possessing "a somewhat more rustic expression." AJD, *Architecture of Country Houses*, p. 276.

23. *Horticulturist* 3 (Jan. 1849): 334; 4 (Nov. 1849): 225; and 4 (Aug. 1849): 77–79.

24. The cottages appeared in ibid. 1 (July 1846), 1 (Sept. 1846), 2 (July 1847), 2 (Dec. 1847), 2 (Apr. 1848), and 3 (May 1849); the cottage villa in 4 (Feb. 1850); the country houses in 4 (Dec. 1849) and 4 (Mar. 1850); and the villas in 3 (Apr. 1849) and 4 (July 1849).

25. Ibid. 1 (Oct. 1846): 153–55; 1 (Mar. 1847): 413–14; and 4 (Apr. 1850): 479–81.

26. Jane B. Davies, "Davis and Downing: Collaborators in the Picturesque," in *Prophet With Honor: The Career of Andrew Jackson Downing, 1815–1852*, ed. George B. Tatum and Elisabeth Blair MacDougall (Washington, D.C., 1989), pp. 93–94.

27. *Horticulturist* 1 (Feb. 1847): 381–82; 3 (Dec. 1848): 287; 4 (May 1850): 516–18; and 4 (June 1850): 563.

28. The four articles presenting English designs for residences included "On the English Rural Cottage," ibid. 2 (Aug. 1847): 66–67; "Design for a Suburban Villa," by E. B. Lamb, from Loudon's *Supplement*, ibid. 2 (Jan. 1848): 328; "A Villa in the Anglo-

Italian Style," again derived from Loudon, ibid. 2 (June 1848): 554–56; and an article describing a small cottage by a Mr. Jackson, originally published in the *London Art Union,* ibid. 3 (July 1848): 47. The two Wheeler plans were "Design for a Villa in the Tudor Style," ibid. 3 (June 1849): 560–61, and "Design and Description of an English Cottage," ibid. 4 (Aug. 1849): 77–79.

29. AJD, "On Simple Rural Cottages," ibid. 1 (Sept. 1846): 105; AJD to A. J. Davis, Jan. 27, 1848, A. J. Davis Collection, Department of Prints and Photographs, Metropolitan Museum of Art, New York (hereafter Davis Collection/MMA). Shortly after the publication of *Cottage Residences,* Downing informed J. J. Smith, "The booksellers all say that now something of a simple character is wanted, on farm buildings, &c." AJD to J. J. Smith, Oct. 21, 1842, printed in "Downing's Landscape Gardening," *Horticulturist,* n.s. 8 (Sept. 1858): 412.

30. AJD, *Architecture of Country Houses,* p. 163.

31. The ten designs that appeared first in the *Horticulturist* were Design I, in 1 (Sept. 1846); Design V, 1 (Sept. 1846); Design X, 3 (Dec. 1848); Design XI, 3 (May 1849); Design XV, 4 (Mar. 1850); Design XXII, 3 (Jan. 1849); Design XXIII, 4 (Nov. 1849); Design XXIV, 4 (Aug. 1849); Design XXV, 4 (Dec. 1849); and Design XXVI, 4 (Feb. 1849). The three other designs from the *Horticulturist* that Downing used were Davis's simple country house (to illustrate the exterior of a southern country house), Penchard's design for a Swiss cottage, and W. A. Nesfield's Anglo-Italian villa. Compare *Horticulturist* 1 (Oct. 1846): 153–55; 3 (Dec. 1848): 287; and 2 (June 1848): 554–56, respectively, with *Architecture of Country Houses,* pp. 316, 123–28, 291.

32. AJD to Robert Donaldson, July 26, 1847, collection of Richard Jenrette; AJD to A. J. Davis, Jan. 27, 1848, Davis Collection/MMA.

33. AJD to A. J. Davis, Jan. 27, 1848, Davis Collection/MMA; Davies, "Davis and Downing," p. 119.

34. AJD, editorial note appended to W. H. Scott, "Notes on the Architecture and Gardening of the Eastern States," *Horticulturist* 3 (Jan. 1849): 326.

35. AJD to A. J. Davis, Jan. 27, 1848, Davis Collection/MMA.

36. AJD to A. J. Davis, May 21, 1849, Davis Collection/MMA.

37. AJD to A. J. Davis, Monday 14 [Aug. 14, 1848], Davis Collection/MMA.

38. AJD to A. J. Davis, Jan. 27, 1848, Davis Collection/MMA; Davies, "Davis and Downing," p. 119.

39. AJD, editorial note, Scott, "Notes on Architecture and Gardening," p. 326.

40. "Domestic Notices," *Horticulturist* 4 (Nov. 1849): 247.

41. AJD to J. J. Smith, Mar. 17, 1850, printed in "Downing's Familiar Letters.—No. III," ibid., n.s. 6 (Apr. 1856): 160.

42. AJD to A. J. Davis, Apr. 12, 1850, Davis Collection/MMA.

43. AJD, *Architecture of Country Houses,* pp. xix–xx.

44. Ibid., pp. xix–xx, 1, 24, and, for references to readers, 10, 281, 378.

45. Ibid., pp. 3–11.

46. Caroline Downing memorandum, Aug. 1852, in John Jay Smith Papers, Library Company of Philadelphia, placed on deposit at the Historical Society of Pennsylvania, Philadelphia; Roger B. Stein, *John Ruskin and Aesthetic Thought in America, 1840–1900* (Cambridge, Mass., 1967), pp. 47–56.

47. AJD, *Architecture of Country Houses,* pp. 28, 38. See also Clifford E. Clark, Jr., *The American Family Home, 1800–1960* (Chapel Hill, 1986).

48. AJD, *Architecture of Country Houses,* pp. 35–36.

49. For example, in 1850 Downing published a design that called for woodwork in the two principal rooms to be "grained and varnished like oak." He also gave readers instructions for staining pine so that it would appear "strikingly like the plainer portions of oak or black walnut." AJD, *Architecture of Country Houses,* pp. 109, 183, 367.

50. Ibid., pp. 383–84, 398.

51. Ibid., pp. 24–25, 30–38, 40.

52. Ibid., pp. 42–43, 51, 71.

53. Ibid., pp. 78, 87, 97, 109, 117–18. Downing had suggested the idea of the arbor-veranda in January 1846, when he wrote, "Let a *veranda* be added, which may be adorned, not so much with expensive pillars, as with beautiful and flagrant [sic] climbing plants." "Hints on the Construction of Farm-Houses," New York State Agricultural Society, *Transactions* 5 (1846): 234–38.

54. AJD, *Architecture of Country Houses,* pp. 135–42.

55. Ibid., pp. 156–59.

56. Ibid., pp. 257–63.

57. Ibid., pp. 263–65, 275–76. Downing also explained the importance of adaptation in his discussion of specific designs. See pp. 304–5, 321–22, 345.

58. Ibid., pp. 267–70.

59. Downing's designs were numbers XIX, XXI, XXV, XXVI, XXVIII, XXXI, and XXXII. Davis contributed designs XXII, XXIII, XXX, and fig. 142, a variation on design XXVI; Wheeler's were XXIV and XXIX, West's XX, and Upjohn's XXVII; Davies, "Davis and Downing," pp. 121–22.

60. These were designs XIX, XXIV, XXVI (bracketed), and XXIII and XXVIII (Rural Gothic). A. J. Davis's design for Lewis B. Brown's small villa in the "classical manner" (XXII) and Downing's villa for a picturesque site (XXXII) have also been included in the counting of bracketed dwellings.

61. Designs XXI and XXVII. Downing's description of the King villa is in *Architecture of Country Houses,* pp. 317–18.

62. Ibid., p. 280. These were designs XX (Norman), XXV and XXX (Pointed Gothic), and XXXII (Romanesque). Design XXIX, Wheeler's "American Country House of the first class," has also been included in the enumeration of Pointed Gothic designs.

Downing considered the Romanesque "a rich field of study for the architect." He expressed hope that "a student of genius might, from a judicious study of it, elicit ideas that could be more easily and harmoniously wrought into a new domestic architecture of a classical character than those from any other transatlantic source" (ibid., pp. 354–55). That, of course, is precisely what Henry Hobson Richardson did later in the nineteenth century, though there is no evidence he was influenced by Downing.

63. Ibid., pp. 364–76.

64. Ibid., pp. 376–97. See also Arthur Channing Downs, Jr., "Andrew Jackson Down-

ing and the American Bathroom," *Historic Preservation* 23 (Jan.–Mar. 1971): 30–35.

65. AJD, *Architecture of Country Houses*, pp. 406–60; Kenneth L. Ames, "Downing and the Rationalization of Interior Design," in *Prophet With Honor*, pp. 191–217. N. H. Eggleston described Downing's chapters on interiors and furnishings as a significant innovation. "As Mr. Downing has shown the man of slender means how he may have a tasteful cottage, architecturally considered, so here he shows him that he can furnish it properly and even attractively without any outlay of money beyond his ability." See Eggleston's review, published in the *New-Englander*, reprinted in *Cultivator*, n.s. 8 (May 1851): 167–69.

66. "Literary Notices," *Harper's New Monthly Magazine* 1 (Sept. 1850): 573–74.

67. N. H., "Architecture of Country Houses," *Home Journal*, reprinted in *Horticulturist* 5 (Sept. 1850): 139–41. Downing was in England at the time this issue of the *Horticulturist* went to press, and the review was inserted by its publisher, Luther Tucker.

68. "Rural Architecture. Downing's Country Houses," *Cultivator*, n.s. 7 (Sept. 1850): 305–7.

69. "Short Reviews and Notices of Books," *Methodist Quarterly Review* 32 (Oct. 1850): 662.

70. N. H., "Architecture of Country Houses," p. 140.

71. "The Architecture of Country Houses," *Literary World* 7 (Aug. 3, 1850): 91.

72. Ibid.; unpaginated advertisement, "Horticultural Advertiser," *Horticulturist* 6 (Apr. 1851), copy in Special Collections Division, Morris Library, University of Delaware. See also "Domestic Notices," *Horticulturist* 6 (Oct. 1851): 487.

73. *Ohio Cultivator* 7 (May 1, 1851): 136.

74. Charles B. Wood III, "The New 'Pattern Books' and the Role of the Agricultural Press," in *Prophet With Honor*, p. 166; Henry-Russell Hitchcock, *American Architectural Books: A List of Books, Portfolios, and Pamphlets on Architecture and Related Subjects Published in America Before 1895* (Minneapolis, 1962), p. 31.

75. Calvert Vaux to Marshall P. Wilder, Aug. 18, 1852, Smith Papers.

76. AJD to A. J. Davis, Jan. 13, 1850, Apr. 4, 1850, Davis Collection/MMA; Davies, "Davis and Downing," pp. 92–93.

77. AJD to A. J. Davis, Jan. 27, 1848, Davis Collection/MMA.

78. Davies, "Davis and Downing," p. 122.

Chapter 7 Downing & Vaux, Architects

Epigraph: Calvert Vaux, *Villas and Cottages. A Series of Designs Prepared for Execution in the United States* (New York, 1857), p. v.

1. AJD to A. J. Davis, July 3, 1850, A. J. Davis Collection, Department of Prints and Photographs, Metropolitan Museum of Art, New York (hereafter Davis Collection/MMA).

2. AJD to Luther Tucker, June 28, 1850, Tucker Papers, Firestone Library, Princeton University.

3. C. Vaux to Marshall P. Wilder, Aug. 18, 1852, John Jay Smith Papers, Library

Company of Philadelphia, placed on deposit at the Historical Society of Pennsylvania, Philadelphia.

4. "Mr. Downing's Letters From England" appeared in *Horticulturist* 5 (Sept. 1850): 117–23, (Oct. 1850): 153–60, (Nov. 1850): 217–24, (Dec. 1850): 264–71, and ibid. 6 (Jan. 1851): 36–41, (Feb. 1851): 83–86, (Mar. 1851): 137–41, and (June 1851): 281–86. The letters were reprinted in *Rural Essays. By A. J. Downing. Edited, With a Memoir of the Author, by George William Curtis; and a Letter to His Friends, by Fredrika Bremer* (1853; reprint ed. with a new introduction by George B. Tatum, New York, 1974), and the descriptions of the places mentioned in this paragraph appear on pp. 499–509 and 532–37 of that volume. All subsequent citations to Downing's letters from England will refer to *Rural Essays*.

Marshall P. Wilder identified the Earl of Hardwicke in "Col. Wilder's Eulogy on Mr. Downing," *Horticulturist* 7 (Nov. 1852): 495.

5. AJD, *Rural Essays*, pp. 483, 512–31, 538–40.

6. Ibid., pp. 485–91, 517–21.

7. Ibid., pp. 543, 533.

8. Ibid., p. 481.

9. AJD, "A Talk About Public Parks and Gardens," *Horticulturist* 3 (Oct. 1848): 153–56.

10. AJD, *Rural Essays*, pp. 548–49.

11. Francis R. Kowsky generously provided this information on Anthony Seddon.

12. C. Vaux to M. P. Wilder, Aug. 18, 1852, Smith Papers.

13. The thirteen include: H. E. Kendall's design for a rural schoolhouse, *Horticulturist* 5 (July 1850); a Mr. Wild's design for a small inn, reprinted from J. C. Loudon's *Architectural Supplement*, ibid. (Aug. 1850); a Tudor suburban residence, reprinted from *Brown's Domestic Architecture*, (Sept. 1850); the entrance to the Derby Arboretum (Dec. 1850); a Rural Gothic church at Bracknell, ibid. 6 (May 1851); a village schoolhouse (Oct. 1851); Horace Walpole's Strawberry Hill (Nov. 1851); the Independent Chapel, Boston, England, designed by Stephen Lewis (Dec. 1851); Hayes Farm, the birthplace of Sir Walter Raleigh, ibid. 7 (Feb. 1852); a design for a free school (Mar. 1852); the Palm House at Kew (Apr. 1852); an English national schoolhouse (June 1852); and a Lombard church (Aug. 1852). Several of these—the entrance to the Derby Arboretum, Hayes Farm, and the Palm House at Kew—were subjects Downing addressed in his letters and can be thought of as illustrations of those essays. The account of Messina was published in the May 1852 issue.

14. Among the excerpts published in the *Horticulturist* were S. H., "The Essence of the Fine Arts," 6 (Jan. 1851): 23–29; H. T. Braithewaite, "A Historical Essay on Taste," 6 (Feb. 1851): 73–78; H. Noel Humphreys, "Notes on Decorative Gardening—Architectural Terraces," 6 (Mar. 1851): 134–37; John M. Ashley, "The Scientific History of a Plant," 6 (June 1851): 267–76; S. H., "On Expression in Architecture," 6 (Sept. 1851): 421–24, and (Dec. 1851): 502–7; and S. H., "The Beautiful in Art," 6 (Oct. 1851): 463–68.

15. The designs for Romanesque and Lombard churches were published in *Horticulturist* 6 (Dec. 1851) and 7 (Aug. 1852); for Downing's intent in presenting designs for schools and churches see "Domestic Notices," ibid. 7 (Jan. 1852): 48.

16. See AJD, "A Country Residence in the Elizabethan Style," ibid. 5 (Sept. 1850): 116–17.

17. AJD, "Hints for Country Houses," ibid. 7 (Feb. 1852): 62.

18. AJD, "Strawberry Hill—A Lesson in Taste," ibid. 6 (Nov. 1851): 510–11.

19. Vaux, *Villas and Cottages*, p. 35.

20. See Constance M. Greiff, *John Notman, Architect* (Philadelphia, 1979); William H. Pierson, Jr., *American Buildings and Their Architects: Technology and the Picturesque, The Corporate and Early Gothic Styles* (Garden City, N.Y., 1978), pp. 159–61; Jill Allibone, "Wheeler, Gervase," *Macmillan Encyclopedia of Architects,* ed. Adolf K. Placzek et al., 4 vols. (New York, 1982), 4:388–89.

21. Pierson, *American Buildings and Their Architects,* pp. 215–19.

22. See Downing's comments in "A Few Words on Our Progress in Building," *Horticulturist* 6 (June 1851): 251.

23. See Jane B. Davies, "Davis and Downing: Collaborators in the Picturesque," in *Prophet With Honor: The Career of Andrew Jackson Downing, 1815–1852,* ed. George B. Tatum and Elisabeth Blair MacDougall (Washington, D.C., 1989), p. 122.

24. Vaux, *Villas and Cottages*, p. 18.

25. William Alex and George B. Tatum, *Calvert Vaux: Architect and Planner* (New York, 1994), pp. 1–31, offers the best summary of Vaux's career. See also Dennis Steadman Francis and Joy M. Kestenbaum, "Vaux, Calvert," in *Macmillan Encyclopedia of Architects,* 4:303–4. Vaux's principal writings, in addition to *Villas and Cottages,* include "Should A Republic Encourage the Arts?," *Horticulturist* 7 (Feb. 1852): 73–77, "American Architecture," ibid., n.s. 3 (Apr. 1853): 168–72, and "Hints for Country House Builders," *Harper's New Monthly Magazine* 11 (Nov. 1855): 763–78.

26. C. C., "A Visit to the House and Garden of the Late A. J. Downing," *Horticulturist,* n.s. 3 (Jan. 1853): 21–22.

27. Vaux, *Villas and Cottages*, p. 61.

28. Benson J. Lossing, *Vassar College and its Founder* (New York, 1867), p. 63.

29. "Domestic Notices," *Horticulturist* 6 (Feb. 1851): 98, which was reprinted as "Ornamental Carriage House and Stable," *Cultivator,* n.s. 8 (July 1851): 241; AJD, *Cottage Residences; Or, A Series of Designs for Rural Cottages and Cottage Villas, and their Gardens and Grounds. Adapted to North America . . .* (New York, 1842), 1852 ed., pp. 186–87. See also Harvey K. Flad, "Matthew Vassar's Springside: '. . . the hand of Art, when guided by Taste,'" in *Prophet With Honor,* pp. 219–57, and Robert M. Toole, "Springside: A. J. Downing's only extant garden," *Journal of Garden History* 9 (Jan.–Mar. 1989): 20–39.

30. Downing and Vaux also prepared plans for a stone porter's lodge, which may well have been intended as the entrance to the cemetery originally proposed for the site. See Flad, "Matthew Vassar's Springside," p. 241.

31. AJD, *The Architecture of Country Houses* (New York, 1850), pp. 83–92.

32. Vaux, *Villas and Cottages*, p. 277.

33. Ibid., pp. 277–80; Flad, "Matthew Vassar's Springside," pp. 244–46, 253.

34. Vaux, *Villas and Cottages*, pp. 277–78; Flad, "Matthew Vassar's Springside," pp. 246–47.

35. *Poughkeepsie Eagle,* June 12, 1852, quoted in Flad, "Matthew Vassar's Spring-side," p. 243.

36. Vaux, *Villas and Cottages,* p. 278.

37. Fredrika Bremer, *The Homes of the New World: Impressions of America,* trans. Mary Howitt, 2 vols. (New York, 1854), 2:628.

38. AJD to J. J. Smith, Oct. 30, 1851, reprinted in "Downing's Familiar Letters.— No. III," *Horticulturist,* n.s. 6 (Apr. 1856): 161.

39. AJD to J. J. Smith, Mar. 29, 1852, in ibid., p. 162. See also Francis R. Kowsky, *Frederick Clarke Withers and the Progress of the Gothic Revival in America after 1850* (Middletown, Conn., 1980).

40. Vaux, *Villas and Cottages,* pp. 187–90.

41. Ibid., pp. 213–18. Vaux also included a plan for the porch, on p. 72, and a sketch of the entrance gate, on p. 274.

42. Ibid., pp. 221–24.

43. Ibid., pp. 241–44.

44. Ibid., pp. 307–8; George Bishop Tatum, "Andrew Jackson Downing: Arbiter of American Taste, 1815–1852," Ph.D. diss., Princeton University, 1950, p. 195.

45. Vaux, *Villas and Cottages,* pp. 227–28, 311–12, 317–18.

46. Ibid., pp. 190, 217–18, 223–24.

47. Ibid., p. iv.

48. Alex and Tatum, *Calvert Vaux,* pp. 5, 52–53.

49. C. Vaux to M. P. Wilder, Aug. 18, 1852, Smith Papers.

50. Ibid.

51. AJD, "A Cottage for a Country Clergyman," *Horticulturist* 6 (July 1851): 313–16.

52. See, for example, A. S. B. Culbertson to AJD, Jan. 7, 1847; AJD to A. J. Davis, Jan. 20, 1847; A. S. B. Culbertson to A. J. Davis, Mar. 2, 1847, all in Davis Collection/MMA.

53. Bremer, *Homes of the New World,* 1:286–88.

54. A. J. Davis offered to adapt existing designs to meet the needs of prospective clients, while Henry W. Cleaveland and the Backus Brothers offered to provide "working drawings and printed specifications" that would enable individuals to erect the designs they published in *Village and Farm Cottages* (New York, 1856).

55. Vaux, *Villas and Cottages,* p. 63.

56. Wilder, "Col. Wilder's Eulogy on Mr. Downing," p. 498. Information on the Dudley Observator, from *Annals of the Dudley Observatory* (Albany, N.Y., 1866), graciously provided by Francis R. Kowsky.

57. Benjamin Silliman and C. R. Goodrich, ed., *The World of Science, Art, and Industry Illustrated* (New York, 1854), p. 2.

58. C. Vaux to M. P. Wilder, Aug. 18, 1852, Smith Papers.

59. Ibid.

60. According to Vaux, at the time of his death Downing was "on his way to Newport, to superintend the execution of Mr. Parish's villa." Downing also made a monthly trip to Washington, D.C. to oversee construction of his plan for the public grounds. See Vaux, *Villas and Cottages,* p. v, and chapter 8 in this volume.

61. C. Vaux, "American Architecture," *Horticulturist* 8 (Apr. 1853): 169.

Chapter 8 The Metropolitan Landscape

Epigraph: Calvert Vaux to Marshall P. Wilder, Aug. 18, 1852, John Jay Smith Papers, Library Company of Philadelphia, placed on deposit at the Historical Society of Pennsylvania, Philadelphia (hereafter cited as Smith Papers).

1. David Schuyler, *The New Urban Landscape: The Redefinition of City Form in Nineteenth-Century America* (Baltimore, 1986), pp. 45–47; Fredrika Bremer, *The Homes of the New World: Impressions of America*, trans. Mary Howitt, 2 vols. (New York, 1854), 1:15.

2. Schuyler, *New Urban Landscape*, pp. 37–56; AJD, "Public Cemeteries and Public Gardens," *Horticulturist* 4 (July 1849): 9–12.

3. Ralph Foster Weld, *Brooklyn Village, 1816–1834* (New York, 1938), pp. 15–28; Henry R. Stiles, *A History of the City of Brooklyn, Including the Old Town and Village of Brooklyn, the Town of Bushwick, and the Village and City of Williamsburgh*, 3 vols. (Brooklyn, 1867–70).

4. Green-Wood Cemetery, *Exposition of the Plan and Objects of the Green-Wood Cemetery, An Incorporated Trust Chartered by the Legislature of the State of New York* (New York, 1839); Nehemiah Cleaveland, *Green-Wood Illustrated. In Highly Finished Line Engravings, From Drawings Taken on the Spot. By James Smillie. With Descriptive Notices by Nehemiah Cleaveland* (New York, 1847), pp. 13–14.

5. AJD, "Public Cemeteries and Public Gardens," pp. 9–10.

6. Ibid., pp. 11–12.

7. AJD to A. J. Davis, Jan. 13, 1850, A. J. Davis Collection, Department of Prints and Photographs, Metropolitan Museum of Art, New York. The likelihood that Davis prepared the finished drawings from Downing's sketches is suggested in the same letter, in which Downing explained that he did not expect to be paid for the designs of the chapel or entrance gate. But from his fees as landscape gardener, Downing added, he would "be glad always to pay in proportion—for you know I often oblige you to do my work at low prices."

8. [S. D. Walker], *Rural Cemetery and Public Walk* (Baltimore, 1835), pp. 6–7 (originally published in the *Baltimore American* in 1833).

9. AJD, "Additional Notes on the Progress of Gardening in the United States," *Gardener's Magazine* 17 (Mar. 1841): 146–47.

10. AJD, "Public Cemeteries and Public Gardens," p. 10; AJD, "A Talk About Public Parks and Gardens," *Horticulturist* 3 (Oct. 1848): 157.

11. AJD, "A Talk About Public Parks and Gardens," p. 158.

12. Joseph Henry, "Locked Book" diary, Nov. 25, 1850; AJD to Joseph Henry, June 14, 1851, Joseph Henry Papers, Smithsonian Institution Archives, Washington, D.C. (hereafter cited as Henry Papers). See also David Schuyler, "The Washington Park and Downing's Legacy to Public Landscape Design," in *Prophet With Honor: The Career of Andrew Jackson Downing, 1815–1852*, ed. George B. Tatum and Elisabeth Blair

MacDougall (Washington, D.C., 1989), pp. 291–311; Wilcomb E. Washburn, "Vision of Life for the Mall," *AIA Journal* 47 (Mar. 1967): 52–59; John W. Reps, "Romantic Planning in a Baroque City: Downing and the Washington Mall," *Landscape* 16 (spring 1967): 6–11; and Therese O'Malley, "'A Public Museum of Trees': Mid-Nineteenth Century Plans for the Mall," in *The Mall in Washington, 1791–1991*, ed. Richard Longstreth (Washington, D.C. 1991), pp. 61–76.

13. Smithsonian Institution, "Annual Report of the Board of Regents of the Smithsonian Institution," in *Senate Executive Documents*, 29th Cong., 2d sess., doc. 211, p. 29; Christian Hines, quoted in John Clagett Proctor, "The Tragic Death of Andrew Jackson Downing and the Monument to His Memory," *Records of the Columbia Historical Society* 27 (1925): 249–50. See also Pamela Scott, "'This Vast Empire': The Iconography of the Mall, 1791–1848," in Longstreth, *The Mall in Washington*, pp. 37–58.

14. Henry, "Locked Book" diary, Nov. 25, 1850, Henry Papers; "Fifth Annual Report of the Board of Regents of the Smithsonian Institution," in *Senate Executive Documents*, 32d Cong., special sess., misc. report 1, p. 63; [A. H. Stuart], "Report of the Secretary of the Interior," *Senate Executive Documents*, 32d Cong. 1st sess., exec. doc. 1, pp. 509–10.

15. AJD, "Explanatory Notes to Accompany the Plan for Improving the Public Grounds at Washington," Records of the Commissioners of Public Buildings, Letters Received, vol. 32, letter 3158 1/2, National Archives and Records Administration, Washington, D.C. This report is printed in W. E. Washburn, "Vision of Life for the Mall."

16. Ibid.

17. Ibid.; AJD, "The New-York Park," *Horticulturist* 6 (Aug. 1851): 346.

18. M. Fillmore, notation added to Downing's plan, National Archives and Records Administration; "Fifth Annual Report of Board of Regents of Smithsonian," p. 63; Schuyler, "The Washington Park and Downing's Legacy," p. 294.

One prominent observer of the Washington scene, Dorothea Dix, denounced Downing as a "landscape manufacturer" and described the sheet of water proposed for the eastern end of the public grounds as "Downing's Death Hole." "All experience shows the certain mischief resulting from such festering pools of rank foul waters," she warned. See D. Dix to Millard Fillmore, Apr. 5, [1852], in *The Lady and the President: The Letters of Dorothea Dix and Millard Fillmore*, ed. Charles M. Snyder (Lexington, Ky., 1975), pp. 128–31. See also Jefferson Davis's more favorable assessment of the plan in his letter to W. W. Corcoran of Mar. 16, 1851, in *The Papers of Jefferson Davis*, vol. 4, *1849–1852*, ed. Lynda Lasswell Crist et al. (Baton Rouge, 1983), pp. 175–76.

19. Alexis de Tocqueville, *Democracy in America*, ed. Phillips Bradley, 2 vols. (1835–40; New York, 1945), 1:299–300; George W. Pierson, *Tocqueville and Beaumont in America* (New York, 1938), p. 667. Downing quoted Tocqueville in "The Influence of Horticulture."

20. AJD to J. Henry, June 14, 1851, Henry Papers; AJD to Millard Fillmore, June 12, 1851, Records of the Commissioneers of Public Buildings, vol. 32, letter 3196, Na-

tional Archives; *Congressional Globe,* 32nd Cong., 2nd sess., Aug. 26, 1852, p. 2374, Mar. 24, 1852, p. 853.

21. AJD to J. Henry, June 14, 1851, Henry Papers; J. Henry to W. W. Corcoran, June 11, 1851, W. W. Corcoran Papers, Manuscript Division, Library of Congress, Washington, D.C.; A. H. Stuart to William Easby, July 18, 1851, Records of the Commissioners of Public Buildings, Letters Received, vol. 32, letter 3204, National Archives; Henry, "Locked Book" diary, July 1, 1851.

Downing was not alone in attracting Easby's censure. According to Robert Mills's biographer, Rhodri Windsor Liscombe, "Easby unremittingly harassed Mills," who was supervising the extension of the U. S. Patent Office building at the same time Downing was directing preliminary improvements to the public grounds. R. W. Liscombe, *Altogether American: Robert Mills, Architect and Engineer, 1781–1855* (New York, 1994), pp. 287–88.

22. AJD to J. Henry, Feb. 23, 1852, Henry Papers.

23. *Congressional Globe,* 32nd Cong. 2nd sess., Mar. 24, 1852, pp. 854–56, Aug. 26, 1852, pp. 2374–76; Constance McLaughlin Green, *Washington: Village and Capital, 1800–1878* (Princeton, N.J., 1962), p. 200.

24. C. Vaux to M. P. Wilder, Aug. 18, 1852, Smith Papers.

25. *Congressional Globe,* 32nd Cong., 2nd sess., Aug. 26, 1852, p. 2375.

26. "The Downing Monument," *Horticulturist,* n.s. 6 (Nov. 1856): 491; Proctor, "Tragic Death of Andrew Jackson Downing."

27. [A. B. Mullett], *Report of the Supervising Architect of the Treasury,* Oct. 31, 1868, p. 11; Green, *Washington: Village and Capital,* pp. 346–54, 400.

28. C. Vaux to M. P. Wilder, Aug. 18, 1852, Smith Papers.

29. AJD, "The New-York Park," pp. 345–49.

30. Ibid.

31. Bremer, *Homes of the New World,* 2:628–31.

32. AJD, "The New-York Park," pp. 345–49; see also Eric Homberger, *Scenes from the Life of a City: Corruption and Conscience in Old New York* (New Haven, 1994), pp. 232–39.

33. AJD, "Hints to Rural Improvers," *Horticulturist* 3 (July 1848): 9–10.

34. AJD, "On the Mistakes of Citizens in Country Life," ibid. 3 (Jan. 1849): 309.

35. See Schuyler, *New Urban Landscape,* pp. 149–53, and Henry C. Binford, *The First Suburbs: Residential Communities on the Boston Periphery, 1815–1860* (Chicago, 1985).

36. AJD, "Our Country Villages," *Horticulturist* 4 (June 1850): 539–40.

37. See the "Map of Village Lots and Cottage Sites at Dearman, Westchester Co., . . .," Archives of the Hudson River Museum, Yonkers, N.Y. I am grateful to John Zukowsky for bringing this map to my attention.

38. AJD, "Our Country Villages," pp. 539–40.

39. [G. W. Curtis], "Editor's Easy Chair," *Harper's New Monthly Magazine* 7 (June 1853): 129–30.

40. H. W. S. Cleveland, "Landscape Gardening," *Christian Examiner* 58 (May 1855): 389; Henry W. Cleaveland, William Backus, and Samuel D. Backus, *Village and Farm*

Cottages, reprint ed., with a new introduction by David Schuyler (1856; Watkins Glen, N.Y., 1982), pp. 24–25.

41. AJD, "Our Country Villages," p. 540.

42. Ibid. The idea of locating a community around a park was not new: the town of Birkenhead, outside Liverpool, had paid for the cost of its park through the sale of adjoining lots, and John Nash's Regent's Park, in London, contained a series of residential terraces. But Downing's application of this idea of the suburb may well have been novel. See [Frederick Law Olmsted], *Walks and Talks of an American Farmer in England,* 2 vols. (New York, 1852), 1:78–83.

43. AJD, "Our Country Villages," pp. 540–41.

44. Ibid.

45. AJD, "Domestic Notices. Suburban Embellishments," *Horticulturist* 6 (Feb. 1851): 98.

46. "Llewellyn Park. Country Homes for City People. A Private Park of 750 Acres; 10 Miles of Drives and Walks; A 'Ramble' of 50 Acres; Only 60 Minutes from New York," undated real estate prospectus, copy in the Frederick Law Olmsted Papers, Manuscript Division, Library of Congress, Washington, D.C.; Howard Daniels, "Villa Parks," *Horticulturist,* n.s. 8 (Nov. 1858): 495–96; "Landscape-Gardening. Llewellyn Park," *Crayon* 4 (Aug. 1857): 248; "Rural Taste in North America," *Christian Examiner* 69 (Nov. 1860): 350. See also Jane B. Davies, "Llewellyn Park in West Orange, New Jersey," *Antiques* 107 (Jan. 1975): 142–58; Richard Guy Wilson, "Idealism and the Origin of the First American Suburb," *American Art Journal* 11 (Fall 1979): 79–90; Schuyler, *New Urban Landscape,* pp. 156–59; John R. Stilgoe, *Borderland: Origins of the American Suburb, 1820–1939* (New Haven, 1988), pp. 52–55.

When Haskell was attempting to sell Belmont Farm, his country seat on the banks of the Passaic River near Belleville, N.J., he advertised its extensive stands of fruit trees, which "have been procured mostly at the Highland Nurseries, of the late Messrs. A. J. Downing & Co." "Horticultural Advertiser," *Horticulturist* 3 (1848–49), copy in Special Collections, Morris Library, University of Delaware. The advertisement was dated Feb. 1, 1849, so the "late" referred not to Downing's death but to his sale of the nursery.

47. N. P. Willis, "Sale of Mr. Downing's Residence," *Home Journal,* reprinted in *Horticulturist* 7 (Nov. 1852): 527.

48. See, for example, Sam Bass Warner, Jr., "If All the World Were Philadelphia: A Scaffolding for Urban History," *American Historical Review* 74 (Oct. 1968): 26–43, and David Ward, *Cities and Immigrants: A Geography of Change in Nineteenth-Century America* (New York, 1971).

49. Calvert Vaux, memorandum, Nov. 1894, Calvert Vaux Papers, Manuscripts and Archives Division, Rare Book and Manuscript Division, New York Public Library, Astor, Lenox and Tilden Foundations, New York.

50. [Frederick Law Olmsted], "The People's Park at Birkenhead, near Liverpool," *Horticulturist* 6 (May 1851): 224–28; Charles Capen McLaughlin and Charles E. Beveridge, eds., *The Papers of Frederick Law Olmsted, vol. 1: The Formative Years, 1822–1852* (Baltimore, 1977), pp. 74–77.

51. Charles E. Beveridge, "Frederick Law Olmsted's Theory of Landscape Design," *Nineteenth Century* 3 (summer 1977): 38–43; Schuyler, "The Washington Park and Downing's Legacy," pp. 306–11; Schuyler, *New Urban Landscape,* pp. 95–100; F. L. Olmsted to Richard Grant White, July 23 [1866], in *The Papers of Frederick Law Olmsted, vol. 6: The Years of Olmsted, Vaux and Company, 1865–1874,* ed. David Schuyler and Jane Turner Censer (Baltimore, 1992), pp. 101–4.

52. F. L. Olmsted and C. Vaux, "Circular Proposing the Erection in Central Park of a Memorial to Andrew Jackson Downing," Apr. 5, 1860, in *The Papers of Frederick Law Olmsted, vol. 3: Creating Central Park, 1857–1861,* ed. Charles E. Beveridge and David Schuyler (Baltimore, 1983), pp. 251–52. Olmsted also described Downing as the *"originator"* of Central Park. Olmsted to Henry W. Bellows, Dec. 22, 1879, Frederick Law Olmsted Papers, Manuscript Division, Library of Congress, Washington, D.C.

53. F. L. Olmsted, Appendix to the *Annual Report of the Architect of the United States Capitol for the Fiscal Year Ending June 30, 1882,* reprinted in House of Representatives, *Documentary History of the Construction and Development of the United States Capitol Building and Grounds* (Washington, D.C., 1904), p. 1187.

54. C. Vaux to James G. Graham, June 17, 1889, in Newburgh, Common Council, *Proceedings* 16 (July 16, 1889): 279–89; David Schuyler, "Belated Honor to a Prophet: Newburgh's Downing Park," *Landscape* 31 (spring 1991): 10–17.

55. "Domestic Notices," *Horticulturist* 7 (Sept. 1852): 431–32.

Chapter 9 Tastemaker to the Nation

Epigraph: Henry F. French's tribute to Downing, published in the *Home Journal* and reprinted in "Tributes to the Memory of Mr. Downing," *Horticulturist* 7 (Oct. 1852): 471.

1. C. C., "A Visit to the House and Garden of the Late A. J. Downing," *Horticulturist,* n.s. 3 (Jan. 1853): 21–27. See also Arthur Channing Downs, Jr., "Downing's Newburgh Villa," *Bulletin of the Association for Preservation Technology* 4 (1972): 5–29.

2. C. C., "A Visit to the House and Garden," pp. 21–27; George William Curtis, "Memoir," in *Rural Essays. By A. J. Downing. Edited, With a Memoir of the Author, by George William Curtis; and a Letter to His Friends, by Fredrika Bremer* (1853; reprint ed., with a new introduction by George B. Tatum, New York, 1974), p. xxxix.

3. See chapter 4 in this volume and Agreement of A. J. Downing and H. Ramsdell, A. Gerald Hull, and Andrew Saul, Feb. 15, 1847, The Athenaeum of Philadelphia; AJD to Cora L. Barton, June 13, 1848, printed in Jacquetta M. Haley, ed., *Pleasure Grounds: Andrew Jackson Downing and Montgomery Place* (Tarrytown, N.Y., 1988), pp. 33–34

4. C. C., "A Visit to the House and Garden," pp. 23–26; Fredrika Bremer, *The Homes of the New World: Impressions of America,* trans. Mary Howitt, 2 vols. (New York, 1854), 1:19; AJD to J. J. Smith, Feb. 19, 1847, printed in "Downing's Familiar Notes and Letters," *Horticulturist,* n.s. 6 (Jan. 1856): 23.

5. AJD, "A Chapter on Hedges," *Horticulturist* 1 (Feb. 1847): 345.

6. AJD, *A Treatise on the Theory and Practice of Landscape Gardening, Adapted to North America . . .* (New York, 1841), 1844 ed., p. 49.

7. C. C., "A Visit to the House and Garden," pp. 26–27; Downs, "Downing's Newburgh Villa," p. 22, n. 40.

8. AJD, "Our Country Villages," *Horticulturist* 4 (June 1850): 538; AJD, "A Reform Needed," ibid. 6 (Oct. 1851): 441–43.

9. Mark C. Carnes, "The Rise and Fall of a Mercantile Town: Family, Land, and Capital in Newburgh, New York, 1790–1844," *Hudson Valley Regional Review* 2 (Sept. 1985): 36–37, 40, n. 49.

10. Mark C. Carnes, "From Merchant to Manufacturer: The Economics of Localism in Newburgh, New York, 1845–1900," *Hudson Valley Regional Review* 3 (Mar. 1986): 46–56.

11. J. D. B. DeBow, comp., *Statistical View of the United States . . . Being a Compendium of the Seventh Census* (Washington, D.C., 1854), p. 193.

12. For Downing's involvement in the establishment of these institutions see chapter 1 of this volume.

13. AJD, *The Architecture of Country Houses* (New York, 1850), p. 8.

14. Calvert Vaux, *Villas and Cottages. A Series of Designs Prepared for Execution in the United States* (New York, 1857), pp. 242–43.

15. These and other properties Downing and Vaux designed are described and illustrated in Vaux's *Villas and Cottages*.

16. AJD to Luther Tucker, Oct. 30, 1851, and Calvert Vaux to Marshall P. Wilder, Aug. 18, 1852, both in John Jay Smith Papers, Library Company of Philadelphia, placed on deposit at the Historical Society of Pennsylvania, Philadelphia.

17. "The Henry Clay Catastrophe," *New-York Daily Times*, July 30, 1852.

18. Bremer, *Homes of the New World*, 1:18.

19. "Dreadful Calamity on the Hudson River," *New-York Daily Times*, July 29, 1852; "The Henry Clay Catastrophe," ibid., July 30, 1852.

20. Ibid.

21. "Burning of the Henry Clay," *Knickerbocker* 40 (Oct. 1852): 343.

22. Amelia A. Bailey statements, from the *Newburgh Gazette*, reprinted in *Horticulturist* 7 (Sept. 1852): 430.

23. Carl Carmer, *The Hudson* (New York, 1939), p. 288.

24. Vaux's testimony before the coroner's inquest was printed in "The Henry Clay Catastrophe," *New-York Daily Times*, July 30, 1852.

25. James Brown, diary, New-York Historical Society, New York, excerpt printed in J. E. Spingarn, "Henry Winthrop Sargent and the Early History of Landscape Gardening and Ornamental Horticulture in Dutchess County, New York," *Year Book of the Dutchess County Historical Society* 22 (1937): 36–70.

26. Rev. John Brown diary, July 30, 1852, St. George's Church, Newburgh, N.Y.

27. "The Real Monument to Downing," *Horticulturist*, n.s. 7 (Apr. 1857): 155–56. Downing's remains were disinterred and reburied in Cedar Hill Cemetery, which was established in 1870 and located several miles north of Newburgh. Charles Downing was one of the organizers of Cedar Hill Cemetery. See David Charles Sloane, *The Last Great Necessity: Cemeteries in American History* (Baltimore, 1991), p. 121.

28. See, for example, N. P. Willis's account of the auction, published in the *Home Journal* and reprinted as "Sale of Mr. Downing's Residence," *Horticulturist* 7 (Nov.

1852): 527–28, and A. J. Davis, diary, Oct. 7, 1852, A. J. Davis Collection, Department of Prints and Photographs, Metropolitan Museum of Art, New York.

29. These and other reactions were collected and printed in "Tributes to the Memory of Mr. Downing," *Horticulturist* 7 (Sept. 1852): 427–30, and 7 (Oct. 1852): 471–72; "Death of A. J. Downing," *Ohio Cultivator* 8 (Aug. 15, 1852): 248.

30. Marshall P. Wilder, "Col. Wilder's Eulogy on Mr. Downing," *Horticulturist* 7 (Nov. 1852): 492–93, 499.

31. "The Downing Monument," *Horticulturist*, n.s. 6 (Nov. 1856): 489–91. See also "Report of Committee on the Downing Monument," *Proceedings of the Sixth Session of the American Pomological Society* (Boston, 1857), pp. 28–33.

32. Thomas Cole, "Essay on American Scenery" (1835), in *American Art 1700–1960: Sources and Documents*, ed. John W. McCoubrey (Englewood Cliffs, N.J., 1965), p. 109.

33. See David Schuyler, "The Sanctified Landscape: The Hudson River Valley, 1820 to 1850," in *Landscape in America*, ed. George F. Thompson (Austin, 1995), pp. 93–109.

34. Henry W. Bellows, "Cities and Parks: With Special Reference to the New York Central Park," *Atlantic Monthly* 7 (Apr. 1861): 416–29.

35. Luther Tucker, "The Publisher's Farewell," *Horticulturist* 7 (Dec. 1852): 538.

36. H. F. French, tribute to Downing, published in the *Home Journal* and reprinted in *Horticulturist* 7 (Oct. 1852): 471–72.

37. The *Evening Post* article was excerpted in "Tributes to the Memory of Mr. Downing," *Horticulturist* 7 (Sept.): 430.

38. Wilder, "Col. Wilder's Eulogy on Mr. Downing," p. 500.

39. Keith N. Morgan, *Charles A. Platt: The Artist as Architect* (Cambridge, Mass., 1985); and Keith N. Morgan, ed., *Charles A. Platt, Italian Gardens, with an Overview by Keith N. Morgan and Additional Plates by Charles A. Platt* (1894; Portland, 1993).

40. See, for example, "Sale of Mr. Downing's Residence," *Horticulturist* 7 (Nov. 1852): 527–28.

41. Downs, "Downing's Newburgh Villa," pp. 77–82.

42. Antoinette F. Downing and Vincent J. Scully, Jr., *The Architectural Heritage of Newport, Rhode Island, 1640–1915* (1952; 2d ed., New York, 1967), p. 193.

43. George B. Tatum, "Andrew Jackson Downing: Arbiter of American Taste, 1815–1852," Ph.D. diss., Princeton University, 1950, p. 195; William Alex and George B. Tatum, *Calvert Vaux: Architect and Planner* (New York, 1994), pp. 5, 7, 57.

44. Harvey K. Flad, "Matthew Vassar's Springside: '. . . the hand of Art, when guided by Taste,'" in *Prophet With Honor: The Career of Andrew Jackson Downing, 1815–1852*, ed. George B. Tatum and Elisabeth Blair MacDougall (Washington, D.C. 1989), pp. 253–57.

45. See, for example, Frederick Gutheim and Wilcomb E. Washburn, *The Federal City: Plans and Realities* (Washington, D.C. 1976); Thomas S. Hines, "The Imperial Mall: The City Beautiful Movement and the Washington Plan of 1901–1902," in *The Mall in Washington, 1791–1991*, ed. Richard Longstreth (Washington, D.C., 1991), pp. 79–99; Jon A. Peterson, "The Mall, the McMillan Plan, and the Origins of American City Planning," in ibid., pp. 101–15.

46. Alan Gowans, *Images of American Living: Four Centuries of Architecture and Furniture as Cultural Expression* (Philadelphia, 1964), pp. 308–13; William H. Pierson, Jr., *American Buildings and Their Architects: Technology and the Picturesque, the Corporate and Early Gothic Styles* (Garden City, N.Y., 1978), pp. 411–13.

47. See AJD, "On the Improvement of Country Villages," *Horticulturist* 3 (June 1849): 545–49; T. H. Hyatt, "Monroe Co. Ag. Society—Rural Architecture, &c.," *Cultivator*, n.s. 1 (Nov. 1844): 354; and Thos. H. Hyatt, "Rural Architecture," ibid., n.s. 3 (Jan. 1846): 24–25.

48. Bremer, *Homes of the New World*, 1:111; Fredrika Bremer, "To the Friends of A. J. Downing," in *Rural Essays*, p. lxiv; F. Bremer letter to AJD, Dec. 2, 1849, reprinted in Adolph B. Benson, ed., "Fredrika Bremer's Unpublished Letters to the Downings." *Scandinavian Studies and Notes* 11 (May 1930): 51.

49. H. F. French, tribute to Downing, published in the *Home Journal* and reprinted in *Horticulturist* 7 (Oct. 1852): 472.

Bibliographical Essay

Although *Apostle of Taste* is based principally on Downing's own writings, I have also had the good fortune to be able to draw upon the works of a talented group of scholars. Any study of the life and significance of Andrew Jackson Downing must begin with George Bishop Tatum's "Andrew Jackson Downing: Arbiter of American Taste, 1815–1852" (Ph.D. dissertation, Princeton University, 1950). Tatum, in this and subsequent works, including introductions to reprint editions of the *Treatise on Landscape Gardening* and *Rural Essays* as well as two essays in *Prophet With Honor: The Career of Andrew Jackson Downing 1815–1852 ,* ed. George B. Tatum and Elisabeth Blair MacDougall (Washington, D.C., 1989), has defined Downing scholarship and provided the essential foundation for this study. Also important are the other contributors to *Prophet With Honor,* Jane B. Davies, Gordon P. De Wolf, Jr., Charles B. Wood III, Kenneth L. Ames, Harvey K. Flad, and Francis R. Kowsky.

Arthur Channing Downs, Jr., an indefatigable researcher, has written several contributions to Downing studies, including "Downing's Newburgh Villa," *Bulletin of the Association for Preservation Technology* 4 (1972): 1–113; *The Architecture and Life of the Hon. Thornton MacNess Nevin (1806–1895),* 2d ed. (Goshen, N.Y., 1972); and *Downing and the American Home* (privately printed by the author, 1988). Other important works include John William Ward, "The Politics of Design," in Ward, *Red, White, and Blue: Men, Books, and Ideas in American Culture* (New York, 1969); Vincent Scully, "Romantic Rationalism and the Expression of Structure in Wood: Downing, Wheeler, Gardner, and the 'Stick Style,'" *Art Bulletin* 35 (June 1953): 121–42, reprinted in *The Shingle Style and the Stick Style,* rev. ed. (New Haven, 1971), pp. xxiii–lix; Richard N. Masteller and Jean Carwile Masteller, "Rural Architecture in Andrew Jackson Downing and Henry David Thoreau: Pattern Book Parody in *Walden,*" *New England Quarterly* 57 (Dec. 1984): 483–510; John Conron, "The American Dream Houses of Andrew Jackson Downing," *Canadian Review of American Studies* 18 (1987): 9–40; and Catherine Howett, "Crying Taste in the Wilderness: Disciples of Andrew Jackson Downing in Georgia," *Landscape Journal* 1 (spring 1982): 15–22. Downing's Newburgh is the subject of two articles by Mark C. Carnes, "The Rise and Fall of a Mercantile Town: Family, Land, and Capital in Newburgh, New York, 1790–1844," *Hudson Valley Regional Review* 2 (Sept. 1985): 17–40, and "From Merchant to Manufacturer: The Economics of Localism in Newburgh, New York, 1845–1900," ibid. 3 (Mar. 1986): 46–79, while Walter L. Creese investigates the Hudson Valley in a superb chapter of *The Crowning of the American Landscape: Eight Great Spaces and Their Buildings* (Princeton, 1985), pp. 43–98. Kenneth B. Hawkins's "The Therapeutic Landscape: Nature, Architecture, and Mind in Nineteenth-Century America" (Ph.D. dissertation, University of Rochester, 1991) places Downing's ideas on landscape within a strong historical context. Joel E. Spingarn's "Henry Winthrop Sargent and the Early History of Landscape Gardening and Ornamental Horticulture in Dutchess County, New York," *Year Book of the Dutchess County Historical Society* 22 (1937): 36–70, is still valuable.

The English background to Downing's writings has an extensive bibliography, one extending back to Kenneth Clark's *The Gothic Revival: An Essay in the History of Taste* (London, 1922) and including such notable works as Christopher Hussey's *The Picturesque: Studies in a Point of View* (London, 1927); Samuel H. Monk's *The Sublime: A Study of Critical Theories in XVIII-Century England* (New York, 1935); B. Sprague Allen's *Tides in English Taste, 1619–1800* (Cambridge, Mass., 1937); and Walter John Hipple, Jr., *The Beautiful, the Sublime, and the Picturesque in Eighteenth-Century British Aesthetic Theory* (Carbondale, Ill., 1957). Among recent works, I am especially indebted to Melanie Louise Simo, *Loudon and the Landscape: From Country Seat to Metropolis, 1783–1843* (New Haven, 1988); John Dixon Hunt, *Gardens and the Picturesque: Studies in the History of Landscape Architecture* (Cambridge, Mass., 1992); and Stephen Daniels, *Fields of Vision: Landscape Imagery and National Identity in England and the United States* (Princeton, 1993).

Writings important to an understanding of Downing's significance for American cultural development include Neil Harris, *The Artist in American Society: The Formative Years, 1790–1860* (New York, 1966) and Roger B. Stein, *John Ruskin and Aesthetic Thought in America, 1840–1900* (Cambridge, Mass., 1967). My interpretation of Downing's efforts to democratize taste has benefited from Richard L. Bushman, *The Refinement of America: Persons, Houses, Cities* (New York, 1992) and John F. Kasson, *Rudeness and Civility: Manners in Nineteenth-Century America* (New York, 1990). Mary P. Ryan, *Cradle of the Middle Class: The Family in Oneida County, New York, 1790–1865* (Cambridge, Mass., 1981) and Stuart Blumin, *The Emergence of the Middle Class: Social Experience in the American City, 1760–1900* (Cambridge, 1989) have helped me understand Downing's audience. Important for delineating the context of Downing's ideas are John Higham, *From Boundlessness to Consolidation: The Transformation of American Culture, 1848–1860* (Ann Arbor, 1969); David P. Handlin, *The American Home: Architecture and Society, 1815–1915* (Boston, 1979); Ann Leighton, *American Gardens of the Nineteenth Century: "For Comfort and Affluence"* (Amherst, Mass., 1987); Tamara Plakins Thornton, *Cultivating Gentlemen: The Meaning of Country*

Life among the Boston Elite, 1785–1860 (New Haven, 1989); Angela Miller, *The Empire of the Eye: Landscape Representation and American Cultural Politics, 1825–1875* (Ithaca, 1993); Clifford E. Clark, Jr., *The American Family Home, 1800–1960* (Chapel Hill, 1986); Gwendolyn Wright, *Building the Dream: A Social History of Housing in America* (Cambridge, Mass., 1981); and Alan Gowans, *Styles and Types of North American Architecture: Social Function and Cultural Expression* (New York, 1992).

Jane B. Davies has devoted a lifetime to the study of Downing's collaborator, Alexander Jackson Davis. Her introduction to the Da Capo edition of Davis's *Rural Residences* (New York, 1980) and her essay "Davis and Downing: Collaborators in the Picturesque" in *Prophet With Honor* constitute the best modern scholarship on Davis and the ways his career intersected with Downing's. Important too is *Alexander Jackson Davis: American Architect, 1803–1892*, ed. Amelia Peck (New York, 1992). The most complete record of the career of Downing's partner, Calvert Vaux, is William Alex and George B. Tatum, *Calvert Vaux: Architect and Planner* (New York, 1994); while Francis R. Kowsky's *Frederick Clarke Withers and the Progress of the Gothic Revival in America after 1850* (Middletown, Conn., 1980) is the standard work on the younger of the two English architects who came to the United States to practice with Downing. William H. Pierson, Jr., *American Buildings and Their Architects: Technology and the Picturesque, the Corporate and Early Gothic Styles* (Garden City, N.Y., 1978) remains the best survey of American architecture of the first half of the nineteenth century.

Several recent works have contributed to my understanding of Downing's relationship with the vernacular tradition. They include Dell Upton, "Pattern Books and Professionalism: Aspects of the Transformation of Domestic Architecture in America, 1800–1860," *Winterthur Portfolio* 19 (spring 1984): 107–50; Sally McMurry, *Families and Farmhouses in Nineteenth-Century America: Vernacular Design and Social Change* (New York, 1988); J. Ritchie Garrison, *Landscape and Material Life in Franklin County, Massachusetts, 1770–1860* (Knoxville, Tenn., 1991); and Fred W. Peterson, *Homes in the Heartland: Balloon Frame Farmhouses of the Upper Midwest, 1850–1920* (Lawrence, Kan., 1992).

Only a small portion of what must have been an extensive correspondence carried on by Downing has survived. Caroline Downing Monell gave some of her late husband's papers to Downing Vaux, Calvert Vaux's son, but these have not come to light, nor have Downing's letters to Fredrika Bremer, though Miss Bremer's letters to the Downings were acquired by Yale University Library in 1927 and published by Adolph B. Benson as "Fredrika Bremer's Unpublished Letters to the Downings," *Scandinavian Studies and Notes* 11 (Feb. 1930): 1–10; (May 1930): 39–53; (Aug. 1930): 71–78; (Nov. 1930): 109–24; (Feb. 1931): 149–72; (May 1931): 187–205; (Aug. 1931): 215–28; (Nov. 1931): 264–74. Excepting several letters to Downing that he forwarded to architect Alexander Jackson Davis, the Bremer letters represent the only substantial block of correspondence addressed to Downing that has survived.

The most important collections of unpublished materials used in this study were the Alexander Jackson Davis papers, most of which are in the Department of Prints and Photographs, Metropolitan Museum of Art, New York City; but other Davis materials in the Print Department of the New-York Historical Society and the Manuscript Room of the New York Public Library were also essential. The Downing letters to Davis cast light on the development of the friendship and professional concerns that united the two men and were essential keys to understanding how Downing wrote the *Treatise on Landscape Gardening, Cottage Residences,* and *The Architecture of Country Houses.* Downing's letters to Philadelphia horticulturist John Jay Smith, which Smith left to the Library Company of Philadelphia but which have been place on deposit at the Historical Society of Pennsylvania, Philadelphia, reveal information on Downing's developing career as a professional landscape gardener in the 1840s and as a practicing architect in the early 1850s, while several critically important letters to Davis's patron Robert Donaldson, recently acquired by Richard Jenrette, reveal how Downing determined the appropriate audience for his books. Jacquetta M. Haley includes ten letters, principally about Montgomery Place, written by Downing to the members of the Livingston and Barton families, in *Pleasure Grounds: Andrew Jackson Downing and Montgomery Place* (Tarrytown, N.Y., 1988). Several letters from Downing to Luther Tucker, publisher of the *Horticulturist,* are located at the Princeton University Library, while correspondence and plans related to Matthew Vassar's estate, Springside, may be studied in the Special Collections Division, Vassar College Library. Essential documents that illuminate Downing's involvement in the design and construction of the park on the public grounds in Washington, D.C., are housed in the Records of the Commissioners of Public Buildings, Record Group 42, National Archives and Records Administration, the W. W. Corcoran Papers, Manuscript Division, Library of Congress, and the Joseph Henry Papers, Smithsonian Institution Archives, all in Washington, D.C. The Reverend John Brown's diary, in St. George's Church, Newburgh, N.Y., was a source of indispensable information on social and cultural life in Newburgh and on the activities of the local horticultural society.

Index

Library of Congress Cataloging-in-Publication Data

Schuyler, David.
    Apostle of taste : Andrew Jackson Downing, 1815–1852 / David Schuyler.
        p.   cm. — (Creating the North American landscape)
    "Published in cooperation with the Center for American Places, Harrisonburg, Virginia."
        Includes bibliographical references (p.   ) and index.
        ISBN 0-8018-5229-3 (hc : alk. paper)
    1. Downing, A. J. (Andrew Jackson), 1815–1852.   2. Landscape architects—United States—Biography.   3. Horticulturists—United States—Biography.   I. Center for American Places (Harrisonburg, Va.)   II. Title.   III. Series.
SB470.D68S38   1996
712'–.092—dc20   [B]   95-33513